D1285621

GIRLS ROCK!

GIRLS ROCK!

Fifty Years of Women Making Music

Mina Carson
Tisa Lewis
Susan M. Shaw

With a Foreword by
Jennifer Baumgardner
and Amy Richards

THE UNIVERSITY PRESS OF KENTUCKY

Publication of this volume was made possible in part by a grant
from the National Endowment for the Humanities.

Copyright © 2004 by The University Press of Kentucky

Scholarly publisher for the Commonwealth,
serving Bellarmine University, Berea College, Centre
College of Kentucky, Eastern Kentucky University,
The Filson Historical Society, Georgetown College,
Kentucky Historical Society, Kentucky State University,
Morehead State University, Murray State University,
Northern Kentucky University, Transylvania University,
University of Kentucky, University of Louisville,
and Western Kentucky University.
All rights reserved.

Editorial and Sales Offices: The University Press of Kentucky
663 South Limestone Street, Lexington, Kentucky 40508-4008
www.kentuckypress.com

04 05 06 07 08   5 4 3 2 1

Acknowledgment is made in the following for permission to reprint copyrighted material: "Girls With
Guitars." Words and Music by Mary Chapin Carpenter. © 1993 EMI APRIL MUSIC INC. and GETAREALJOB
MUSIC. All Rights Controlled and Administered by EMI APRIL MUSIC INC. All Rights Reserved. Interna-
tional Copyright Secured. Used by Permission. "It's Alright." Words and Music by Emily Saliers. © 1997
EMI VIRGIN SONGS, INC. and GODHAP MUSIC. All Rights Controlled and Administered by EMI VIRGIN
SONGS, INC. All Rights Reserved. International Copyright Secured. Used by Permission. "The Ones Who
Aren't Here." Words and Music by John Calvi. Used by Permission of John Calvi.

Library of Congress Cataloging-in-Publication Data

Carson, Mina Julia.
Girls rock! : fifty years of women making music / Mina Carson, Tisa
Lewis, and Susan M. Shaw ; with a foreword by Jennifer Baumgardner and
Amy Richards.
p. cm.
Includes bibliographical references (p.   ) and index.
ISBN 0-8131-2310-0 (hardcover : alk. paper)
1. Women rock musicians. 2. Feminism and music. 3. Rock
music—History and criticism. 4. Music—Social aspects. I. Lewis,
Tisa. II. Shaw, Susan M. (Susan Maxine), 1960- III. Title.
ML82.C37 2004
781.66'082—dc22
2003024592

This book is printed on acid-free recycled paper meeting
the requirements of the American National Standard
for Permanence in Paper for Printed Library Materials.

Manufactured in the United States of America.

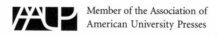   Member of the Association of
American University Presses

To Mina McDaniel—my partner, my co-parent, my love.
—M.C.

To Courtney and Lindsey.
—T.L.

To Alma Johnson, my grandmother.
—S.M.S.

In Memory
of
Rana Ross
1969–2003

CONTENTS

FOREWORD

Jennifer Baumgardner
and Amy Richards

Rolling Stone recently made one of their typical pronouncements: a list of the "100 all time best guitarists." Unsurprisingly, 98 percent of the list was men—Joni Mitchell and Joan Jett had made it, while Bonnie Raitt had not. But more shocking than the low XX turnout were our low expectations. It didn't occur to either of us that any chick guitarist would break the top one hundred. In our brainwashed heads, the word *guitar* was still synonymous with *male.* If it had been the hundred best singers, we could have named dozens of women. If it had been the hundred best groupies, we would have listed *only* women.

Why couldn't we imagine that women might be ax-masters, even in boy-friendly *Rolling Stone?* We are feminists, after all—even the kind of feminists that promote pop culture as part of feminism. Amy may have been the only child asked not to sing but rather to interpret in American Sign Language in her third grade choir, but she loves discovering new musicians and faithfully supporting their careers. Jennifer once aspired to be a singer and eventually channeled that into dating only musicians. By far the best guitarist she has dated—the only one to be in *Rolling Stone,* in fact—is a woman.

As our examples attest, you don't have to be a musician or a *High Fidelity*–level collector to know that music profoundly affects our lives. Music is in our cars, in the movies we love. Music has been there to comfort us during breakups, to motivate us to keep writing, to tune out a noisy neighbor, or to perfectly sum up something we have been trying to convey for paragraphs. For instance, Joan Jett's line "I love rock 'n' roll" says more about women's audacious claim on rock than pages from us could. Music is ubiquitous—which makes it all the more crucial that we recognize it, as the writers of *Girls Rock!* have, to be a political force as much as it is entertainment.

What we share with the writers is that we are music fans independent of our politics, but our politics inspire us to seek out women musicians and to uncover their role in the history of music. We got to know the authors, Mina Carson, Tisa Lewis, and Susan Shaw, when we visited their schools after our first book, *Manifesta,* was published. Carson, Lewis, and Shaw are so sensitive to the magical elements of both music and feminism—you sense they love both forces so much—that they take care not to kill either by adding stodgy theory. ("Not one reference to Levi-Straus!" they proudly claim.) For instance, they refer to the interviewees as "informants," not subjects, underscoring the musician's role as a storyteller. Meanwhile the interviews were conducted while *experiencing* Lilith Fair and Lady Fest, while going to concerts and crying with women as they told of the bad shit that had happened in their careers, while shining a light on the huge successes that have gone almost unarchived. They stop short of apologizing for being middle-aged academics, the unlikely authors of such a hot book, and what is clear from the book is that they want to delve into music's female side to sate their own curiosity, not to lecture to others.

Thus *Girls Rock!* is told through the lens of female musicians themselves, although you feel the presence of millions of other women: female fans, critics, and connoisseurs. For instance, when they talk about the phenomenon of Lilith Fair, they don't directly cite the thousands of women who attended, but it's implied that these women are mostly the reason for its success. Conversely, when they address the remaining inequalities for women—access to radio play, money, press coverage—they don't point fingers at *Rolling Stone* for, for instance, mostly hiring male writers or at Clearchannel for heavily larding the playlists with male rockers. In other words, the book is positive. It doesn't dwell on blaming but rather explores what has been, what is, and what could be.

Girls Rock! lays out three intersecting elements of women's relationship to popular music: historical, practical, and artistic. In terms of history, the women's music movement, well known to insiders but hardly part of the official story of rock, is given its due here. So are the stories of individual innovators, such as Wanda Jackson, a peer of Elvis Presley's, and Ferron. Perhaps most importantly, the authors tell the stories of artists who didn't achieve the kind of commercial success that will lead them into any mainstream documentation. Some women in this book are much more famous than others, but the authors wisely and generously treat them all as equals, because each artist has a following and is an artist, whether or not she is famous. They emphasize the power of knowing the nuts and bolts of the business, citing Martha Reeves's (of Martha Reeves and the Vandellas) assertion that the Motown experience was akin to a university for performers. Finally, every woman interviewed is asked about her first instrument and her influences, which grants each of them the seriousness of being a masterhand rather than a "woman in rock" obligated to comment on Britney's influence on kids or explain why she's not a feminist.

That last point gets to a central paradox of this book: the double edge of being identified as a "woman rocker." When is the label "woman in rock" defiant and when is it relegating oneself to the margins? The writers reconcile this paradox thus: "While [many] artists shun the label 'women in rock,' they have no difficulty identifying times in their lives and careers when gender skewed their experiences." In other words, you don't have to be a "womon" to know which way the wind blows. Drummer Kate Schellenbach is a case in point. She established her career as the only girl in the Beastie Boys, a fact that gave her a certain amount of credibility when she went on to play drums in the all-female group Luscious Jackson. Yet the reason she left the Beastie Boys was a classic example of the misogyny of rock. According to Schellenbach, the Beastie Boys' manager pushed them (and they acquiesced) to embrace a more sexist, homophobic form of hip-hop. In that story and others, you get the sense that not only rock is a "male" form, success is—the Beastie Boys were getting huge when Schellenbach was pushed out.

Even those musicians who eschew the feminist label acknowledge that women artists who were drawn to rock 'n' roll knew that they were doing something inherently feminist, even if they weren't calling it that. As Etta James said in an interview: "When I found out about the feminists, the women that were for women, I felt real connected to that. Women in this business have to take care of themselves, make their own living and be their own boss. I'm just happy that women are where they are today, where they can say, 'no, man, that ain't what I want.' "

And one thing that is clear in this book (and a bit controversial among feminists) is that these women don't want to take the sex out of rock 'n' roll. Rock's *sexiness*—which is different than its *exploitativeness* in the form of thirteen-year-old groupies and beauty double standards—is a dive into the freedom of male privilege. The writers don't attempt to desexualize rock or overanalyze sex in rock. They acknowledge its potency and appeal and expose the complexity of it. One particularly useful piece of history: several of the women who performed in the R & B girl groups of the fifties and sixties had to downplay any raw sexiness and felt compelled to be perfect ladies, replete with gloves and charm school. Their example shows that being al-lowed—feeling free—to be sexual is a sign of privilege. The writers note progress by describing today's young black female artists, such as Queen Latifah and Da Brat: "For these women, equality has meant the ability to be strong and in control and as sexy as they want to be."

This points to the fact that music has been able to deal with race in ways that politics—and feminism—has not. Even the *form* of rock has been a response to life in white America. And rock now is, as the writers point out, a convergence of white and black, male and female, made manifest es-pecially in its audience: "Communities of kids created their own sounds, neither black nor white, but a mash of American popular styles that issued in something a little bit new under the sun." What this book does beauti-fully, but implicitly, is show us what *could* happen for gender, using the ex-ample of race.

While it's not a polemic, *Girls Rock!* asserts that music changes the world in political terms. The writers paint this picture over and over, with-out dropping the anvil of Marxist-feminist-vegan theory on your head. The real story of rock music has never been about the guys or even the few girls who made it to the major labels, the stadiums, or the cover of *Rolling Stone.* They seem to say that the power of that music has to do with the event of coming together to make (or hear) live music. One example: during the segregationist sixties, Dick Clark took racially mixed groups of pop and rock musicians on the road through the Jim Crow South. Even with Clark's fame, hotel clerks often shut the door in his face when he arrived with his interracial bus. Shirley Alston Reeves (of The Shirelles) recalls that when the black bands were turned away at venues and hotels, Clark would cancel the whole show and they'd get back on the bus. "Thank God things have changed!" Alston Reeves told one interviewer of this book. "But you know what? That's what I was going to tell you. Music is what changed it. Music has so much to do with change."

We agree. "Survival" is the name of the final chapter. In it, Melissa Auf der Maur says, "If I can be a role model to young women who are trying to be honest, strong, brave, and independent, that would be . . . it's as simple as it gets, I think." This year we had four interns working with us. Two were high school seniors from Ohio—best friends—and two were Barnard Col-lege sophomores, also best friends. We always ask our interns not only how they found us, but how they came to feminism. Three of the four came to the movement through rock music. For the high schoolers, it was by read-ing a Courtney Love interview in a mainstream magazine. Love talked about reading Susan Faludi's *Backlash,* and the girls went and read it themselves.

From this, they went on to seek out dozens of feminist books and articles and to teach a course in their high school called "Chick Lit" (which eventually led them to us). Meanwhile, Liz, our college-age intern, went to a Veruca Salt concert in high school. The very second that Louise Post stepped on the stage, Liz knew both that she wanted to play guitar—and she does now— and that she was a feminist.

Music will continue to be an entry to feminism—and artists like Auf der Maur simply playing contributes to that process. Whether they call themselves riot grrls, feminists, female musicians, or just musicians, these women rockers will continue to demonstrate just what feminism looks—and sounds—like. The writers of this book understand that—and embrace it. More to the point, they believe it has revolutionary power.

By the way, by the time we finished this book, we could name dozens of incredible female guitarists.

PREFACE

In an interview with the *Cleveland Scene* on her way through town in August 2002, Kathleen Hanna lamented that interviewers never ask her about her music. "A lot of times, we get long runs where like every single question is, 'Why do you like being a feminist?' Sometimes I'm like, 'Is it because I'm a woman that I never get asked about my music? Is it something that really freaks people out—that we actually sit down and make this stuff?' " Catching the theme, and honest in his trade, the reporter acknowledged that three-quarters through the interview he had not asked about the music.[1] That reporter is not alone.

Our research grew out of a recognition that, while much has been written about women in rock (to the point, Lucy O'Brien reports, that during a 2000 concert members of Le Tigre chanted, "Not another book about women in rock!"), little has been written about women's relationship to their music—in particular how, given rock's male identification, women have come to construct identities as rock 'n' roll artists.[2] *Rolling Stone* and other popular magazines seem much more interested in the love lives, wardrobes, and offstage escapades of women performers than their music. Serious examinations of women in rock have yielded impressive volumes such as Gillian Gaar's *She's a Rebel,* a lively and thorough history of women in rock, Barbara O'Dair's *Trouble Girls,* a collection of essays by prominent rock critics, and Lucy O'Brien's *She Bop* (and now *She Bop II*), an excellent thematic analysis of various eras and genres of women's rock. While these works and others have provided crucial background for our research, we have shifted focus a bit to look quite bluntly at the processes of identity and music making that we find intriguing. And so we set out to find out how women put themselves upon a course to become rock musicians, how they learned to play and perform, how they write, what their music means to them, and what they hope their music means to their audiences.

Starting in the spring of 2001, we spent a year and a half interviewing women musicians. Some filled out an email form; others talked to us by phone; others we met in person. We traveled to Washington, D.C., to interview the Indigo Girls in the green room before their concert at Wolf Trap, and we spent a week in New York attending Ladyfest East and interviewing Paz Lenchantin, Deborah Frost, Bitch and Animal, and Erin O'Hara just days before the terrorist attack of September 11. Susan went to Divafest in the Bay Area, sponsored by the Institute for the Musical Arts, and interviewed June Millington. Mina attended Ladyfest Midwest in Chicago, where she talked with Rose Polenzani and Ellen Rosner. Janis Ian enjoyed Tisa's phone interview and invited her to come backstage after her concert in Asheville, North Carolina. We attended the unveiling of the girl groups stamps at the Rock and Roll Hall of Fame and Museum and got to hear performances by Martha and the Vandellas, The Crystals, The Chantels, The Cookies, The Shirelles, The Dixie Cups, Sarah Dash, and Mary Wilson. We met artists embarking on their careers and professionals whose songs have topped the charts. All together, we interviewed more than fifty musicians.

Obviously, we define rock broadly to include a wide range of voices and experiences, and we have elected to privilege these voices in our analysis. The primary data for *Girls Rock!* comes from our interviews. This information is supplemented by published interviews from these artists as well as from others we were unable to interview, and by the profiles and analyses of women in rock written by other scholars and rock critics. In writing about women in rock, we have chosen to focus on the self-perceptions of musicians rather than on external assessments of their music and careers. Often we quote these women at length. We privilege their words because their stories are so compellingly told and because they have so seldom been asked about their own music.

Because there are good chronological accounts of the history of women in rock, we have focused on broad themes that move through (and change and are changed by) rock's chronological history. As we listened to women tell their stories, various themes emerged, and these are the themes we have tried to capture in this book. In some sense, the story does move chronologically. We begin with Wanda Jackson and the revolutionary act of picking up a rock instrument; we end with the ways musicians are making careers during the digital revolution that is putting so much control back into the hands of artists. Within each chapter, we move across time, exploring common themes in their various historical contexts and examining what changes, if any, have occurred for women since rock's beginnings in the 1950s.

We acknowledge that any exploration of "women in rock" is, at its outset, problematic. Many women in rock eschew the label, preferring to be known simply as great musicians. We have to admit that we believe this position can overlook the obvious ways in which gender influences these performers' lives, which these same women eloquently identify. We also came to understand much better the passion for recognition for sheer and simple *excellence* that animates that aversion to the "woman musician" label. We acknowledge that differences among women play an important role in women's experiences in music, and we seek to pay close attention to difference and avoid lumping all women into a single inchoate category.

We have also elected to tell a story of women in rock that includes the broad spectrum of women performers. Many histories tell about the rich and famous, the headliners playing stadiums and large concert halls. We feel that the story of women in rock also includes those women just starting a band, playing the local coffeehouses, or traveling a regional circuit. In writing about these women, we have not distinguished in the text between the superstars and the lesser known. For one thing, the superstars usually came from a somewhere that is no-particular-where; further, the lesser known may well be on their way to being better known and then notorious. Finally, music making is a gift the musician gives her audience, big *or* small; in art as in many theologies, numbers do not count in any way central to the art itself. Each musician has something to teach us about women's experiences becoming rock musicians.

We believe that the knowledge gained from studies of popular culture is an important contribution to scholarship and society. Popular culture exerts an enormous amount of influence on people's inner and outer lives, and thus on social dynamics. As feminist scholars, we believe that understanding this influence is an important piece of any movement toward a more just and equitable society. Because we are writing about figures from popular culture, many of our sources are themselves artifacts of pop culture: *Rolling Stone, Billboard, Performing Songwriter, Curve,* and other magazines and Web sites. Not only are these sources rich in primary material—direct quotations from the musicians themselves—but they also provide us with insights into how pop culture views itself and how the discourse of pop culture constitutes part of the story of women in rock.

We believe that accessibility of feminist scholarship is a crucial issue. We have chosen to write a book that is accessible to the general public and informed by feminist scholarship and theory. We have tried to write in an entertaining style and have taken the welcome opportunity to try to use "plain" language—usually the best kind—in integrating relevant theories. In her introduction to *We Gotta Get Out of This Place: The True, Tough Story of Women in Rock,* Gerri Hirshey castigates the "earnest academics" who "burden their subjects with a gravitas that would horrify [rock's] impulsive, lightning-thighed perpetrators" and deconstruct "Madonna's bustier sequences with shadings of Barthes, Foucault, and, yes, Lévi Strauss." She concedes, "That's fine if it gets your tenure-seeking ya-yas out," although she prefers a more "fluid" approach—listening to the music and talking to musicians.[3] While academia is certainly all about getting one's "tenure-seeking ya-yas out," we have tried to create a balance between the words and stories of our subjects and the scholarly analysis we offer. And not once do we refer to Lévi-Strauss.

We do approach our task from a social construction perspective. We assume that identity is fluid and is constructed and reconstructed in a complex interaction of personal experience, choice, and social context and experience. That process of constructing identity is at the center of our research. While we examine the words of the musicians themselves, we set their stories in the social and historical contexts that helped to shape these women's experiences and identities, in order to create a larger narrative that both encompasses shared themes and takes note of the significant differences in individual experiences. And each of us brings a different disciplinary perspective to this book.

By working closely together (almost daily emails and phone conversations for the past two years), we have created a work that is truly collaborative and interdisciplinary. Mina is a historian, Tisa teaches human development, and Susan teaches women studies. This book is a product of the interweaving of these disciplines and a collaboration of ideas and effort. While we each wrote sections of every chapter (in our first draft, Mina's words were in black, Tisa's in blue, and Susan's in red), the end product reflects a thorough melding of each author's contributions. Most sentences were written and rewritten by all three of us.

And we were not alone as collaborators. The musicians themselves, folks who work in the music world, academic colleagues, and friends and family all played an important part in creating this book and richly deserve our gratitude. First, we would like to thank the musicians who participated in interviews: Amy Emerman, Bitch and Animal, Brenda Lee, Brita Rae Borough, Carey Colvin, Carol Kaye, Claire Anderson (Vimala), Deborah Frost, Ellen Rosner, Emily White, Erin O'Hara, Ferron, Holly Near, Indigo Girls Amy Ray and Emily Saliers, Janis Ian, Jann Arden, Jean Millington, Jill Gewirtz, June Millington, Jill Sobule, Jonatha Brooke, Kate Campbell, Kate Schellenbach, Kathy Fleischman, Kitzie P. Stern, Lalo, Laya Fisher, Leah

Hinchcliff, Lynn Ann Witting, Lynn Frances Anderson, Madeline Puckette, Magdalen Hsu-Li, Martha Reeves, Mary Wilson, Melissa Auf der Maur, Michelle Malone, Niki Lee, Paula Spiro, Paz Lenchantin, Rana Ross, Robin Renee, Rose Polenzani, Sarah Dash, Scarlet Rivera, Shirley Alston Reeves, Stacey Board, Tret Fure, Wanda Jackson, and Wendy Profit.

We would also like to thank those who helped us make connections for interviews and who have provided input and support for the project: Jennifer Baumgardner and Amy Richards; Howard Kramer of the Rock and Roll Hall of Fame and Museum; Carla DeSantis, editor of *Rockrgrl* magazine; Diane Gershuny of Fender Musical Instruments; Ann Powers of Experience Music Project; Candice Pedersen, formerly of Experience Music Project; Dana Powell. We would also like to thank the women studies office coordinator, Lisa Lawson, who made travel arrangements and filed reimbursement forms and in general made life easier by doing her job so very well; the intelligent, funny, and long-suffering History Department staff—Ginny Domka, Marilyn Bethman, Christie Schwartz, Jodi Mahoney, and Rachel Lilley—who processed Mina's forms and listened to her stories; staff members at Oregon State University's Valley Library, particularly Lorraine Borchers, who made arrangements for Mina and Susan to share a research study during the many months of this book's composition; Montreat College librarians Elizabeth Pearson, Judi Bugniazet, and Sue Diehl, who provided moral support and tracked down elusive books and citations; Montreat College and Oregon State University students, who listened with interest to interview stories and the progress of our research; Evy Cowan and Tracy Clow, the graduate students who assisted with library research; colleague and blues harmonica player Jeff Hale, who provided encouragement, information, and support; and Dean Kay Schaffer, who provided financial support through the College of Liberal Arts' Summer Faculty Research Grant. We offer special thanks to Carlie and Dave Krolick, who hosted us outside New York City in the last golden days before the dark. We also appreciate the support of colleagues who read drafts, offered suggestions, and provided general moral support: Grace Aaron, Nancy Breaux, Vicki Ebbeck, Paul Farber, Steve Hackel, Mo Healy, Mary Jo Nye, Bob Nye, and Patti Watkins. In the "without whom" category, we thank those who put up with us, cheered us on, took care of the kids and collected the mail while we traveled, and listened to our endless stories: Mina McDaniel, Donna Champeau, Janet Lee, and Heather Ferguson. Thanks and love to Lyn and Ricky, the next generation of rock artists, who moved through a significant portion of their lives during this book's research and writing. Thanks to Gena Henry, who came to the project in the very last stages, and David

Cobb, who oversaw it. And finally, we offer special thanks to our editor, Jennifer Peckinpaugh, who encouraged us, extended our deadlines, and made sure this book came to be, even as she moved through morning sickness and delivery. A big ol' welcome to Jackson Edward Peckinpaugh.

Mina Carson
Tisa Lewis
Susan M. Shaw

CHAPTER 1

GIRLS WITH GUITARS

Guitar stores are the worst, always. There were never any women working in them and still rarely are. I worked in a guitar store for a while, and none of the customers took me seriously until I started talking about gear. It's always that way—whether you're playing or recording or selling or buying, you always have to prove yourself.

—*Emily White*

There's just no stopping those girls with guitars.

—*Mary Chapin Carpenter,*
from the song "Girls with Guitars"

Wanda Jackson built her career on a dare. When she was twelve, her church friends dared her to try out for *The Local Talent,* a fifteen-minute radio spot hosted by Jay Davis on KLPR in Oklahoma City. Scared to death, Wanda hauled her guitar to the station and won the tryout. "One thing led to another," she recalls. She began winning local contests, and when the radio station announced a contest to win a daily quarter-hour slot for six months, Wanda won that one too.

At the end of six months she was not ready to give up her show. "Every day after school, I carried my guitar up to the radio station, and kids would laugh at me and everything. Country wasn't cool, you know, but it never mattered to me. And they said well, we'll tell you what: if you can keep a sponsor for that fifteen-minute time slot, you can keep that show." A local lumber company stepped up, and Wanda Jackson had her show. While her

1

high school classmates joined clubs and played sports, Wanda honed her chops on Oklahoma City radio every day.

That persistence fueled her big break. Hank Thompson, leader of *Billboard*'s fourteen-time number one country and western band, moved home to Oklahoma City and heard Wanda on KLPR. He called her up. "I couldn't believe I was actually talking to Hank Thompson." She said sure, she could sing with him at the Trianon Ballroom that Saturday as long as it was all right with her mother. "Since it was a nice ballroom, it was OK with her."

Wanda had been playing guitar and singing since she was a little girl in Bakersfield, California, where her parents had moved so her father could go to barber school. Homesick, her mother prodded him to move the family back to Oklahoma. ("As soon as the gravy has to be made out of water," her husband told her, "we're coming back to California.") Wanda took some piano lessons but could not settle in with a teacher, so she continued with guitar instead. Passionately focused, she would practice until her mother begged her to go outside and play. "My world was, I guess, pretty small; I just lived and breathed music. I never joined any clubs or anything at school. If I went to a ballgame and got excited and screamed and hollered on Friday night, I couldn't sing Saturday night with Hank Thompson, so I never went, you know—it was just music."[1]

After she connected with Hank Thompson, Wanda zoomed quickly from local hero to national star. Decca Records signed her at sixteen, and her first release, "You Can't Have My Love," recorded with Thompson's bandleader, Billy Gray, hit the country Top 10 in 1954. She toured with Elvis Presley during his early fame, when no other opening act could command his audience. She and Presley became close, and he persuaded her to try rock and roll. In 1956 she signed with Capitol and worked with Ken Nelson, an A&R man ready to follow his protégée in the new direction. Just out of high school, Wanda Jackson was one of the biggest stars of "rockabilly," a wildly popular mating of rock and country.[2]

Unfortunately, the United States in the 1950s was not ready for women who could growl, shake, moan, and demand their share of the fun (sexual or otherwise) with the best of male rock 'n' rollers.[3] Rejecting postwar notions of femininity, rockabilly women asserted themselves in both their lyrics and their performance. They were sassy, sexy, aggressive, and decidedly "unladylike." "America just wasn't ready for a female screaming, hollering, twisting and singing like that," Wanda says.[4] In Europe and Japan, however, Wanda was hugely popular. Her 1959 "Fujiyama Mama" was a big hit in Japan, staying at number one there for six months. One American music magazine called it "probably the best female vocal ever done in rock & roll."[5]

After a few years in the spotlight, Wanda struggled to find her musical niche. She landed back in country music and then in gospel. Today her avid international audience draws her back to Europe sometimes twice a year, and she has come full circle in the rockabilly revival, sharing the stage with Pam Tillis and another young admirer, Rosie Flores. Though her career is unique, the steps Jackson took to a life in music have been retraced by many younger women rockers: that passion for music that made it seem inevitable, the recruitment of family and friends, and the long hours of solitary practice that taught her about her own creative flow.

Playing the Chosen Instrument

We begin our tour of women rockers' collective history with that bold and basic gesture: learning to play an instrument. Of course learning an instrument is more than a gesture; it is a *practice,* a tedious, physically challenging, and sometimes emotionally painful routine in which the aspiring musician repeatedly wraps her fingers around a stiff, inert, often heavy machine and coaxes it beyond thuds, squeaks, and squeals to something like intentional music. The "natural" musician is not the one who avoids this process because she is so talented she "gets it" without work. Rather, the natural is the one for whom the *practice* is so necessary, so thrilling, and so unavoidable that she pushes on from level to level, through the frustration and muscle cramps and split fingertips, until one day she *is* a musician. She can play.

For women, learning to play a rock instrument is an especially bold gesture because of rock 'n' roll's usual association with masculinity.[6] From its beginnings, rock music was generally male terrain. On those occasions when women were allowed entrée into this masculine domain, only the role of vocalist was truly open for women's participation. On the whole, men just didn't want to listen to women play bass, drums, or electric guitar. Women were welcome only on the sidelines—as fans and groupies.[7] When Hole lead singer Courtney Love was asked about differences between male and female groupies, she responded, "There certainly wasn't a line of 16-year-old boys in little bondage outfits waiting for me, OK? But interestingly—interestingly—there was a line of 16-year-old girls in little bondage outfits waiting for me. I just wanted to spank them and give them all guitars and tell them to go start bands. It's a bummer that girls have to respond to rock artists sexually, rather than like, 'Wow, me too.' Guys come backstage and they're like, 'Dude, like wow, what kind of guitar is that?' "[8]

Many cultural constraints have discouraged women from picking up rock instruments. As electric guitarist and rock historian Mavis Bayton notes, even to begin to play guitar forces women to break with at least one of the norms of cultural femininity—they have to cut their fingernails short.[9] Playing rock music also demands that women break with a number of other cultural constraints of femininity. Rock musicians sweat; they get calluses; they work with equipment and technology; and they are loud. On the whole, playing rock music has itself been an expression of masculinity. In particular, the electric guitar and electric bass have been perceived as extensions of the male body, and the instruments have been held and played low on the body, despite the fact that playing the instruments at waist or chest height is actually easier, especially for women. Bass player Rana Ross acknowledges this tension: "I play my bass a little, not that high, but in the middle here, so it's enough for jazz playing and it's enough that you can play different styles. . . . There's no way to be a great player with your bass down here. . . . I mean, if you're standing up onstage and your bass is down here, you know, it looks really cool . . . but the truth is that you can't play."[10] So, women are left with the dilemma of either "looking good" and playing in a masculine way or looking "sissy" and playing in a way that is more comfortable and offers the opportunity for better technique.

Knowingly or not, when women take up rock instruments they enter into a domain in which they may not be welcome and in which they may have to challenge their own notions of self, particularly as women. Gender identities are created in the interplay between social expectations and institutions and individual expressions.[11] Every day, each person performs a gendered identity in behavior and self-presentation; in fact, this performance of gender is what maintains gender as a social reality.[12] And, of course, these gendered identities are shaped by race and sexuality. In addition, society enforces gender, and to choose not to enact gender-appropriate identities often leads to censure, if not worse.[13] Nonetheless, many people do refuse complete compliance with gender norms and actively resist institutional and individual constraints. Because of cultural expectations of femininity and rock's masculinity, women who construct identities as rock musicians must negotiate a resistant identity—one that claims women can sweat, jump, shout, *and* play rock music in ways that do not simply mimic traditional male forms of playing.[14]

Vibraphonist Lalo says she has always fought "the self-deprecating urge to be timid or hold back." She says going electric has made this easier for her. "I feel free and have a blast when I'm onstage, and I think that being an electric, uninhibited female in a predominantly male world makes the experience even more potent. I'm crossing an additional boundary (female stereotypes and society-encouraged behavior) to get to an amazing place."[15]

When Leah Hinchcliff played her guitar in a fourth grade talent show, a male classmate said, "You can't play guitar because you're a girl." But, Leah says, at the time she was "into 'anything boys can do, girls can do better.' That was our mantra . . . and if they told me I couldn't do it, I was gonna do it. If they said you can't play guitar, I'm gonna play guitar."[16]

Joan Jett's all-women 1970s band, the Runaways, showed the same determination. The Runaways were largely dismissed as a novelty. "I mean there wasn't anything that we got because we were girls that I remember in a positive sense. Everything was, 'You're weaker 'cause you're girls. You can't take it because you're girls. You can't do it because you're girls. But you're cute to have around, so come in and get drunk.' "[17] After Jett's subsequent band, the Blackhearts, released several commercial hits such as "I Love Rock 'n' Roll" and "Bad Reputation," the jeers mostly subsided, and Jett became an inspiration for many aspiring women rockers. "After all," she says, "one of the goals of the Runaways was to make it normal for a girl or woman to write and play rock 'n' roll and sweat onstage, and we seem to be getting closer to that."[18]

First Instruments and First Lessons

Many girls learned to play band instruments, such as flutes or trumpets, before or alongside folk and rock instruments. Many rock musicians are classically trained. Though few tell stories of being forced into lessons, virtually all refer to a moment, or a growing feeling, of breaking out of the prescribed boundaries of classical pedagogy and repertoire—much like Tori Amos, a child prodigy on piano who was kicked out of Baltimore's Peabody Conservatory at the age of eleven for preferring rock music and her own technique.

Having grown up in Argentina in a musical family, Paz Lenchantin of A Perfect Circle and Zwan recalls that around the age of five she discovered music as something she could do. "My parents were always playing the piano and I was always fascinated by what they were doing. It was like magic. . . . So I remember asking my mother, 'How do you do that?' So she put me on her lap, and she started playing. And I put my hands on top of her hands. And that was my first sensation. It was like magic, magician, musician feeling," she says, playing with words as she remembers. In the lobby of New York's Chelsea Hotel on a sunny late summer afternoon, Paz recalls her family: the quartet made up by her violin, her brother's viola, her sister's cello, and her mother's piano. From Argentina, the family moved to Los Angeles. From the violin, Paz moved to the bass. She quietly borrowed her mother's classical guitar and took off the treble strings, tuning down the bottom four. Soon she found she could integrate both instruments into her musical life, just as a young classical musician she "exploded" inside when she first heard punk music. "I started seeing the relationship between the two but in extreme opposites." Which does she prefer? "It hit me one day that it's like saying what would you prefer, your left eye or your right eye. It's like you need both of them to kind of keep you focused."

A boyfriend gave her an electric bass when she was fifteen. A few years later she chose her own bass. "I saved up for it." She remembers the transaction as "scary" because it was "almost like getting into a relationship with someone. You know, you're just kind of committed to this instrument now. This will be it, this instrument."

Paz Lenchantin is not the only musician to combine violin and bass in that counterintuitive marriage of big and small, high and low: the "learned and schooled" violin, says Paz, groping for the nuanced description, versus the "explosion of inwards" that characterizes the bass. Playing bass is like "connecting with the ground and the earth and the rumblings of the ground, and just letting yourself go without judgment."[19] Bitch (yes, her real name) of the group Bitch and Animal also migrated to the bass from her classical training in violin. All she needed to follow an earlier whim was a chance encounter with a stranger at the Michigan Womyn's Music Festival who told her she could "see a bass player" in the formally schooled violinist. "And so literally after the festival, me and my friend who had gone to the festival together went to a music store and bought a bass."

Like Paz, Bitch found solace in the bass's deep, more intuitive complement to her violin training. As a child she was good enough to get deep into the classical world but also felt "repelled" by it. At college in Chicago, she gave up violin, then returned, then gave it up again. "I had such a critic on my shoulder about it that I knew how much I had regressed by not playing for a few years." She finally broke the impasse by changing her style, taking lessons from a fiddler, and escaping to another set of rules, styles, and practices. Like Paz, Bitch found liberation in a different approach to the same instrument, and then she was able to return to classical lessons without being seduced into the world of rigid rules and competitive self-criticism that had put her off before.[20]

Touring and recording with artists ranging from Bob Dylan to Tracy Chapman and the Indigo Girls, Scarlet Rivera played a huge role in legitimizing the violin as a rock instrument. She too was trained in classical music as a child, beginning lessons in first grade. Her sister took piano and her brother took trumpet, at their parents' urging, but it was Scarlet who loved the music. Eventually, much as Tori Amos reports scandalizing her conservatory teachers by messing around with the piano repertoire, Scarlet just got tired of "playing the same old piece that every violinist in history had ever played. You know, just the same way." And the part of herself that tried to interpret the repertoire she discovered was "frowned upon. . . . If I veered off a notation to what I felt, [my teachers] didn't really like that." Like Bitch she turned to the fiddle, learning styles from Vassar Clements to Stuff Smith and the jazz patriarch Stephane Grappelli. She also began playing along to records of her favorite rock artists. Moving from Los Angeles to New York in the 1970s, Scarlet forged a career as a popular musician, at one time juggling gigs with a Latin band, a rock band, and a jazz ensemble. Walking down the street in lower Manhattan one day—at Thirteenth and First, as she recalls—she was approached from behind by a man interested in her violin case. It turned out to be Bob Dylan. "Can you play that thing?" he asked.[21]

Carey Colvin started out with flute lessons on her father's Air Force base in Miami because the family spent a few years without a piano and her hands were too small for her father's guitar, her first passion. "At the age of four I used to sneak and open up my father's guitar case and strum the strings of his guitar back and forth."[22] After starting out as a young child on her grandfather's guitar and mandolin, in fifth grade Lynn Frances Anderson sneaked her brother's trumpet out to the doghouse, then smuggled it onto the bus the morning of band practice after her mother refused to let her sign up. Her mother proved flexible. "She thought if I went to that much effort she may as well let me learn."[23] Lynn Ann Witting, of Gate 18, started out on accordion just because that was what was in the house; her mother played. She would later visit friends' houses and "I'd just sit at their family's piano and pick out melodies and, like, ignore my friend."[24] Madeline Puckette's house was full of art and music. Her father played guitar and mandolin (for which he sold his motorcycle); her mother, also an artist and a pilot, played piano and harpsichord; and her older sister played harp. Madeline started on the piano but at age five, after hearing a sax player at a local deli, she decided she wanted to be a professional saxophone player. Thinking her daughter too small for a sax, Madeline's mother bought her a flute, and then later Madeline "upgraded." In middle school she started playing mandolin, and when her friends suggested they form a girl band, she offered to play mandolin. Her friends didn't like that idea and told her she should get a guitar; so she started playing her dad's guitar.[25]

When Kate Campbell was four years old, her parents gave her a ukulele. "I really couldn't even read, but I could look at the pictures [in the teach-yourself-to-play book], and I figured out how to play the little chords and sing along." When Kate turned seven, her mother enrolled her in piano lessons, and her parents told her that if she would learn to play piano they would always give her any other instrument she wanted. In fifth grade Kate joined the school band and started playing clarinet. But, in high school, when she refused to play in the marching band ("I didn't want to wear the uniform. I thought it looked stupid."), the band director told her she couldn't continue to play in the concert band. So, much to the band director's surprise, she gave up her first-chair clarinet position, quit band, and traded her clarinet for a new guitar.[26]

Guitarists often remember minute details of their first instruments—what the guitar looked like, what it felt like, what it smelled like, and how it came into their hands. Carol Kaye, the legendary bass player, started out on a steel guitar her mother bought from a traveling salesman with the struggling family's pin money in the 1940s.[27] During the '60s British Invasion, Heart's Nancy Wilson recalls, "I, in particular, just flipped for the Beatles. [Ann and I] just had to get guitars right away and be as much like them as we could."[28] Michelle Malone remembers her mother's husband, a music teacher, lending her a twelve-string guitar when she was about eleven. She sat in her room with her ear against the stereo speaker, learning riffs from Rolling Stones records.[29] Bonnie Raitt got her first guitar for Christmas when she was eight years old, and she taught herself to play it at summer camp while listening to a counselor's Odetta records.[30] Tracy Chapman wanted to play drums, but her mother, fearing the drums would be too loud, bought her a tinny twenty-dollar guitar.[31] June Millington's first guitar was a gift from her mother on her thirteenth birthday, just before the family moved to the United States from the Philippines. It was a handmade Filipino guitar with mother-of-pearl inlay. Rana Ross also received her first guitar as a gift, and learned only later that her young benefactor had stolen it from a music store.

Emily Saliers of the Indigo Girls sees the guitar as fate. After trying drums as a very young child, she saw a flyer for guitar lessons at the YMCA and asked her parents if she could go. "Of course they said 'yes.' And I got my first guitar; it was twenty-four dollars. I can remember what it looked like. It was small and had gut strings . . . and from the very first it was just like, OK, this is what I am supposed to be playing. And I loved it like no other thing I've loved in my life, you know? It was just like finding something that's completely undeniable to your nature."[32]

Leah Hinchcliff, bass player for Swamp Mama Johnson and SoulJonz, saw her first guitar when her aunt, barely older than she was, got one for her birthday. "I thought that was the coolest thing ever, that a person I knew could play an instrument and make music." She begged her parents for one and got her wish at Christmas. "I don't think it left my hands or my sight. . . . I used to sleep with it. I would put it in bed with me."[33] Amy Emerman says she slept with her guitar and "even draped an arm or a leg over it once."[34] When Wendy Profit got her first electric guitar ("a shiny red squire tele [sic] for $99"), she slept with it for the first week. "I'd heard Jimi Hendrix slept with his guitar, and I wanted to infuse it with my love and energy . . . OK, maybe that is a little wacko, but, hey, when you're that passionate about something, you know you're on the right path."

Wendy started out playing the acoustic guitar, but "it always felt a little wrong. I'm not Jewel. Not that there's anything wrong with Jewel. I love and respect her music. But I have a Joan Jett soul." Then Wendy and her best friend quit their corporate jobs in the record industry and "headed west in the true spirit of American freedom and rock 'n' roll" to "be on the other side of the fence as artists." They stopped in Austin, Texas, to stay with a friend, who set Wendy up in his home studio "full of amps and guitars." He went out for groceries and told her, "Play whatever you want as loud as you want. Have fun. Bye." She says she "picked up his old Fender telecaster, cranked it up to eleven, and played an open A chord. Rwaaaaaaggggghhhh! My whole body vibrated with the sound. Something electric went through me, a thrill to the bone. I was transported in my imagination to Madison Square Garden, bright lights, screaming fans, my sold out concert. I played a D chord, E, then A again. I was Lou Reed, Joan Jett, me. A song came pouring out [of] me like water, complete before my friends returned from the store. I hadn't felt such pure childlike fun playing since I was eight years old building forts under the oak trees. I will never forget that day."[35]

Jann Arden made her parents furious when shortly after she graduated from high school she bought her first guitar on credit. "I think I paid this man ten dollars a month for five years," she says. A couple of years later she was playing the Washburn cutaway in a bistro when a fight broke out. Two drunken men fell into her and broke her guitar in half. She did get it fixed, but then she loaned it to a friend in Vancouver—twenty years ago. "I should get it back, actually," she muses.[36]

When she was eleven, Michelle Malone got a Sears Silvertone twelve-string hand-me-down guitar from her stepfather. "I don't think he had changed the strings on it since he got it . . . and [the strings] were all rusty, you know, and I would just cry, I would be so annoyed, [but] I guess it's a good way to learn if you want some strong hands."[37]

Melissa Etheridge started strumming a tennis racket when she was a toddler. "I was way into the Archies, but I didn't want to be Betty or Veronica. I wanted to be Reggie, and I never thought I couldn't."[38] She got her first guitar when she was eight years old. "I learned three chords, and that was it," she says.[39]

Emmylou Harris discovered her love of the guitar when her cousin got one for Christmas. She spent the entire visit playing it. "Apparently I had a talent for music, but before that I never really shook hands with an instrument. I mean, I was one of those people who hated piano lessons. And when I got into late grade school, I dutifully went to clarinet lessons, but my fingers were too small to close the holes, so they put me on saxophone. And I did it, but I didn't love it." Her grandfather bought her her own guitar for thirty dollars from a pawnshop in Birmingham, Alabama. "The strings were about an inch and a half off the fret-board. So I had to love it because it was extremely painful to make a C chord."[40]

This refrain of pain gladly or obliviously suffered runs through some of our informants' stories. Ellen Rosner tried to learn guitar as a nine-year-old, then gave it up when she wasn't the best in the class, she told us, laughing. Four years later she fell for a camp counselor who played and sang. "I wanted to be just like her. . . . I was obsessed, I was on fire, I had to play guitar." She borrowed her brother's Fender Stratocaster and would lock herself in his room and play. "No amp. And I played until my fingers bled. It's very clichéd," she said, "but it's true."[41]

During each performance on a tour in Australia, Hole's Courtney Love gave a guitar to a girl in the audience. At one concert, Courtney handed her guitar to a young girl, dressed in black, who had made her way to the front of the mosh pit. A nearby man tried to take the guitar away from the young girl, and Courtney called in security to make sure the girl got her guitar. Then she instructed the girl, "Play it loud, and don't give it to your boyfriend."[42]

Janis Ian reports that as a result of a burglary in 1972, she lost the only material thing that ever mattered to her, a 1937 Martin D-18 that her father had bought for twenty-five dollars from the widow of a farmer in 1948. Growing up with that guitar, she says it trained her and she wrote her first song on it. After "Society's Child," two albums, her appearance on the *Tonight Show,* and concerts across the country, her dad gave her the guitar for her sixteenth birthday. Even though other artists offered her thousands of dollars for the instrument, which she describes as having the best bass tone she had ever heard, she held on to it, and it became her dearest companion. So the loss of this guitar was devastating. Not even the death of family and friends affected her as much as losing her beloved Martin. For twenty-six years Janis mourned its loss until one day she received word that the guitar had been located. She notes, "How do you thank someone for giving back your dreams? How do you thank someone for filling a hole in your heart?"[43]

The Evolving Guitar

Women's relationship to the guitar has ebbed and flowed throughout modern history. A popular European parlor instrument during the Renaissance, the guitar lost favor among northern European elites in the eighteenth century, and then reemerged in the nineteenth century. The new guitars sported six strings and a repertoire sparked by the brilliant Spanish composers and advocates Fernando Sor and Dionisio Aguado. Small (at that time), lovely to look at, and easy to coax pleasant sounds from, the guitar proved unobjectionable as an instrument for genteel young women in their own circles. As in earlier times, women taught as well as studied the instrument. The Englishwoman Catherine Pelzer (later Madame Sidney Pratten) was a wunderkind of the midcentury who popularized guitar for bourgeois London families.[44]

Though the guitar traveled to North America as a parlor instrument for both men and women, it was the hardier steel-stringed folk guitar that moved west with Euro-American settlers and found dispersion among African Americans during slavery. By the 1920s steel-stringed guitars most often accompanied country blues, and transmogrified into jazz instruments.[45] Though relatively few women played the steel-stringed guitar, recent musicologists have reconstructed a tradition of black women blues guitarists in midcentury to stand beside the better-known white women of country music.[46] "Memphis Minnie" (Lizzie Douglas) made a career in guitar-and-voice country blues from the 1930s through 1960. As bold and assertive as any blues singer, female or male, she also stood her ground as a guitarist, reputedly dueling with Big Bill Broonzy as well as playing lead guitar with her own band. Among white country artists, Maybelle Carter of the Carter Family has often been acknowledged for influencing popular guitar technique, with her thumb-plucked melodic lines driving the up-and-down brushed rhythm kept by the fingers. [47]

While the guitar began as a predominantly female instrument, its popularity in jazz, country, and big band music moved it more and more into the hands of men.[48] And as the guitar became an increasingly male instrument, it also grew from its original eleven- to twelve-inch width to the massive sixteen-inch dreadnought introduced by Martin Guitar in 1916. The increased size made the instrument more difficult for women to play. Guitarist Diane Ponzio notes, "If you have appreciable breasts, it's just uncomfortable to play."[49] Kristin Hersh of Throwing Muses started learning to play guitar from her father when she was nine. "At first it was hard on my fingers," she says. "Changing chords was really hard. I had little, tiny nine-year-old hands, and my father's guitar was this nylon-stringed Yamaha, which has a big fretboard. So I'd be sliding my hands up against the strings. That's probably why I started making up my own chords."[50] Janis Ian's beloved Martin D-18 "was miles too big" for her, and she remembers, "My small fingers could barely get around the neck. As I began learning chords, I discovered new ways of fingering them to compensate for my size. To this day I play a D chord 'wrong,' but it works for me."[51]

When we were in New York conducting interviews for this book, Mina (the only one of us who is a musician) went in search of finger picks for her guitar. "They do not make finger picks that fit these fingers," she lamented later as we talked to Erin O'Hara about guitars and masculinity. "I had to go into every guitar store, *every* guitar store, and the guys are totally unapologetic for the fact that they don't carry the right finger picks—they say, 'Oh, bend them. Heat them and bend them.' Why should I have to heat and bend my guitar picks? Why can't I just go to the store and buy them?"[52]

When more girls and women began to play guitars in the late 1990s and early 2000s, guitar manufacturers at last turned their attention to this market segment. In 1997 Martin launched a limited edition acoustic guitar with a smaller body, slender fingerboard and narrow neck, and in 2001 Los Angeles bass player Tish Ciravolo introduced Daisy Rock Girl Guitars, a line of brightly colored daisy- and heart-shaped guitars with smaller bodies. By 2002 several guitar companies had begun to market signature lines for women, bearing the names of such musicians as Melissa Etheridge, Shawn Colvin, Emmylou Harris, and Sheryl Crow.

With a Little Help from My Friends

Smaller than most eight-year-olds, Leah Hinchcliff was also clearer about how to get what she wanted. She began taking lessons from a thirteen-year-old she remembers as "an absolute prodigy." A child of the seventies, her teacher brought songs by Joni Mitchell and Bob Dylan and other classic rockers and singer-songwriters. "I was like, 'Well, how do you know all these songs? And how do you learn songs?'" Her teacher told her that she listened to the records to figure them out. "I was like, 'I can do that!'" She chose the Rolling Stones' version of "As Tears Go By." "And I learned it, and I was so excited. . . . And the next time my guitar teacher came, I played it for her. And she started crying. She said, 'You don't need me any more!' 'No, no, I do. I do!'"[53]

Most women performers quickly acknowledge that need for other musicians. They cultivate connection. Girls as well as boys participate in the hallowed garage-band tradition: kids teaching other kids, some getting better, others creating a public nuisance. Many of our women informants lingered over their early experiences of support from family and friends. Sometimes it was mother or father, a brother or sister, sometimes a boyfriend, sometimes girlfriends. Paz Lenchantin mentions getting her first bass from a boyfriend. Rana Ross remembers that her boyfriend helped her learn to play, and more importantly, to listen to music as a musician. "You don't realize that people don't separate different instruments when they listen to music. So . . . I can listen to the bass line throughout the whole song and not really hear anything else that's going on."[54]

Rose Polenzani says a high school best friend jump-started her music career. One day this friend heard Rose playing "Olga's Birthday," a song Rose had written, and asked, "When are you going to take this career seriously? That's a really good song. Are you just going to play open mics the rest of your life?"[55]

As a child, Luscious Jackson drummer Kate Schellenbach played piano and then guitar, but the turning point in her musical life came when as a young teenager she fell in with a group of friends whose lives revolved around music. "We went to different schools, but we all went out to see the same bands." Together they discovered the New York underground scene around 1980 at clubs like CBGB and Max's Kansas City. "It wasn't about dating. . . . It wasn't about doing drugs and drinking. It was seeing bands that we were in love with. So that felt like a really safe and productive group of kids to be around." Though it felt like the end of an era, the musicians were accessible, and Schellenbach gradually imagined making music herself. "One of the bands I went to see was a band called Stimulators. And they were a punk band, and they had like a twelve-year-old drummer, this boy playing drums, a girl guitarist and bassist, and a guy singer, which was really cool because it seemed like this was really all-inclusive."[56]

Lynn Witting of Gate 18 put in hours of solitary practice sitting on the family's backyard picnic table before she got up the nerve to join the regular jam in Forest Park in Glendale, Queens. Two or three guys were always there, and they welcomed her. "I think the dudes considered me somewhat of a novelty at first, but soon enough I was accepted among them as a serious musician. They started phoning and asking me if I was coming up to jam, etc. That was a great feeling."[57] Like Kate Schellenbach, Lynn doesn't remember making musical choices relating to gender; the musicians she hung out with happened to be guys. Jill Gewirtz, a New York musician transplanted from Chicago, entered the music scene through Chicago open mics, which attracted mostly men. She got used to hanging out with the guys and also found that they roused her competitive instincts. Thinking that they found her songs more "feminine," she began developing her guitar playing to "compensate for my voice"—meaning not that her voice was weak, but that it was *stronger* than her guitar playing in a male world that appreciated technical instrumental excellence.[58]

Almost all of our informants pointed to the importance of other women performers in their development and survival as musicians. Melissa Auf der Maur calls Courtney Love her mentor. Before joining Hole, Melissa had never toured before. She says Courtney took her "under her wing and said, 'Come on, come explore the world with me.'"[59] Melissa's experience of another woman's friendship and mentorship seems to be typical for women musicians. Other women performers show them the ropes, encourage them, support them, and create for them a community in which to grow and thrive. We will explore the importance of mentoring in chapter 8.

Family Ties

Rock music has often been perceived as rebel music, the driving sound of the outsider, living beyond the boundaries, outside convention. As rock enters its sixth decade, most of us recognize the ironies and half-truths in that characterization. Rock has not just made room for big money and big crowds (throwing into question its edgy outsider status), but also has found a medium in the bosom of the conventional Western family. The centrality of family for so many of the women we interviewed may reflect several things. Even today, girls are often more sheltered and closely supervised than boys. Our culture still nourishes expectations that girls will stay more connected to family and will accept more family responsibilities for daily household maintenance and childcare. These assumptions were particularly sharp in the first decade of rock.[60] For several of our informants, staying close to family took a poignant turn when their music promised to be lucrative. Not only did Wanda Jackson receive her parents' permission to play a downtown ballroom; her career also moved to the center of her family's life when her father became her manager and her mother her costume designer.[61] Brenda Lee loved singing as a child and remembers enjoying the spotlight from the age of two or three, but for her, another big draw of the musical life was the chance to help her family financially after her father's death when she was nine.[62]

But the centrality of family, the crucial role family support has played in allowing young women to build their musical skills, has persisted over the decades. In late August 2001 a hundred girls aged eight through seventeen gathered nervously in the courtyard between two brick classroom buildings on the campus of Oregon's Portland State University. Bleary-eyed, heavy-laden, shy, noisy, they had all the earmarks of young teenagers reporting for the first day of camp, and indeed, they were. Only instead of tennis and canoeing, these girls would be studying rock music—specifically, how to make it—at the first-ever Girls Rock and Roll Camp. Instead of hefting their daughters' footlockers and backpacks, Mom and Dad were carrying newly bought electric guitars, basses, and drumsticks. A week later, at the camp's final performance gala at an all-ages nightclub in northeast Portland, families were even more in evidence than on that first morning, waiting patiently in a line stretching around the corner for the club to open its doors, chugging sodas in the stifling heat of the packed club interior, shooting home movies, and cheering at their daughters' amped-up debuts as rock divas.

Many of our respondents came not only from supportive families but also from musical families. Paz Lenchantin grew up with musical parents. So did Carol Kaye. "My mother was a piano player for a lot of the silent films . . . and my dad was a trombone player that played in the theaters around [Everett, Washington]."[63] Kitzie Pippin Stern, a rock and jazz vocalist, also recounts that her grandmother played organ for silent films. Her musical lineage goes back at least to her great-grandmother, also a singer. Her mother and father were singers, her mother professionally. The family, she remembers, always sang at home, and so it was a natural transition for her to form a madrigal group with her brother and sisters during the Philadelphia Bicentennial celebrations.[64] Emily Saliers also comes from a musical family. Her grandfather was a professional musician, and her parents are both musically accomplished. "When first I could remember anything, there was music. You know, we grew up listening to it in the house, listening to records, listening to the radio, public radio, and going to concerts and singing in the choirs and then taking lessons. I mean, it was just always there, like food. It fed us."[65]

Michelle Malone's mother and grandmother were singers. "I never really gave it much thought," Michelle says. "I was just going into the family business, you know." Her mother took her to her shows at clubs, and, on her nights off, they would see jazz shows.[66] Kate Schellenbach's mother was a singer-songwriter, and Kate not only took piano lessons but also picked up her mother's acoustic guitar. In addition, she and her sister immersed themselves in choir from age six through early high school. Even more remarkably, when a drum set happened into her life (a friend stored it in their apartment), her mother encouraged her to play. "My mom is pretty tolerant, and she was just happy that I was doing something musical or creative, and I was excited about it and I was sort of self-motivated." The neighbors too refrained from complaining. Soundproofing helped, as did the local ambience. "It was kind of a funky, artsy building, and everybody . . . you know, thought it was cute." [67]

Mary Wilson of the Supremes remembers her stepfather as her first musical educator. "From the time I can remember, probably 1950, all I ever heard was music. And . . . the earliest songs I remember were songs like LaVern Baker, 'Jim Dandy to the Rescue,' like Lloyd Price." This was her critical introduction to R&B (rhythm and blues). "My daddy was like an avid listener to all of it. You know, I virtually grew up with it in the household." [68]

Family encouragement can flourish even for a child who shows the only musical interest in the family—in fact, for her, it will be even more important for parents to support her talent and hard work. Rana Ross was the only musical person in her family, but her mother gave her a nylon-stringed guitar when she asked for it at age four, and sent her off for lessons at the Brooklyn Conservatory of Music. Her mother, young and single, also introduced her to the music of Led Zeppelin, Jimi Hendrix, and Elton John. [69] Rana exemplifies the artist growing up in a culture where rock has matured—a second-generation rocker schooled in the classics by parents whose youths were shaped by the alternative culture that took rock as its sound track. Similarly, Melissa Auf der Maur, bass player for Hole and Smashing Pumpkins, grew up in Montreal with a mother who was a rock journalist and a disc jockey. She immersed her daughter in the lore of classic rock. "She'd tell me all these great stories and show me the record covers." Like Kate Schellenbach, Melissa grew up in a neighborhood friendly to an alternative musical culture. "We lived in like a Bohemian kind of multicultural area in Montreal, and everybody just seemed to love music and . . . poetry." Melissa went to an experimental arts school and took trumpet, piano, and dance lessons. She remembers that her mother "made me feel like I could do anything." The arts felt open to her as living possibilities. "My mother was always inviting me into that world." [70]

Sisters and brothers have been as important as parents to a number of women artists. Kitzie Pippin formed a singing ensemble with hers. After gravitating to piano and then violin as a young child, in high school Tret Fure took over her older brother's guitar; now he tells the story, "I taught my sister how to play guitar and then the next week she started teaching me," she recalls. She and her brother later formed a coffeehouse duo and played around their Michigan hometown.[71] Jonatha Brooke attributes her first musical influence to her brothers, who brought home records by the Rolling Stones, Stevie Wonder, Joni Mitchell, the Who, Loggins and Messina, and the Mamas and the Papas.

Ann and Nancy Wilson grew up in a musical family. Nancy says, "We were from a military family, so we were always driving across the country singing songs in the car."[72] After being inspired by the Beatles to get guitars, the girls began to put bands together. "We come from a family that had no brothers, so we didn't really relate to boys at all. So we would get these girlfriends and teach them how to be in our band: 'Here. Here's a guitar, here's how you play it, go be in our band.' We had quite a few different bands, folk rock bands, playing all kinds of Simon and Garfunkel and Beatles songs, at churches, schools, and living rooms. We did a lot of living rooms—including our own!"[73]

June and Jean Millington, just a year apart, were connected by music very early. They both remember starting out on ukulele as kids in the Philippines. Then June moved on to guitar. "It was a neighborhood gang," Jean recalls, "friends that we were hanging out with." After they moved to the United States when June was thirteen and Jean twelve, the girls continued to play guitar, in part to assuage their loneliness and anxiety about not fitting into the junior high culture of Los Angeles. "Here we are from another country and we're half this and half that. . . . So June and I felt very much on the outside, and actually music ended up, I think, really saving us." They entered a talent contest with one of June's first songs, "I'm Miss Wallflower of 1962." In a nicely cinematic twist, that talent show was the sisters' social turning point. "A lot of people started paying attention to us." Their talent allowed them to ride the rising wave of the folk movement. A couple of years later, at fourteen and fifteen, they went electric against their father's wishes, sneaking out of the house with their mother, who signed for them at the store to buy their instruments.[74]

The Music Store: Friend or Foe

The music store seems to be a peculiarly active site for the gendering of rock 'n' roll. Many women guitar and bass players relate tales of being ignored, harassed, and insulted by the young male clerks who typically populate music store staffs. In the mid-1960s Jean Millington was "completely intimidated" when she went into a music store to buy her first bass. "At that point, you know, women just didn't do that. If you were a folkie, that was more or less acceptable. You went in there and you bought an acoustic guitar." But, she explains, if a woman picked up an electric instrument, "Of course, all eyes in the store are on you. 'What's she think she's doing?'" Now, she says she is still a little intimidated when she goes into a music store, but the difference is that now she actually knows she's a great bass player. "So when I pick [a bass] up [in a music store] and do something, people kind of go, 'Oh, shit! She actually knows what she's doing.'"[75]

Theorists have argued that the creation and use of space is a key factor in the construction and maintenance of gender.[76] Male spaces, such as music stores, define and reinforce male identity, especially through its opposition to women.[77] Erin O'Hara describes music stores as "a very masculine environment."[78] Bitch explains, "You've got like a thousand guys sitting there doodling around. And they're all taking themselves very seriously. And so for a long time I would never play in the store."[79] In most human cultures men have dominated public spaces, while women have been relegated to the private sphere of home and family. Even in the last half-century of rapid social change in the United States, when women have attempted to enter male spaces, they have faced great resistance. Erin tells a story of going to a music store with her husband. Each time she asked a technical question, especially about studio equipment, the clerk responded to her husband. At last, he told the clerk, "I don't work in music. Tell her."

At that first Rock and Roll Camp for Girls in Portland, Carla DeSantis relayed a similar music store experience. "Trying to purchase gear in the music store wasn't much better. Whenever one of us would try to get a clerk's attention, we were asked, 'Are you getting this for your boyfriend?'" She adds, "I remember one time I went into a music store with a male friend of mine to buy a bass. There were some teenage boys playing really, really loud. I reached to get a bass off the wall to try out, and the clerk ran over to me and shouted, 'Don't touch that!'" Carla was twenty-seven at the time and had been playing professionally for about eight years. "It was clear that the reason he didn't want me to touch it was because he didn't think I knew how to handle it. My friend and I both left the store surprised and a little bit shocked that the clerk didn't mind the kids playing but wouldn't let me touch the merchandise."[80]

Male spaces also reinforce male dominance by using exclusion as a means to minimize competition and increase men's likelihood of success. By denying women access to male spheres, men ensure their continued dominance over women.[81] When Jill Sobule entered the exclusive back room of the Guitar Center in Los Angeles, where the "fancy-ass" guitars are kept, the young male clerk approached her and said, "You know these are for professionals" (at the time, Sobule had a Gretsch endorsement).[82] Singer-songwriter

Emily White explains, "Guitar stores are the worst, always. There were never any women working in them and still rarely are. I worked in a guitar store for a while, and none of the customers took me seriously until I started talking about gear. It's always that way—whether you're playing or recording or selling or buying, you always have to prove yourself."[83] Ani DiFranco concurs. "For many, many years, simply walking into a guitar store was almost an act of courage, because it was very much a boys' club. They would kinda look you up and down and say, 'Hi, honey, are you here to get something for your boyfriend?' "[84]

Kate Schellenbach says she was terrified to go into Manny's or Sam Ash to buy drumsticks. "I resisted buying drumsticks for the first four years that I played. I would just find them on the stage or under the stage, or if somebody threw them [into] the audience, I'd make sure to get them because I just couldn't deal [with having to go into a music store to buy them]. I think part of my fear was that they would find out that I didn't know what I was doing, because, you know, you're constantly feeling defensive as a woman about your craft, especially if it's something male-dominated."[85]

Beth Rippey, co-owner of Jackson's Music in Winston-Salem, North Carolina, tries to ensure that girls and women like Jill, Emily, Ani, and Kate feel welcome in her store. Realizing that the music store can be an intimidating place for females, she and her business partner Mari-Jo Dryden insist that their employees treat customers equally and with respect, regardless of gender, no matter if they are buying a twenty-five-cent pick or a $2,500 guitar. Beth believes the mindset of the management sets the tone, and she loves when customers come in and want to cross stereotypical gender lines. Approaching one older woman browsing the guitar section, Beth assumed the woman was looking for a guitar for herself. When asked what kind of guitar she would like, the woman responded that it was for her grandson who was in another part of the store.

Not only are Beth's female patrons buying music, they are also taking private lessons in her store. Of 309 weekly students, 120 are female, and many of those are learning to play guitar or drums. Fifty-eight percent of their piano students, 30 percent of their guitar students, and 18 percent of their percussion students are female. As a sixth grader in a private school without a band program, Becky Dickson decided that she wanted to make the prestigious drum line at a local public school, Mt. Tabor. She took private snare drum lessons at Jackson's and not only made the percussion line but also became the drum captain of this award-winning group of musicians.[86] Unlike a young Kate Schellenbach, she will not be looking under the stage for drumsticks, at least as long as Jackson's is in business.

015 Waltrip H.S. Library

In quiet Corvallis, Oregon, a haven for musicians of all genres, Kurt and Guy of Valley Music have maintained Mina's (unimpressive) guitar collection for a decade. They tolerate her regular visits to the Larrivee of her dreams, and they do not hesitate to tell her honestly when they believe she has made a bad gear choice—which she has been known to do. All three of the music stores in Corvallis are women-friendly, and parents will have to take their girls out of town if they are looking for the traditional misogynistic experience. Times have changed, at least in these stores in Oregon and North Carolina, from the days when female customers stayed at home, dreading scorn and intimidation.

Bitch says that now when she goes into a guitar store, she plays. "I started to realize that part of so much of what we are doing and what our success has been comes from us being women because I think that we do have a new voice." So now, she says, when she takes down a bass in a store, "I like sort of puff up my feathers a little, and I feel really proud."[87]

In the face of cultural expectations, social constraints, and active opposition, many women have laid claim to the right to identify themselves as rock musicians, and for many of them, the first movement toward that resistant identity has been to pick up a rock instrument. As they have developed proficiency with their instruments, they have been able to say, sometimes with the help of friends and sometimes at first only to themselves, "I am a drummer," "I am a bass player," "I am a guitar player." In the next chapter, we look specifically at how these gendered identities are shaped and complicated by intersections with race and sexuality.

CHAPTER 2

SEX, RACE, AND ROCK 'N' ROLL

Why don't we just say it? Men are still ruling the world.

—*Mary Wilson*

A visionary promoter, Dick Clark combined what was right with what sold. Running mixed-race caravans of "stars" through the segregated South in the early 1960s, he pushed the edges of America's rigid racial envelope. Some performers paid a higher price than others. Mary Wilson of The Supremes remembers one of Clark's Southern bus tours around 1964. "Many places we were not allowed to come in. They said that the white groups could come in, but the black groups would have to go. So Dick Clark was really a great guy.... And he said, 'Well, if you can't take everybody, we'll all go someplace else.'" The Supremes were already veterans of Southern touring, participating in the earlier Motown Review tours, which came with no protection but luck and the growing reputation of the Detroit music powerhouse. One night in the Carolinas, Wilson remembers, "we were all getting on the bus, and there were gunshots. So everyone started scrambling to get on the bus. . . . And once we got out of that proximity . . . everyone started singing, and then finally we stopped and looked and there were definitely gunshots on the windshields." She shrugs off the chilling memory. "The majority of us were from the South and obviously had been to the South, and you knew of all these things anyway."[1]

In the 1950s, rock 'n' roll, like its enveloping culture, was men's terrain. Rock was also, ironically, white terrain—ironically because, of course, the musical and lyrical languages of rock were those of the rebel and the outsider, and the building blocks of rock 'n' roll were jazz, blues, and gospel

music—all written in the syntax of black American experience. While dominant social groups may appropriate, recombine, and redefine cultural expressions like jazz and blues music, subordinate groups—and this is
somewhat odd—find themselves assigned the cultural task of carrying certain attributes that are in fact logically, and by definition, universal. Thus in
American society blacks, not whites, have *race,* women, not men, have *gender,* and gays, not straights, have a *sexual orientation.* By this rule, women in
rock have been forbidden to sidestep daily decisions and rationalizations
about how they construct themselves as racial and sexual beings, and how
they negotiate and understand the peculiar intersections and interactions
of race, gender, and sexuality. This chapter explores that story, or those overlapping and intertwined stories, from the early days of Motown and Scepter
Records through DaBrat's platinum breakthrough, and from Brenda Lee's
innocent years as a child pop star through the playful and celebratory sexuality of Rana Ross and The Butchies.

To return to the road—veterans of the black girl groups tell depress-
ingly similar touring stories, stories that echo the tales of itinerant blues
players and jazz bands of earlier years. Shirley Alston Reeves recalls The
Shirelles' early touring, sometimes with the Dick Clark Caravan of Stars
and sometimes on their own. The stars of Florence Greenberg's Scepter
Records, based in New Jersey, The Shirelles had a couple of big hits with
Luther Dixon songs (including "Tonight's the Night," written by Shirley
Owens—later Shirley Alston Reeves—and arranged by Dixon), and then in
1960 went over the top with the Gerry Goffin/Carole King song "Will You
Still Love Me Tomorrow." Even after charting with "Mama Said," "Baby It's
You," and "Soldier Boy," they continued to play out-of-the-way Southern
venues hosted by college kids.[2] "This is just the way it was," Alston Reeves
recalls. One Georgia fraternity rented a remote tobacco warehouse for one
of these wet parties. While the white male guests started drinking, the black
women artists changed in a dressing room rigged of sheets hung over wires.
Their powerful bodyguard, Ronnie, stood outside. Two college men wan-
dered back and demanded to enter the dressing room. Ronnie blocked the
way. The trio argued. Hearing trouble outside, the women started pulling
their clothes on as fast as they could. They heard the boys say, "Oh, the hell
with it. Let's charge him. We can take him." Alston Reeves recalls that the
boys "didn't know what they were running into. Like a brick wall. So he
takes 'em both, grabs 'em by the back, and cracks 'em. Cracks 'em. Cracks
their heads together like that. And they're like, boom, on the floor."[3] Alston
Reeves remembers big Ronnie in a kind of trance. Strong enough to kill the
young men, he had hoisted one of them over his head when Shirley begged

him, crying and screaming, to just put the kid down. There was more fear than charity behind her plea. "I said, 'If you don't put him down we may get killed or something down here. . . . We're way back in the woods!' " The bodyguard finally set the boy on the floor, just as their hosts returned. When they apologized to the Shirelles and sent the drunken attackers home in a van, Shirley remembers thinking, "Well, maybe things are looking up." Yet on another horrific occasion on a Southern highway at night, the group's car was followed out of town and repeatedly edged off the road by white men who pulled up beside them and aimed a pistol at their windows. In an episode of terrorism so familiar in the Jim Crow South, "they just held that gun on our car it seemed like for the longest time." Finally, the white men drove away, leaving the women huddled crying in their own car. "Aw, I said, 'God, I never want to come here again.' . . . Probably the next week we were down South again. We used to play the South a lot. Yeah, because they liked it."[4]

Martha Reeves reminded us that the Motown tours coincided with the Freedom Rides, aimed at desegregating interstate bus terminals. "Same scenario. Black people on a bus. So they figured we were the same people, ones that came to picket or march or whatever. And they turned us around at different facilities." She too tells the story of a gun. "One gas station attendant put a shotgun, I'd never seen the barrel of a shotgun, but he put it right up on the bus and told us, 'Don't get off.' And that's a horrible thing, looking down the barrel of a shotgun. You can see it in the movies, but it's not the same as when it's right up in your face."[5]

Sarah Dash of Patti LaBelle and the Bluebelles (later LaBelle) recalls her parents packing lunches for her when she was going to be on the road because they knew she couldn't eat in a restaurant in the South. "We'd have to stay in the black side of town in black hotels, whereas we watched the white groups go off and stay at the better hotels. And we'd have to go sometimes staying in rooming houses that people just provided for artists who were coming to town." When they played the all-white colleges, the only "black people you see [were] serving the food." Sarah tried not to let segregation embitter her. "It didn't affect my thinking because I came home to a minister's home that [welcomed] black, white, all kinds of people. . . . There was always different people sitting at our table."[6]

Mary Wells first confronted overt Southern racism in New Orleans in the Freedom Rides era. In city hall on a hot day, she stopped to drink from the water fountain. "All these people started lookin' at me. And me, so much a fool. I say to myself, 'Oh, they know who I am, I'm Mary Wells.' Then I look up and see the sign. Yeah, you got it. WHITE ONLY. Me in my little Motown star bubble. All of a sudden everything kind of crushes."[7]

Of course, the South was only the flagship of white American racism. At the high tide of the Civil Rights Movement of the 1960s, the music of the black girl groups played a part in changing the racial landscape of the United States. Though most of these women sought artistic expression, stardom, security, and a good time, rather than social change, they put themselves in the public eye, and on the white-controlled public highways, in acts of personal courage that deserve recognition. Though it took more than R&B to erode white-imposed racial barriers, early rock music profoundly affected the ways both white and black American teenagers constructed their identities. Teens imitated rock 'n' roll singers in their dress and demeanor; they challenged and annoyed their parents by attending concerts and events like Alan Freed's Moondog Coronation Ball; and of course they filled the coffers of the music and movie businesses as they pursued the sounds and images of their idols. Popular music, economic change, and intentional reform movements symbiotically pushed American society closer to accepting racial equality as a social goal.

Rock 'n' roll was a commercial phenomenon, but it was also a story of convergences. Charismatic white disc jockeys Dewey Phillips of Memphis and Alan Freed of Cleveland put black R&B on the radio where white kids could hear it. Jerry Leiber and Mike Stoller, Jewish city boys whose families had relocated to Los Angeles, teamed up to write rhythm and blues songs that stood on the shoulders of the jazz, blues, and boogie they had both loved since they were kids.[8] Black songwriters like Holland/Dozier/Holland were joined by white songwriters—Gerry Goffin and Carole King, Barry Mann and Cynthia Weil, Ellie Greenwich—in creating R&B and doo-wop hits.[9] And while accounts of rock history rightly showcase these innovators and rule-breakers, communities of kids simultaneously created their own sounds, neither "black" nor "white," but a mash of American popular styles that issued in something a little bit new under the sun.

At the same time *Brown v. Board of Education* (1954) declared school segregation unconstitutional, doo-wop groups multiplied in the streets and stairwells of black communities in New York, Chicago, Detroit, and other American cities.[10] In her memoir *Dreamgirl*, Mary Wilson describes the scope of the phenomenon: "Every local street corner was occupied by trios, quartets, and quintets of kids teaching themselves the intricate harmonies they picked up off current hit records by the Platters, the Drifters, the Coasters, the Cleftones, the Flamingos, Mickey & Sylvia, Elvis Presley, and others.... By 1956 every major city's black ghetto housed hundreds of young singing hopefuls, the vast majority of whom, I thought, were living in the Brewster Projects."[11] Kids were doing it for themselves. Often well-taught in school, at church, and at home, they took their formal and informal musical training into new or "morphed" musical forms. Most groups were male, but by the late 1950s girls had eagerly joined the competition. Sometimes they followed the "women's auxiliary" model, taking a boys' group as their patrons or companions. In eighth grade, Mary Wilson jumped at her friend Florence Ballard's invitation to start a "sister" group to the Primes, a male group that became the Temptations. The Supremes began their musical lives as Primettes.

Church and Family Influences

The Supremes' early history underlines these vocal harmony groups as a creative outlet many families encouraged. When Mary Wilson sought her mother's approval to join Florence and two other girls, Betty McGlown and (then) Diane Ross, she was pretty confident she would get it. "My mother was relieved that I would have my free time occupied by something constructive. This would keep me off the streets, and she would know where to find me at all times."[12]

Many families not only welcomed but hosted their children's musical beginnings. For Ronnie Bennett Spector, music was definitely a family affair. She and her sister Estelle and cousin Nedra Talley began singing to entertain their huge clan at family get-togethers. In *Be My Baby*, Ronnie recalled childhood weekends at her grandmother's with her aunts and uncles "stag[ing] little amateur shows." Harmony singing, accordion, ballet, and comic routines filled the house. When Ronnie was eight, one of her uncles shined a makeshift spotlight on her as she sang "Jambalaya."[13] "I looked around the room and saw all my aunts and uncles smiling and tapping their feet to keep time. . . . When it was over I got down and sat on the rug between my sister and Nedra. That's it, I thought. That's the feeling I want for the rest of my life."[14]

Thus like other women we interviewed, the women who formed the "girl groups" of the fifties and sixties remember family influences at the core of their early music education. In addition, their churches, schools, and especially peers, created an atmosphere saturated with music.

Many commentators have noted the centrality of sacred music in black communities. Churches hosted the crucial intertwining of musical exposure and performance, community solidarity and creative individuation, and spiritual and secular languages.[15] For many women, this institutional venue has made it possible to *imagine* musical careers. While women have been silenced or suppressed in many churches' ministries, they have often found a voice in church music.

For Martha Reeves, church and family were inseparable. "My grand-father, being a Methodist minister, made sure that we were always at church. And at the age of three, me and my two older brothers won some candy singing in a competition." Earning her mother's praise by remembering the carefully taught words and music, "I knew I had something."[16] Church provided an opportunity for that "something" to shine. Sarah Dash, the daughter of a Pentecostal minister, grew up with the music of Sister Rosetta Tharpe and the Clara Ward Singers. "My father didn't really want us to have any-thing but gospel music . . . [but] my brother at times would play different kinds of music when my father wasn't around." Sarah moved on to rock 'n' roll as part of a teenage rebellion. "You know when they tell you you can't have that ice cream over there, you're sure to do that." She listened to records of The Shirelles, The Del Capris, and Brenda Lee at friends' houses and sang rock 'n' roll songs in the junior high locker room.[17]

Recognizing the appeal of black gospel music to audiences beyond churchgoers, record producers saw a financial opportunity in the music that had been performed primarily in churches. John Hammond organized "From Spirituals to Swing," a 1938 musical extravaganza at Carnegie Hall featuring Mitchell's Christian Singers and Sister Rosetta Tharpe. Until then, Tharpe had performed only in black churches, with the exception of one performance at the Cotton Club in Harlem, but she excited the Carnegie Hall audience and began to appear regularly in nightclubs and theaters.[18] Ignoring disapproval from her church, in the 1940s Tharpe combined gos-pel and popular music in songs that appeared on the "race" (later renamed R[hythm] & B[lues]) charts.[19] Tharpe was an original, a deft and lively guitar player, and a compelling popular interpreter of formerly "sacred" music.[20]

Gospel's first female group formed in 1934, when Gertrude Ward or-ganized herself and her daughters Willa and Clara into Gertrude and Daugh-ters. The group eventually became the Famous Ward Singers, with a changing lineup behind Clara as the frontwoman.[21] Like Sister Rosetta Tharpe, Clara Ward and her Singers performed in secular venues. "Although perhaps there are many people who would not share my feelings on the subject," Ward declared, "I now feel that God intended for his message to be heard in song not solely by those who attend churches, but also by the outsiders who in many cases never attend a house of worship."[22]

One of the greatest gospel singers chose not to cross the line between sacred and secular.[23] A secret devotee of blues singer Bessie Smith, Mahalia Jackson insisted that her own music was not meant for nightclubs. "I felt all mixed up," she recalled, when a music teacher told her to change her vocal style to appeal to white audiences. "How could I sing songs for white people to understand when I was colored myself? It didn't seem to make any sense. It was a battle within me to sing a song in a formal way. I felt it was too polished, and I didn't feel good about it."[24] And so Jackson continued to sing in her unique voice, moaning, shouting, growling, singing the blues in gospel.

"Honey, there ain't no difference" between blues and gospel, the great Sippie Wallace declared. "In the church we say Jesus, and in the blues we say baby."[25] Both Clara Ward and Mahalia Jackson frequently called on Pastor C. L. Franklin of the New Bethel Baptist Church in Detroit, where they joined other musicians in mentoring his young daughter, Aretha. [26] Aretha Franklin became one of the seminal musicians who carried sacred music into the popular realm. Her hit tunes were essentially gospel, bringing all of its passion, strength, and soul to lyrics about earthly love and black women's self-determination.

Melding gospel with rhythm and blues, soul music became a liberatory artistic response to white racism. Within a couple of years in the mid-1960s, a climate change overtook American racial discourse. Black Power activists challenged the suddenly old-line civil rights leadership. Inner cities exploded with riots sparked by long-suffered police brutality, business "red-lining," unemployment, and the daily indignities of being black in white America. Many whites suspected that the Vandellas' joyous hit, "Dancing in the Streets," called angry blacks to revolution. As Aretha spelled out "R-E-S-P-E-C-T," *Ebony* writer David Llorens called 1967 "the summer of 'Retha, Rap and Revolt."[27]

With Aretha Franklin, however, soul music crossed over to white audiences. While "I Never Loved a Man" reached number nine on the pop charts (number one on the R&B charts), "Respect" quickly climbed to the top of both. In the next two years, Aretha had another twelve Top 40 singles and four Top 20 albums. The early gospel influences and unending hard work blossomed into a now-legendary career.

School Days

Pop singers of the fifties and sixties were also fundamentally influenced by school music programs. "I always was in musical classes at school," Mary Wilson tells us. "From the time I was in kindergarten I was in . . . the choirs and the glee clubs and all that in school." She recalls a school choir competition in Detroit when she was about eight: the imposing "museum type" Ford Auditorium, the excitement. "We were one of the choirs that were chosen, and that was my first experience . . . singing publicly and knowing that this was something different than what I had been doing at home."[28] Martha Reeves recalls being singled out by the church "elders" and encouraged by her public school teachers. In elementary school Mrs. Wagstaff chose Martha to teach the other children the patriotic anthems. At Northeastern High School in Detroit, she studied music with Abraham Silver, who also taught Mary Wilson and Florence Ballard as well as Bobby Rogers, later of the Miracles. "He taught all of us . . . basic vocal and taught us all to read [music], which I think was the best thing that ever happened with my public education because it gave me a career."[29]

For Shirley Alston Reeves both church and school singing created a comfort level with music. She also remembers the fun of singing with her friend Beverly Lee when they were babysitting together. They listened to the Chantels and Little Anthony and the Imperials—groups that had cut singles and made it onto radio. "We wanted to . . . get a sound like this group sound." To achieve the harmony they were after, they drafted two more childhood friends: Micki Harris, and then Doris Jackson, the daughter of a preacher who developed her "real strong voice" in church choirs. Their first big break came in school when they were singing together, "fooling around," and one of their teachers recruited them for the talent show.[30]

Their new group, The Shirelles, soon influenced other girls singing after school and in the hallways between classes. Inspired by the success of other groups their age, Mary Wilson and her friends became emboldened to take the next step to professionalism. "1956," she recalls, "we started going to the rock 'n' roll movies and started seeing the people like Little Richard, and there were the Clovers . . . the Skylarks and all these different people. And I started just looking at music differently than I had before. . . . This was the first time I saw people who were not so far ahead of me."[31]

Ronnie Bennett Spector brushed up against young fame in the flesh when she learned that her idol, Frankie Lymon, also lived in Harlem and ate at the diner where her mother worked. Her mother inveigled the fourteen-year-old Lymon into coming to Ronnie's thirteenth birthday party. He arrived late, smelling of alcohol, and sat down close to her on the couch. She fled and waited out his visit in the bathroom. Even his precocious depravity (poor Lymon, out of the spotlight by eighteen, died of an overdose in his twenties) failed to put Ronnie off his incredible voice. "In spite of how Frankie turned out, I still loved his singing. I played his records and sang along with them until I knew every note by heart."[32]

Gordy's Girls

"Until Motown," Mary Wells once said, "there were three big careers for a black girl. Babies, factories or daywork. Period."[33] Yet before her death in

1992, Mary Wells spent years in court trying to recapture money from her brief and spectacular career at Motown. Berry Gordy, Motown's founder and a commercial genius, created opportunity. Yet he also, in a sense, took it away. At sixteen, Mary Wells found her way to Gordy hoping to sell him her tune "Bye Bye Baby." Instead he signed *her* to sing the song, and from 1962 to 1964 she worked with producer Smokey Robinson and became Motown's first woman star. At twenty-one she left, seeking greater independence. She confessed to Gerri Hirshey in 1984 that no other record company offered her Motown's tight creative "family" feeling.[34]

In her fluent history of women in rock, *She Bop*, Lucy O'Brien also portrays the ambivalent and charged relationships of the Motown women singers with Gordy and his empire. First of all, Motown was a *black* company. Though whites also figured on Gordy's management team, as Gerald Posner deftly recounts, Motown was essentially owned, operated, and creatively driven by black individuals.[35] In its early years Motown offered an open door to kids wandering in and hanging around, hoping to catch somebody's attention. Martha Reeves came wanting to sing and ended up the A&R secretary before she worked her way into the artistic lineup. Mary Wilson and her friends dogged Gordy and his producers until they signed the young, talented group.[36] Motown operated from a house—literally, a house in a black Detroit neighborhood—where black kids could walk in the front door. "We tried to learn as much as we could," Mary Wilson recalls, "and in those days there were plenty of people to watch; young performers seemed to find their way there in droves. The negative rumors about Motown deterred very few; it was still one of the few places in Detroit a young musician or singer could make a buck or get the chance to really succeed."[37]

Performers had mixed experiences with Motown founder Berry Gordy. On the one hand, he had opened up opportunities for black musicians. Motown created hugely successful stars with crossover music that appealed to both black and white audiences. On the other, Gordy exacted a high price, controlling his performers' names, image, music, and money and dropping them when his attention turned elsewhere. "Of course other labels treated their artists badly," Mary Wilson writes in her preface to *Supreme Faith;* "we all knew that. We also thought Motown was different."[38]

Gordy controlled both his female and male performers. Even the names of the groups belonged to Motown, and when performers left the label, they left their names. Gordy also controlled their money, providing performers with only a portion of their earnings and requiring them to seek permission to buy cars or real estate. In 1977 Mary Wilson sued Motown for taking advantage of her in those agreements made when she was a minor. As part of the settlement, Wilson won 50 percent of the rights to usage and interest in The Supremes' name.

More Education: "Class" Not Dismissed

Perhaps one of the most innovative ways in which Gordy controlled Motown artists, especially the women, was through Artist Development. For the Motown women this was the famed charm school in which young black female performers learned to stand, walk, sit, eat, dress, talk, and perform like "ladies." If Gordy were to achieve his crossover goals, he knew that these lively, spontaneous young women, many of them high school kids, had to be acceptable to the bourgeois pretensions of a white-dominated society. They had to be "classy." According to Diana Ross, during the first Motortown Revue in 1964 "they wouldn't let us off the bus until everybody had their makeup on. It was the day of the beehive, and your hair had to stay teased up like that for days."[39] Notably, the performers speak fondly of their "charm school" teacher Maxine Powell, who left her own business to work at Motown, and they express appreciation for the doors the charm school opened for them. These young women found themselves whisked from the projects to the sometimes glitzy, sometimes grueling routines of international performers in New York, California, London, and Paris. Nothing in their lives had prepared them to go so far in so short a time. In *Dreamgirl,* Mary Wilson recalls, " 'Young ladies always . . .' was the stock opening phrase for Mrs. Powell's direction. Hats and gloves were mandatory attire for the girls around Motown, and she often lectured us about clothes. Since Flo, Diane, and I already had devoted years to creating our own unique and sophisticated style, we quickly became Mrs. Powell's star pupils. Attendance in Artist Development was never mandatory. We went because we loved it."[40]

Martha Reeves concurs. She once told Lucy O'Brien: "I remember Miss [*sic*] Powell gave a speech to all the girls in the class—The Marvelettes, Mary Wells, Claudette Robinson, us, and The Supremes, we were all gathered together. 'You're not the prettiest girls in the world,' she said. 'You're not the best singers. But what I'm going to teach you will give you all the charm, finesse and glamour you need to take you through the rest of your life.' We rolled around on the floor with laughter. She stayed firm. 'It'll take you all over the world, if you apply yourself.' "[41] Reeves said she "loved" the "Motown experience," akin to a university education for a performer. Music, choreography, deportment, it was wraparound mentorship. Of course, another time, Reeves told Gerri Hirshey, "Now we were doing just fine before all this. I mean, I don't think I ever offended anyone with my *eating* habits."[42]

Perhaps most problematic for the girl groups was Gordy's willingness to drop girls when his attention turned elsewhere in the quest for the perfect group. While the Vandellas, Marvelettes, and Velvelettes turned out hits for Motown, no one of these groups measured up to Gordy's ideal. Despite The Marvelettes' run of Top 10 hits in the early 1960s, they quickly lost Gordy's attention. Marvelettes founder Gladys Horton attributes Gordy's change to his perception that the girls from Inkster, Michigan, were "hicks from the sticks." "We weren't pretty city girls from the projects like The Supremes, with nice clothes and make-up on and long nails."[43] Martha Reeves recalls, "Nobody was competing at first. We were all hopefuls, all wannabes. We were sisters, and the early Motown Revues were like camping tours or girl scouts. . . . The rivalry started when the groups were separated off, and Berry selected Diana Ross and The Supremes as his favourite [*sic*] pet group."[44]

Within The Supremes, Gordy eventually focused his attention on Diana Ross. This favoritism redounded most poignantly on Florence Ballard, the group's founder. Ballard's deep, bluesy voice could easily dominate the other Supremes, and in order to highlight Ross's thinner, higher, poppy voice, Motown producers downplayed Ballard's, eventually forcing both Ballard and Mary Wilson into essentially backup roles for Ross. Ballard began to express her resentment, drinking heavily and showing up late for rehearsals and press conferences. She had to be replaced in one show when she was too drunk to perform. In 1967 Gordy fired Ballard, replaced her with Cindy Birdsong, and changed the name of the group to Diana Ross and The Supremes, emphasizing the extent to which Ross had really become the act.[45]

Ballard's initial settlement with Motown provided her with only $2,500 a year for six years. She gave up any claim on The Supremes' name, and she no longer received royalties. An attorney helped her gain a larger settlement. She signed with ABC records, but her singles did not do well, and about that time her attorney cheated her out of most of her money. She lost her home and had to go on welfare to support her three children. In 1976, at the age of thirty-two, Ballard died of a heart attack.

Sexuality: Subtle but Salable

Like Phil Spector, Gordy built girl group images that relied on particular intersections of race and gender. In an acutely race-conscious society, whites' reception of the black girl groups was shaped by stereotypes, including culturally transmitted ideas of black sexual behavior as wild and uninhibited. While the (white) Shangri-Las could pout for and flirt with the audience, The Supremes, Crystals, Dixie Cups, Marvelettes, Ronettes, Velvelettes, and others experienced greater constraints on their personae. Their producers—and they themselves—chose to project more subtle, often more mature, feminine sexual images. In earlier decades, when black blues singers performed primarily for black audiences, they could overtly express sexuality. Angela Davis suggests that the blues music of the 1920s and 1930s differed from other American popular music in its explicit attention to sexuality (including homosexuality).[46] She argues that the representations of love and sexuality in the blues performed by black women contradicted dominant notions of love, sexuality, and woman's place in the domestic sphere. In the blues, black women asserted their right to independence, fulfillment, and sexual desire.

But when blacks began to perform for whites, they had to subdue the sexual elements of their performances. Diana Ross thinks, for example, that Gordy made a wise decision in limiting the overt sexuality of the girl groups. Perhaps the more restrained Motown style had the paradoxical effect of licensing white fantasies. "Someone said," Ross comments, "and I agree with him, that The Supremes were such a crossover for young black and white males in our country because there were three black girls and they could openly enjoy them and even lust for them—without thinking what color they were."[47]

Sexual Personae

As a very young girl from Lithonia, Georgia, Brenda Lee believes she escaped being sexually objectified, at least in conventional ways. "I started out so young that I was insulated from a lot of that because of my age."[48] Performing and recording before puberty, she appealed to her audiences as a cute little kid with a load of talent: a kind of novelty act. Lee's managers initially hesitated to let her release "I'm Sorry" at the age of fifteen. Despite their fears that the ballad was too mature for Lee, the record reached number one, selling more than ten million copies.[49] In the midst of her success, Brenda Lee avoided sexual exploitation, but she was one of the fortunate ones.

To a great degree, the (white, male) sexuality of rock 'n' roll results from the social processes and relationships that construct gender and sexuality. As Judith Butler suggests, gender itself is performative.[50] Gender exists only in combinations of gestures, acts, clothes, and other signifiers that *rep-*

resent "male" and "female." On the whole, rock 'n' roll has provided a stage on which masculinity and male sexuality have been enacted. Bearing out Catharine A. MacKinnon's argument that "[a] woman . . . identifies and is identified as one whose sexuality exists for someone else, who is socially male," not only women as depicted by rock music, but also women rock performers, have generally been sexual objects rather than sexual actors.[51] Kate Campbell believes that musicians "have to have a certain sexual persona."[52] June Millington, whose all-women rock band Fanny reached international prominence in the early 1970s, says that the difference for her between playing in Fanny and then women's music (code term for "lesbian" and generally acoustic) later in her career was that she "didn't feel objectified sexually onstage. I mean I know that that goes on, certainly. But I didn't feel it coming at me in the same way."[53] Her sister Jean Millington puts it more bluntly. The record companies, she says, "wanted to emphasize the tits and ass."[54] And, of course, for the half-Filipino sisters, their sexual objectification was complicated by racial stereotypes (exotic and erotic).

In the late 1960s some feminists argued that the sexual revolution of that decade added up to male access to unlimited numbers of women sexual partners. The sexual revolution affected women and men quite differently, because the "new" sexual codes perpetuated gendered sexual scripts, including the one that privileged male sexual pleasure. On the whole, rock 'n' roll continued to follow this script, with brutal results for many women trying to break in. "Dyke. Whore. Slut," Joan Jett remembers being called. "The women were like, 'Get away,' and the men were like, 'Dyke, whore, slut.'" The *Rolling Stone* reporter asks why this cascade of abuse? "What do you think?" she asks wearily. "Let me try to explain. Say that you were a guy, and we're sitting here having drinks and talking. And you start coming on to me. You're the guy that thinks I'm a whore or a slut. But I rebuff you. So what am I now? A dyke."[55]

In the 1980s, male rockers' lyrics and performances were captured and intensified in the new music-video format, which soared in popularity with the launch of MTV (Music Television) in 1981. Music video overwhelmed viewers with largely gratuitous images of scantily clad women. It has always been difficult to choose which is more offensive: videos that show women in submissive sexual poses for no reason related to the song's narrative, or videos in which women act out a song's misogynistic lyrics. In the documentary film *Dreamworlds II,* filmmaker Sut Jhally argues that music videos connect these hyper-sexualized images of women to sexual (and racially based) violence against women.[56] Women performers feel pressure to shape their images to fit the gendered script of women's sexuality and thus often position themselves not as sexual actors but as sexual objects for the gaze of male fans.

Of course, many women performers refuse to accept these gendered scripts and instead construct themselves to perform and defy gender at the same time. While sexuality seems to be one of the defining characteristics of rock, some women experience its sexual messages as liberating rather than confining of self and desire. Indigo Girl Emily Saliers traces her sexual awakening to Heart's "Magic Man":

> Emily Saliers: It was the first song that ever scared me, I think. It was like in eighth grade. . . . It was awesome. It was awesome.
> Amy Ray: It was a sexual awakening.
> Emily Saliers: It was, no doubt! Like, "Oh, what do I do? This song is making me feel weird."[57]

Kate Schellenbach argues, "It's really empowering to see a strong woman who's like sexy and rocking and all that. I mean, I don't think you could ever desexualize rock 'n' roll."[58] And Melissa Auf der Maur contends that rock allows her to express both her masculine and feminine sides. She compares playing rock music to sex: "The most intimate thing I will ever do is to play music with people and in front of people, other than making love to somebody." On the one hand, she suggests, rock "definitely brings out the male in me" because rock is an aggressive form that has typically been defined as male. On the other hand, she argues that rock music is feminine because it draws on emotions and the subconscious. Playing rock music, she says, is "letting out your demon sometimes and letting out your sexual side sometimes. . . . I'd say there's definitely some masculine and sexual and spiritual stuff going on all at once."[59]

Women rockers have dealt with sexuality in a variety of ways, from overtly embracing their identity as sexual actors, to intentionally defying the beauty norm, to coming out of the closet, to ironically exaggerating stereotypical female sexuality. Rana Ross, the (tragically) late, quite great bassist, acknowledged that she enjoyed the way audience members—male and female alike—looked at her in a sexual way. She said rock breaks down walls by blurring the lines of sexual desire: "When you're a female and you're standing onstage, you know there's not just guys looking at you; there's women looking at you. There's women looking at you in a sexual way. There's women looking at you in a way of awe. . . . Men to men, women to women, everybody, all mixed, everything mixed. And that's the beautiful thing about it.... It crosses all ... gender stratifications and all racial stratifications.... That's what I love about it. You know, it just breaks down the walls, and it brings people together. And if I can do that for one second, then I've done my job."[60]

Many women rock musicians, especially young alternative rockers, have chosen to flout beauty conventions as a feminist political statement or as simply another way to rebel against the dominant culture. Even the Butchies' name points to their refusal to conform to stereotypical feminine images. The cover of their 1998 album "Are We Not Femme?" exemplifies their desire to parody "feminine beauty" with their short skirts, bobby socks, and pink wigs, a look that belies the identity of the group. Even their coquettish posture in the photo intentionally exaggerates the flirtatious image projected by so many women performers. Neckties, combat boots, work suits, and "masculine" uniforms are more typical of the group's look, and they appeal to many young lesbians seeking identity outside the mainstream.

Many feminist theorists argue that lesbian sexuality challenges patriarchal norms by refusing to define women in relation to men.[61] For lesbians in rock, the terrain has been tricky. According to Janis Ian, "If sexual orientation is a factor at all, it's because it makes you more of an outsider to have a different sexual orientation. And being an outsider is what most artists are."[62] While lesbians in the women's music scene have pretty much always been out, mainstream performers mostly stayed in the closet, fearing the loss of their sales, popularity, and careers, until the early 1990s when k. d. lang and then Melissa Etheridge came out publicly. Coming out has always been a commercial risk for lesbian performers because rock 'n' roll is not only predicated on male sexuality but also on heterosexuality.

While the Indigo Girls had a large lesbian following from their earliest days playing Eddie's Attic in Decatur, Georgia, and the Uptown Lounge in Athens, they did not come out publicly until the early 1990s. Although Amy Ray was willing to be out, Emily Saliers initially worried about the consequences of public statements of their sexual orientation. Like Melissa Etheridge, they wrote songs that obscured the gender of the person to whom the song was addressed, but, as they came out, their lyrics began to reflect their sexual orientation and eventually took on a political tone, as in Emily's "It's Alright" in which she says, "It's all right if you hate that way, hate me 'cause I'm different, hate me 'cause I'm gay. Truth of the matter come around one day, and it's all right."[63]

A final strategy that women rockers have employed to control their own sexuality has been, according to Luce Irigaray, "mimicry."[64] Irigaray contends that exaggerated gender behaviors can undermine gender stereotypes by making the performative nature of gender itself visible. "One must assume the feminine role deliberately. Which means already to convert a form of subordination into an affirmation, and thus to begin to thwart it." Playing with mimicry allows women to expose their exploitation without being reduced to it—"to make 'visible,' by an effect of playful repetition, what was supposed to remain invisible."[65] Courtney Love's use of gauzy feminine dresses in contrast to her sexually raw performance and overtly feminist lyrics exemplifies such mimicry.

The career of 1960s British singer Dusty Springfield illustrates the complicated intersection of sexuality, race, and rock music. Springfield's sexuality occasioned speculation and rumor. Modeling herself on drag queens, she presented herself in excessive femininity, with dramatic black eyeliner and bouffant hairdos.[66] Rumors about her sexuality preceded her move to the United States in the mid-1970s. By the late 1970s Springfield spoke out on gay issues, although she herself never publicly came out. A white woman, Springfield wanted to capture in her music the sounds of black blues performers. Her unique sound was so rooted in soul music that many black singers, including Martha Reeves and Mary Wells, thought Springfield was black.[67] Occasionally referred to as "the white Aretha Franklin," Springfield recorded her Top 10 hit, "Son of a Preacher Man," after Aretha turned it down, and when the Motown Revue arrived in England in 1968, Springfield hosted the British television special "The Sounds of Motown."[68] In 1969 she was dubbed "the blue-eyed soul singer." In the United States her career stalled under poor management. "Springfield suffered from being a trail-blazer," Lucy O'Brien contends, "trying to articulate R&B torch songs in an era when white girls were not supposed to express raw 'black' emotion."[69]

A black woman who calls her alternative rock/new wave music "Bohemian Glam," Robin Renée had the opposite experience. "I think that race has been a factor for me because a lot of people expect that my music should be something other than what it is. . . . They say, 'Oh, so you're a musician. What do you sing? Jazz? R&B?' And I'm like, 'No, actually.'" She adds, "So a lot of assumptions are made about what a black woman should be doing in music. I know that a couple people at record labels have felt that they can't market a black rock 'n' roll woman" because "it doesn't fit one of their boxes necessarily."

Growing up, Renée got a lot of harassment, often from black people who "felt I was too white or inappropriate or whatever." She was not their idea of a black woman. "And because of that I think I went through a lot of pain," she confesses. "I tried to denounce the music that I loved." She felt bad about herself until she was able to *name* her identity struggle. "I really have come to understand that my experience, my family experience, my cultural experience, was very much multiracial." Proclaiming her identity as a strong black woman, she adds, "To try to change that or cater it to make some particular group of people like me more is not what I need to do."[70]

The Asian-American singer-songwriter Magdalen Hsu-Li has also mapped her own path by refusing the racialized scripts available to Asian women. "There are a lot of advantages to being Asian-American and a woman in the music industry. I get lots of gigs and press with hardly any effort because I really stand out as one of the first Asian women to come out with songs and an image that do not fit into the clichés and stereotypes. . . . I am a real person who is a minority in this country who has assimilated to American culture, who is redefining her own identity by writing deeply personal and universal original songs. While pop artists do this all the time in America, it's no small feat for an Asian."[71]

Particularly in the world of rap music, African American women struggle to maintain control of their sexuality and position themselves as strong black women. While hip-hop's roots can be traced back through black poetry, the blues, and ancient African oral traditions, contemporary African American rap music emerged in the late 1970s with the recording of the Sugarhill Gang's "Rapper's Delight."[72] Tricia Rose defines rap music as "a black cultural expression that prioritizes black voices from the margins of urban America" and "a form of rhymed storytelling accompanied by highly rhythmic, electronically based music."[73]

The familiar critiques of rap music indict it for violence and misogyny, coarse and offensive language, and glorification of bad actors of various persuasions.[74] But rap also provides an alternative discourse from socially marginalized perspectives. Rap speaks of the poverty, despair, violence, and hopelessness at the core of black urban experience.[75] Yet while rap offers a critique of racism and classism, like other forms of popular music, it has generally been defined, developed, and controlled by men.

Women have been on the rap scene since the beginning, although rarely acknowledged. In the 1980s women participated in mixed-gender groups such as the Funky Four Plus One More and in all-women groups such as Sequence and the Mercedes Ladies. Unlike the men, these early women rappers did not receive major label contracts and, unable to support themselves, dropped out of the rap scene. A few cultural critics have identified the dilemmas of black women rappers developing their art in a booby-trapped popular culture. Marla L. Shelton sees them trying to function in a commercial no-woman's land caught between the "predominantly white and patriarchal culture industry" and a "management system" controlled by black men.[76] This has been a hard place to stand for black women artists struggling to be true to *all* aspects of their experiences "living as African-Americans and women and, in many cases, in poverty," as Patricia Hill Collins writes.[77]

Eventually a first generation of commercially successful women rappers did emerge: Queen Latifah, Salt-n-Pepa, MC Lyte, and Yo Yo. In many ways, these pioneering women modeled themselves on their male counterparts. They wore baggy clothes and heavy boots and presented themselves with gangster attitudes. But their message challenged the intertwined racism and misogyny they experienced daily both from the dominant white culture and from black male culture. In her 1994 Grammy Award–winning record, "U.N.I.T.Y.," Queen Latifah challenged the misogynistic language of the rap industry and the larger culture. "Bitch" and "ho" were *not* synonyms for "woman," as Judy Neubauer of Tempo Records distilled her message.[78]

These first women rappers gave voice to young, urban black women and to their sexuality. Tricia Rose contends that these women rappers differed from their male counterparts in focusing on sexual politics.[79] Their lyrics were both sexually progressive and anti-sexist, equally pro-women and pro-black. Recognizing that some women do play the roles described in many male rappers' lyrics, Sandy Denton (Pepa of Salt-n-Pepa) says that her group wanted to counteract negative images. "We're not trying to judge the women that hard core rappers are talking about. What we are doing is sharing things we've witnessed regarding some men's treatment of women, trying to set an example of independence, and let [women] know they shouldn't be giving those guys so much to talk about."[80] Salt-n-Pepa's manager Carol Kirkendall says, "Through all the changes [rap] music's gone through over the course of their careers, they've maintained a strong sense of independence and continue to be committed to addressing social conditions in the community such as AIDS, single parent households, and female self-respect."[81]

While Queen Latifah and Yo Yo expressed control of their sexuality through their lyrics, they did not present themselves in hyper-sexualized costumes. Salt-n-Pepa, however, were much more explicit in their performance of sexual freedom onstage and in music videos. Asserting their right to sex and sexiness under their control, Salt-n-Pepa also challenged male sexuality and sexual entitlement.[82]

Many feminists found the next generation of women rappers more problematic. While Queen Latifah and Salt-n-Pepa promoted pro-woman, woman-controlled sexuality, these new women approached rap by being as raunchy as the men. The first woman rapper to have a platinum premier album was not Latifah or Yo Yo, but DaBrat. Unlike earlier women performers whose sexuality had been exploited by the men who produced and managed them, the new generation of women rappers have created and controlled themselves—and sold their music by flaunting their assertive, and to many offensive, sexuality. Most of their lyrics are rated NC-17, and the clothes they perform in leave little to the imagination. For these women, equality has meant the ability to be strong and in control and as sexy as they want to be.

"Females in this business aren't taken as seriously as we should be," says Missy Elliott. "So in order to be heard we often assume a character and give off what one would call a 'diva' or 'bitch' attitude. A bitch is what they call a woman who knows what she wants."[83] Elliott's lyrics reflect this strength. She followed her own dream through a childhood plagued by genuine, not-enough-fruits-and-vegetables poverty, sheltered by a loving mother and, when it came time to leave dad, a life near aunts and cousins with plenty to eat and plenty to share. There was more poverty when she finished school and took off for New York to make it in show business. This fairy tale, like many other real-life ones, is driven by talent and that mysterious confidence that burns under all the apparent fears, doubts, and insecurities. No wonder she tells Gerri Hirshey, "Women seem strong in [my] songs because that's not just a song anymore. . . . Females are starting to be a lot stronger and have self-confidence. Like 'I don't need you, I'm going to get my own—my own job, my own money. You want to leave, leave. You cheating on me and you think I'm going to stay here? No! I have my own stuff now, so you gotta go.' "[84] For Elliott, being labeled a bitch is evidence of her success.

Solé claims, "Back in the days of Latifah, you had to be one of the boys to be taken seriously. You couldn't use your femininity. Now it seems like the more feminine-looking you are, the more attention you get."[85] No longer restricted by gender expectations, as Joan Morgan points out, many of these young women rappers choose to empower themselves by doing what the men do and exploiting their own sexuality.[86]

An Uphill Climb

Brenda Lee's personal journey was starkly different from these young rappers. A little white kid coming up in a different era, she does not believe she was sexually exploited nor did it occur to her to exploit her own sexuality to catch the public's eye. She certainly did not experience the fear most of the black girl groups experienced down South due to the "double jeopardy" of being black and female. But she observed it at close quarters on Dick Clark's Caravan of Stars. "It really saddened me" when her black friends had to stay at different hotels in the South. A Southerner herself, Lee already knew about racism, though she herself seems to have grown up protected from at least some of its pernicious manifestations. "I grew up playing with black children and going to black children's homes and eating with them. And I didn't see the big deal about it. I knew that it was happening, but for me and my world, it wasn't happening."[87]

While she did not experience sexual or racial exploitation, Brenda Lee recognizes the difficulty women have breaking into the business. She does not dismiss her unique status as the only woman ever inducted into both the Country Music Hall of Fame and the Rock and Roll Hall of Fame. When we congratulated her on her induction to the Rock Hall in 2002, she thanked us graciously, then added, "You know, you're talking about a Hall that has very few women in it. . . . And it's awfully hard for a woman to get in, much less a woman of the '60s because . . . the people that vote are getting younger and younger. And it's not their fault that they don't know our body of work. . . . I think I got in just under the wire."[88]

In August 2002, at the invitation of Rock and Roll Hall of Fame and Museum associate curator Howard Kramer, Mina and Susan attended the unveiling of a series of Girl Group stamps at the Hall. The result of Mary Wilson's tireless work and promotion, the stamps, released by the Caribbean nations of Nevis, St. Vincent, and the Commonwealth of Dominica and the African nations of Ghana and Liberia, honored a dozen girl groups: The Supremes, The Crystals, The Ronettes, The Chantels, Martha and the Vandellas, The Velvelettes, The Angels, The Dixie Cups, The Shirelles, Patti LaBelle and the Bluebelles, The Cookies, and The Marvelettes. Members from each group, and entire groups in some instances, attended the ceremony. Much to our delight, they sang. More than thirty years since their girl group days, these women still had it going on. And as they sang their most famous songs, we all cheered and sang along. A young woman of about eighteen stood behind us in the crowd. She didn't know much about the musicians and certainly didn't remember their music. But she was impressed. "Wow," she said as The Crystals finished "Da Do Ron Ron." "This music is great." Up on a balcony, a man in his seventies nodded and swayed next to his young grandson. The majority of the audience members were middle-aged women and men who had grown up listening, dancing, and falling in love to the sounds of these groups. The crowd was racially diverse, squeezed together in one wing of the Rock Hall's lobby, which is lofty but not wide.

While the walls built by racism in this country have not entirely come down, this crowd's enthusiastic embrace of these performers certainly suggests that the music they gave the world did do something to remove a brick or two.

Women constructing identities as rock musicians must negotiate the intersections of gender, race, and sexuality. While all women in this culture are sexualized, their sexual identity is also racialized. This makes rock an especially hazardous terrain for women of color who may get caught between racist assumptions about the sexuality of women of color and their own desires to present themselves as sexual agents. After all, rock 'n' roll is bound up if not *quite* coextensive with sex, sexiness, and sexuality. And, of course, rock music and identity are constructed against changing backgrounds that provide performers opportunities to re-create themselves and enact their own sexual agency. Some women choose to conform to the sexual stereotypes; some choose to subvert them; others embrace them, flaunt them, and throw them back in the face of the culture that created them. Some of these responses are problematic from certain feminist points of view, although not surprising in a masculinist arena such as rock music. Nonetheless, women continue to create identities as rock musicians that embrace their racial and sexual selves and challenge the white male paradigm of rock 'n' roll.

CHAPTER 3

THE SINGER AND THE SONG

Do they call Dylan cranky for making social commentary?
It's like an angry man is an angry man, and an angry woman
is a bitch.

—*Joni Mitchell*

Every so often *Rolling Stone*, that notoriously and sometimes hilariously misogynistic publication, feels compelled to recognize that women play rock music. The magazine does it by constructing women as a special group in rock. In a recent nod to the ladies, the 2002 "Women in Rock" issue, Joni Mitchell was asked to respond to Bob Dylan's years-old comment—to the same magazine—that "chicks" who perform "whore themselves." Joni, he had struggled to explain, was "almost like a man. . . . Joni Mitchell is in her own world all by herself, so she has a right to keep any rhythm she wants." Mitchell was thoughtful and kind, as she seems invariably to be when confronted with that old and weird runaway train of a "thought" from a notoriously weird cultural icon. She assumed that Dylan meant his pronouncement as a compliment—to be a man in this culture is, she reflected, to be eligible to be a "member of the academy," instead of just an associate, as women have been in other civil organizations and arts establishments.[1] Indeed, Joni Mitchell holds unique and fundamental status in creating rock. She also has maintained an ambivalent relationship to feminism as any kind of formal doctrine. In her 1994 interview with Alice Echols, Mitchell disavowed feminism but voiced her resentment of sex-based exclusion, discrimination, and gratuitous sexualization ("the madonna-whore thing is never going to disappear").[2] Compassionately, Echols puts Joni Mitchell's discomfort with the feminist label into the context of her artistry. Mitchell accepts compliments that take her outside the categories of race and gender, into a realm of sheer terrific art-making.

Cutting short an interview with the new magazine *Women Who Rock*, Michelle Shocked protested that the magazine ill serves musicians who are women. "If this is just more of me being genrefied [*sic*] as a woman first and a musician second, I don't really need the space. . . . I'd love for my fans to read about me in a '*Men Who Rock*' magazine."[3] An electrifying performer and brilliant songwriter with a fierce fan base, Shocked was taken to the cleaners by a profiteer who stole a Walkman recording of her campfire performance at Kerrville, the great Texas folk festival. (She has since recaptured rights to the tape.) She has been homeless, institutionalized, raped, exiled, and a college student majoring in oral interpretation of literature. Held in bondage by a major label (Mercury), she had to fight for her freedom in court and by selling her own music at gigs. If Michelle Shocked speaks bluntly, who can be surprised? "Quite honestly," she told *Women Who Rock*, "you embody everything that I've fought so hard against—not only for myself, but for women musicians to come."[4]

"Women in Rock"

The *Rolling Stone* "Women in Rock" issue evokes a wide variety of responses among women musicians. Certainly, they all want to be known as good musicians. Period. For some, to attach the label "woman" to "rock musician" somehow marginalizes their talents. "You're pretty good, for a girl" is about as generous as the dominant social discourse gets toward women rock musicians. Other scholars have noted that often women musicians feel the need to " 'erase' their gender to do the work they [choose] to do."[5] Patti Smith says, "As an artist, I don't feel any gender restriction. When I'm performing, it's a very—for me—transcendent experience. I can't say I feel like a male or a female. Or both. What I feel is not in the human vocabulary."[6] Artists like Ferron and Ani DiFranco resist being labeled as "feminist" because it "ignores or wrongly characterizes the universal nature of their creative output."[7] Likewise, Queen Latifah says, "I'm not a feminist. I'm not making my record for girls. I made 'Ladies First' for ladies and men. For guys to understand and for ladies to be proud of." At this point the interviewer asked her "So, if you're not a feminist, what do you call this powerful attitude you convey?" Latifah replied, "I'm just a proud black woman. I don't need to be labeled. My mother is the same way. That means that I care about other black women. I speak to sisters and brothers; that's just how it is."[8] Alanis Morissette suggests that gender is not a primary factor in musicianship. "Even if the covers of a million magazines say 'Women in Rock' or 'New Women Artists,' at the end of the day I have to believe that most people are buying a record because they want to listen to it, and they forget about the gender as soon as they've put it in the CD player. I've always believed that it's 'the best person for the job.' Whether you're Leonard Cohen or whether you're Joni Mitchell or whether you're Liz Phair or whether you're Wyclef, you're expressing yourself. You are what you are, and you're a human being."[9]

While these artists shun the label "women in rock," they have no difficulty identifying times in their lives and careers when gender skewed their experiences. By appealing to "universal" human values, these musicians recognize the appeal their music has across differences—racial as well as gender. But simultaneously, by distancing themselves from the labels "women" or "feminist," they inadvertently gloss over the material differences gender makes.[10] Norma Coates suggests that the moniker "women in rock" is an "egregious example" of othering. She says the phrase itself implies that " 'Rock' is separate from 'women.' 'Women' are only related to 'rock' by being allowed 'in.' " She adds, however, that "women in rock" may be a politically useful term "as a way to designate rock as contested ground."[11] Me'Shell Ndegeocello makes this point with a bit of sarcasm. When asked if she has experienced any career advantages from being a woman, she responded, "Yeah. We get the Women in Rock issue."[12]

When performers at Lilith Fair shied away from calling the event feminist, Indigo Girl Amy Ray said, "Look, I don't mind being specified by gender; I'm proud to be a woman." She later added, "I can't separate being gay or being a woman from anything that I do, because it influences everything I do."[13] Mary Wilson says gender is the "big issue that no one really addresses." She acknowledges the work many women artists do to create and control their own music, but she does not see much outward discussion of the issue. "Why don't we just say it?" she asks. "Men are still ruling the world. James Brown says it's a man's world. And it really is."[14] Etta James, who says she was a feminist before she knew what the word meant, explains, "When I found out about the feminists, the women that were for women, I felt real connected to that. Women in this business have to take care of themselves, make their own living and be their own boss. I'm just happy that women are where they are today, where they can say, 'No, man, that ain't what I want.' "[15] Likewise, Ruth Brown proclaims, "I've been a feminist all my life. A feminine feminist. I've always been a strong woman; I've worked all my life. I think I've been a good mother on top of all that. I've tried to be a good wife, but like I've always said, I could always pick a good song, but I could never pick a good man."[16] Courtney Love calls herself a "militant feminist."[17] Bonnie Raitt says, "Any guy who has a problem with feminists is signaling a shortage in his pants. If I had had to be a woman before men and women were more equal, I would've shot somebody and been in jail."[18] Kathleen Hanna, formerly of Bikini Kill and now of Le Tigre, stopped playing in 1998 and then started again, partly because she felt a debt to earlier feminists: "Sure, I thought about giving up sometimes. But then I think about those feminists in the seventies. They created phrases like 'sexual harassment' and 'domestic violence.' They started rape crisis centers in their apartments. They fucking got abortion legalized. How can I give up? I haven't even gotten started yet."[19]

Women rock musicians, like women in general, demonstrate a huge range of relationships first to the concept of feminism, and second and more fundamentally to the creative and performative implications of gender identity. Women musicians have bucked stable though often counterintuitive prohibitions against women relating to instruments. (If women are the "feeling" part of the species, why are they denied the emotional expression of music and art? Gender rules are complicated and hard to learn.) The "girl groups" penetrated the sex barriers of early rock by traveling in gangs and relating to each other onstage as girlfriends talking girl talk, which the culture understood. Women broke into popular songwriting like men did: by following the conventions closely enough to be able to violate them to make hits. For women singing their own songs, there continues to be a special set of challenges, internal and external. Like men, women songwriters struggle primarily with issues of authenticity. "Is this good?" gets articulated more often than "Is this real?"—but keeping it real is generally, for the artist, what makes it good. What *genders* the creative struggle of songwriting is the burden of voice.

A Voice of Her Own

For many women, the burden of voice has a flip side. Speaking in a woman's voice violates years and centuries of training.[20] But speaking of a woman's experience can create a lightness, and a power, that heals and liberates. Like Michelle Shocked, the Canadian singer-songwriter Ferron found her voice as she emerged from a pain-filled childhood. Her mother had played the guitar, then put it away when the children came— seven, eventually. When Ferron found the neglected guitar in the basement, "I started plunking around on it. I had a difficult childhood, so the guitar really was something that I used to kind of drape over and play. And it would ease my anxieties." Yet Ferron conscientiously resisted her poetic voice, the music welling up inside. "I actually come from a working-class family, and I really thought that there was nothing more important than having a job. So in fact, trying to play the guitar, I guess it would be a calling in a way because I tried to put it down many times and always went back to it." To "be normal," as she says, meant holding a job—"and stop daydreaming and stop fiddling around with music." But her music was inescapable. "I guess I was fiddling around with a world that I could stand by writing, you know?"[21]

When Ferron was twenty-one or so, a friend submitted a tape of her songs to the organizers of a benefit for the Press Gang, a Vancouver women's press. They invited her to play her first gig. "You could have heard a pin drop. And I think people were just kind of surprised." She laughed at us, not unkindly, when we asked her how she developed an audience from there. "You're an American; I can tell. It doesn't work that way," she maintained, denying a systematically constructed career. "What happened was someone asked me to play somewhere else, and I went." She began packing local coffeehouses and theaters. In retrospect, she cannot see her appeal. "Maybe what they saw was just a broken bird."

A few years after Ferron's first stage performance, an American film producer, Gayle Scott, sought her out and challenged her to be serious about her art. "I had no idea a person could make music for a living. I think I was holding down three jobs when I met her. And maybe the more jobs I had, the more good I would be. . . . But she asked me some really probing questions—like it was deep. 'Do you think that you could live the life of a writer?' And I knew that she was talking about some kind of moral integrity, and because I was trembling when she asked me, and I thought that I would. . . . So right from the beginning it seemed like the life was not so much about fame . . . it was a spiritual journey." Her music, she believes, was both therapy and politics, for herself and for her growing audience. "It fit in with what I wanted to do, which is nonviolence. It seems to me that you can get tenderness and all your ideas across with music, and it's very healing."[22] Ferron's autobiography is written through her oeuvre: the lost and wandering child, the seeker for home, the joyful and jilted lover, the spiritual seeker, the wise woman.

Tori Amos also experienced her voice as a force not to be denied, and her music as a vessel of healing, both for herself and for others. She had to put aside her career once before claiming it back again. Her first recording venture with her band, Y Kant Tori Read, failed miserably. Around the same time, she reached a point in her life in which *she* felt like a miserable failure.

In a 1994 interview, Amos described an epiphany after a humiliation: the worst kind, in a restaurant. All punked out with hair "6 feet high," plastic boots and a miniskirt, she approached an acquaintance, only to be ignored and then laughed at (at least as she imagined it) behind her back as she walked out. She fled to a friend's house and played the piano for four hours straight. It changed her direction. If she was going to fail as a musician, she might as well fail doing the thing she had been doing since she was two years old: playing her own music on a piano. "This is what you are," her friend reminded her. A year later, in 1991, she issued *Little Earthquakes* and, miraculously, her same record company, Atlantic, backed it, and her, sending her on tour in England to give this new sound a chance to emerge.[23]

The new sound was the sound of inner, violent, painful experience. The best-known song on *Little Earthquakes* is "Me and a Gun," about her rape by an acquaintance. Just about too painful to listen to, this song has reached incalculable numbers of women listeners with similar traumatic memories. Amos remembers a letter from a fourteen-year-old girl that read, as she reported, "I'm coming to your show tonight, can I just come by and say hi, because I know that when I'm finished here, I know I have to go home to my stepfather. He molested me last night, he's gonna molest me tonight."[24] These responses galvanized Amos to join the twenty-year-old movement against violence against women by founding RAINN (the Rape, Abuse & Incest National Network) in 1994.[25]

Melissa Etheridge has become as celebrated a voice for those who hurt as Tori Amos. In the late 1990s Etheridge became a cynosure of the new, hip, out lesbian—the lesbian out enough to survive, artistically, her own revelations about the biological paternity of her two children (David Crosby), the end of her long-term relationship with Julie Cypher, and the couple's post-breakup parenting arrangements. Through her struggles, inside and in the world, Etheridge's audience stuck, and with good reason: her talent rang through the 2001 album, *Skin*, which shared her feelings of abandonment, betrayal, anger, and then recovery, hope, and renewal. In an interview with *Lesbian News*, Etheridge talked about the roots of her songwriting in her otherwise silent survival of abuse by a sibling. "Nothing was expressed. So as a child I was just filled with all this stuff—and where was I going to put it? Some children get angry and they do drugs and rebel. I went in the basement and wrote songs. I cultivated this anger and this fear and this sadness and longing into music." On *Skin*, she insisted, she was writing for herself, about herself. But she also believes that "the reason I write so autobiographically is because the closer I get to my truth, the more it speaks to more people."[26]

"My identity as a woman is absolutely central to my work," Jonatha Brooke commented in 1998. "I'm a girl. That fact flavors everything, and it's a strength."[27] In the same conversation, she grappled with the family influences on her songs—her grandmother and her mother, as well as her father. She finds that the women in previous generations seem to have been, not abused, but "stifled." Her grandmother was a pianist and a naturalist—but, Brooke mourns, "her passion and talent never went further than the living room or perhaps the backyard." "Amelia," Brooke's song about her grandmother, "questions the notion that long-suffering patience, kindness, and virtue are the attributes most appropriate for a woman and wife." "Angel in the House" addresses her mother's similar self-sacrifice—and the legacy of that womanly message for Jonatha herself. "When I sing 'I cannot kill the angel in the house,' I mean that I can't escape this notion of femininity that makes me 'clean the house' before writing a song. . . . It's still there."[28]

The Writing Process

We learned in talking with Jonatha Brooke several years later that part of that urge to clean the house before writing a song comes from the "torture" of writing itself. Brooke's laugh as she confessed the "nightmare" of the creative process scarcely undercut the strength of her statement. "It's just this hell. . . . It sucks every time, and you think that I've made six records now, and you'd think I'd be kind of in the saddle and I'd know how to get the juices flowing. It's worse and worse and worse. Like every time it's like, 'I'm such a loser, such an idiot. I suck. I suck. I suck.' . . . And I avoid it. I do laundry. I go crazy." On a good day, she says, she wakes up with a song in her head. But that's rare. "I have ten notebooks going at once usually. It's just like a jigsaw puzzle. So I'll finally, what I have to do actually is sequester myself. I have to make myself go away where there's no phone, not many cafes, and nowhere to run. And then just stick with it for hours and hours at a time because otherwise I just won't do it."[29]

Those "good days" Jonatha Brooke talks about are the times songwriters live for. In fact they are so good, they seem to be part of a parallel universe, to which access is magical and for which responsibility cannot be taken. Many songwriters talk about their material coming from somewhere else. "Usually what happens," says June Millington, "is I put the time aside, then I doodle on the guitar until I get this feeling. . . . It's like the angels and the muses, they come into the room, and I have to be very careful that no one disturbs me at all, no one talks to me, no one even taps me on the shoulder when I'm completely to myself because it's just us. . . . It's just channeling whatever they give me, and so I'm just really thankful that I happen to be some sort of a divining rod for music, for vibrations, for songs."[30] Jonatha agrees that sometimes her songs are "a total gift." She says that for some songs, "I just sat down and BOOM; there it was on the page. I was like WOW! Where did this come from. . . . Who wrote this?"[31]

Many writers describe making themselves available to *hear* the riff, the phrase, even, in those blessed moments, the full-blown song. Leah Hinchcliff says she sometimes dreams a song. "It's fully formed, all the in-strumentation. And it's amazing because I never can think that way when I'm awake. And I wake up and I'm like, 'Oh, that was the best thing I ever heard in my life.' And I get up, and I write it down."[32] Scarlet Rivera's best composition leads come from her unconscious mind and happen when she's just waking up or doing something she does not have to think about, like riding a commuter train at off-peak times. She says when a song comes to her, she grabs a piece of paper, draws the five staves, and writes down the exact notes she hears. Sometimes, she says, a note may be off by a half step or so, but usually it's not wildly out of key.[33]

Emily Saliers works with her guitar, just sitting and playing "some chords or a picking pattern and [I] start sort of channeling lyrics about stuff that I've been thinking about recently. . . . Usually it starts with the music and then it sort of all comes out together. . . . The music comes pretty easily, and the lyrics are really hard. So you spend a lot of time sitting, and you can't get it out, and you put it away, come back to it." In the last few years the computer has added a dimension to her lyrical development. "The editing process has become a lot more expansive with having a computer."[34]

Chrissie Hynde eschews both computer and tape recorder, as often do Bitch and Animal, who describe a very fluid writing process. Bitch explained, "There are some times that she'll leave a poem out that she wrote, and I'll put it to music. There's times where I've written music that she's put words to. There's times that we've written music together and put words to it . . . and we get into a zone sometimes." "Is the tape running?" we asked. "No," Bitch said in a deadpan, "We just remember and write it down. We've lost a lot of hits."[35]

Emily Saliers's partner in the Indigo Girls, Amy Ray, describes a differ-ent writing process, whose struggle seems to share something with Jonatha Brooke's tortuous way. "Music is a little harder for me," says this gifted and charismatic artist. "Just finding the chords . . . I'll have a melody, and I'll try to figure out what chord it's supposed to be. Sometimes it takes me a long time. . . ." Like Brooke, she keeps a notebook of "just everything. And I just read it periodically, write everything down on a piece of paper that struck me about what I wrote, and see if there's a song there." She uses a tape recorder. "I basically record everything that I'm doing all the time and go back and listen to the tapes all the time. I do use a computer . . . the computer's like my prize at the end of the song where I get to put it on to the computer because it's finished."[36]

Likewise, Kate Campbell keeps a notebook. "I'm very visually oriented, and I often work off of titles or phrases. And I collect them in my notebook. I've kept notebooks since I was a little girl. But they're not journals. I don't do journals. I write down stories that I hear that interest me, but usually it's a phrase initially."[37] During a recent concert in Minneapolis, Kate told the story of how her song, "Jesus and Tomatoes," came together. Kate had seen a sign advertising "Jesus and tomatoes coming soon" along a roadside in North Carolina and had written the phrase in her notebook. A while later, when Kate heard news of the "nun bun"—the pastry that looked like Mother Teresa found at the Bongo Java coffee shop in Nashville (true story)—she found a way to use the phrase; her song tells the story of a woman who raises a tomato that looks like Jesus and then builds a whole enterprise around it. For Kate, the key is to wait for the song to come to her. She says that "The Yellow Guitar" woke her in the middle of the night. "The song was literally coming to me. And I had to get out of bed, and I had to write it down." But, she's quick to add, she also spends a lot of time rewriting, editing, and structuring her songs and CDs. The former history graduate student says, "I begin to have themes, and it's kind of like writing a history essay for me."[38]

Amy Ray's insistence on steady, regular work, on the persistence involved in finding the songs (rather than waiting for them?) has a number of advocates among songwriters, including Carole King, a hero to many of her musical colleagues. The prototypical "Brill Building" writer, King teamed up with Gerry Goffin, her then-husband, to write songs under contract with Don Kirshner's Aldon Music in New York. (Aldon Music was actually located around the corner from the Brill Building, at 1650 Broadway.) The two met as teens and hung around with Neil Sedaka, Paul Simon, and other Queens College students interested in making popular music. In their heyday, they developed hits for groups from the Righteous Brothers to Aretha Franklin to Blood, Sweat, and Tears. The Beatles told the couple that they had aspired to be the next Goffin and King, and they covered "Chains."[39] King's song "You've Got a Friend" has been covered by many artists, most famously James Taylor. Battling stage fright, King cultivated a performing persona in the late sixties and early seventies. Her 1971 album *Tapestry,* featuring King's vocal and piano work, became one of the biggest-selling albums of recording history, wrapping songs of tender intimacy in her sharp pop sensibility.

King too has reported both the "inspiration" and "perspiration" routes to a finished song. "You've Got a Friend," she recalls, "wrote itself. It was written by something outside of my self through me." But in a 1991 interview with Paul Zollo, a journalist and music historian, she struggled to deliver what she felt was a more urgent message. "I have found," she said, "that the key to not being blocked is to not worry about it. Ever." For her, getting up and moving around—the "doing the laundry" stage of the process that Jonatha Brooke describes—is a natural part of the writing process. "When the channel wasn't open enough to let something through, I always went and did something else and never worried about it and it always opened up again."[40]

The Muse Within

Tori Amos agrees that songwriting is about receptivity as much as activity. In a 1997 interview she insisted, "The songs are alive in themselves; I always feel like I'm trying to translate. I'm only a conduit—a scribe. I could just be walking, sort of having no destination, and I'll sense this presence. The music really comes from the ethers. It's not an intellectual process." But the activity is there as well. "I believe that you must keep bringing grapes and gifts to the muse or the muse stops coming. I argue with her, and I laugh with her. . . . Even if I'm arguing, she knows I recognize that she's there. I'll manipulate a song the way I want to 'cause I just like it that way. It's like I'm saying to the muse, 'Look, if you don't want my input, go to Jewel.' "[41]

In an interview from 1991, Rickie Lee Jones spoke of her conversations with the creative source—she called it a spirit—that delivers fragments of songs. "Gee, that doesn't really make sense. *Okay, I'll write it,* if that's what you want, but . . . . And then when it's done, you find out, as long as you don't interfere, somebody knows what they're writing. You know what I mean? You just listen. 'Cause your logic will tell you, or your rhyme scheme will say, 'You know, I want this to be this other way,' but you mustn't interfere with the spirit that's writing. Once in a while, I write one. But . . . most of the time I don't write them."[42]

Jones also talked about persistence, and the penalties of not persisting. For her, not persisting meant being critical too soon in the writing process. Of that song spirit, she cautioned, "You have to be really quiet and careful with it when it's first being born, and you can't tell it it's wrong, 'cause it will just die. . . . You have to keep going back and playing 'em over and over again and listening to them." She speaks of the "torment" of entering the song, which for her involves leaving "the life you know." "It's really alchemy," she concluded.

Jonatha Brooke's songwriting began, oddly enough, with an assignment in a music composition class in a "very classical department—They didn't have any pop stuff." The professor told students to put an e.e. cummings poem to music. Jonatha chose "Love is More Thicker Than Forget," and it became her first song and appeared on her first record. She says, "all of a sudden it was this explosion because I got an A first of all (I was always like rabid for approval). And then it was just like this door being completely blown open. And I started writing like crazy."[43]

In a conversation in 1998, Mary Chapin Carpenter said, "Being a woman definitely informs my songwriting. Being a woman is a central fact of my existence." But she also embraced those songs that were not about herself, or about being a woman. "I believe that it's in the explorations of what you *don't* know that exercises your mind." She expressed particular pride in her songs "John Doe No. 24," inspired by a newspaper obituary of a ward of Illinois and written in his imagined voice, and "I Am a Town," whose lyrics and lush, flowing melody paint the poignant self-portrait of a Southern town.[44] Lynn Witting of Gate 18 wrote one of her favorite songs in her husband's voice. "Chris and I were getting ready to go out to a party or somewhere, and I was verbally stressing about being late and meanwhile, I wasn't even dressed yet and he was waiting on ME, he's sitting there dressed and ready and sipping a beer. So he says to me: 'Hey, will you PIPE DOWN? At least I'M fully dressed and drinkin'. My head just spun around and I was like: 'WHAT did you say?' And then we ended up being REALLY late, because of course I had to sit and write down all the lyrics for this new song ['Fully Dressed and Drinkin']."[45] Kate Campbell wrote "Tupelo's Too Far" in the voice of Elvis Presley, and her "Signs Following" raises questions about the limits of faith by telling the story of a snake-handling preacher who was sentenced to ninety-nine years in prison for attempting to kill his wife by forcing her to put her hands in a rattlesnake's cage.[46]

Singer-songwriter Holly Palmer has also talked about "go[ing] past that impulse" to write autobiography. Her song about "Sal, the Gardener" came from three weeks of listening as the fictional character's voice found its way through her. "The story told itself to me: 'Singing songs Sinatra sang/ Sal the gardener is drunk again/She is gone but he remembers/Polka dots and breathing hard/He dances with an angel in the yard.' Even though I hadn't experienced what Sal had and despite the fact that he isn't someone I knew in a literal sense, I understood what I needed to say about him. I tried to see through his eyes and to live in his skin."[47]

In the dominant culture, songwriting is less difficult for women to claim than actually playing rock music; somehow it seems more accessible, more acceptable for women. It is, after all, behind the scenes and builds on several centuries of women's literary accomplishments and identities. Nonetheless, for women to create authentic music, music that is in their words "real," they have to learn to speak in their own voices. Whenever women speak their own truths, either in the speaking itself or in the content or in both, they challenge the norms that constrain them, and they give voice to the experiences, concerns, and joys of other women who are constructing their own voices.

Talkin' 'bout a Revolution

While the Women's Movement first collectively asserted "the personal is political," many folk, rock, and pop singer-songwriters of the 1960s instinctively interwove public life and private experience in their music and musical performances. Already the Civil Rights Movement had demonstrated the power of music to unify and inspire social and political activism.[48] Uplifted by black spirituals, often adapted to contemporary situations, and gospel-style tunes of protest and determination, civil rights activists marched, rode buses, and went to jail to create a more just society.

By the early 1960s a number of social and cultural forces, in addition to the Civil Rights Movement, merged to create a context in which music and movement could combine indistinguishably.[49] The Baby Boom's maturation into adolescence and young adulthood in the bosom of the politically absurd Cold War set the stage for a social movement that both gave shape to and was shaped by expressions of popular culture, especially music.[50] Musicians involved in the folk music revival found receptive audiences among demonstrators and youthful social critics. "The songs, and the singers, formed part of the process of collective identity formation of the movement, just as the 'freedom songs' had in the Civil Rights Movement."[51]

In particular, folk music provided a genre in which intentional text dominated catchy tunes that were "easy on the ear."[52] These tunes then lent themselves to sing-alongs and were easily learned by any teenager sitting on a bed plunking away at an acoustic guitar. The melodies were simple and emotive, the lyrics easily memorized and highly political. Singing them functioned as a form of consciousness-raising and community-building that helped energize a social movement.[53]

Women musicians' involvement in protest movements, however, did not begin in the 1960s. As early as the 1920s and '30s, women folk singers like Aunt Mollie Jackson, the daughter of a Kentucky coal miner, were singing about poverty and exploitation in Appalachia.[54] Balladeer Ella May Wiggins sang her protest songs in the coal mines of Kentucky and was shot to death for her activism.[55] Malvina Reynolds, who earned a Berkeley Ph.D. in 1936, was a social worker, journalist, and assembly-line worker at a World War II bomb factory. She met Pete Seeger and other folk singers in the late 1940s and began to write her own songs, which were later recorded by Harry Belafonte, Joan Baez, Judy Collins, and Pete Seeger, among others. The majority of Reynolds's songs dealt with pressing social issues such as nuclear war ("What Have They Done to the Rain?") and tenants' rights ("The Faucets are Dripping"). Pete Seeger recorded her most popular song, "Little Boxes," which critiqued cookie-cutter housing developments and suburban values.

Similarly, Peggy Seeger has devoted her songwriting talent to thoughtful considerations of social issues. Seeger says, "I get ideas from many places and from a lot of other people's ideas. I take them from conversations, from magazine articles, or from cartoons. Then I expand them into songs."[56] The idea for "Everyone Knows" came from a cartoon through what she calls "creative plagiarism": "Everyone knows you can't trust a woman whenever that time rolls around." The song juxtaposes this common bit of "wisdom" with the suggestion that neither can a man be trusted when "that time rolls around"—that time when "He's a walking, talking divining rod ten thousand times a year."[57] Seeger notes that she also works hard at her instrument—her voice. "Some singers seem not to have to work at singing," she says, "—they just open their mouths and that glorious sound comes out. But I have had to work as I don't have that beautiful almost hypnotically lovely voice. So as a singer, I try to give folks something else: my mind and my political approach. It is possible that people who come to hear me come away exhausted. But I try to send them away thinking deeply and feeling deeply, hopefully at the same time."[58]

Joan Baez came to epitomize women protest singer-songwriters. Baez first appeared at the Newport Folk Festival in 1959 and quickly found commercial success, with nine records hitting the Top 40 albums list. In 1961 she met the aspiring young folksinger Bob Dylan, whom she invited to join her at the 1963 Newport Folk Festival. The two, who became involved in a short-lived romantic relationship, were soon dubbed "The King and Queen of Folk Protest."

Baez had not started out to make protest music. In her 1987 autobiography, *And a Voice to Sing With*, she explains that the first time she traveled in the South in 1961, she was barely aware of the Civil Rights Movement.

But as she toured, she realized that there were no black people at her concerts, and so the next summer she wrote into her contract that she would not perform unless blacks were admitted. By then she was singing "Oh, Freedom" and "We Shall Overcome," but still no blacks came to her concerts because they had not heard of her. The next time she toured in the South, she sang at black colleges. She became increasingly active in the movement, lending her voice and presence to demonstrations. She attended the Selma-to-Montgomery march in 1965.

As the peace movement birthed itself in 1964, Baez encouraged President Lyndon Johnson "to quit meddling around in Southeast Asia," and she refused to pay the portion of her taxes that went to fund the military.[59] She married antiwar activist David Harris in 1968 and focused on peace actions as he served a three-year prison sentence for draft resistance. (The couple divorced in 1971.) In 1973 she released *Where Are You Now, My Son?*, which documented her 1972 visit to Hanoi shortly after its fierce bombing. She became the first musician since Marian Anderson to be denied use of Constitution Hall in Washington, D.C., by the Daughters of the American Revolution.[60]

Many women had participated in both the Civil Rights Movement and the antiwar movement. Like their male counterparts, they had risked their lives on the front lines yet were consistently marginalized in the movements, outside the spotlight and outside power. But their participation had taught them some things. One was that they did have the power to effect social change. Another was that they had the skills to organize effective protest. And so these women who had marched beside Dr. King and had sat-in on college campuses began to discover their own second-class citizenship. On the shelf beside Betty Friedan's *The Feminine Mystique* (1963), nascent feminists propped that potent trio of books published in 1970: Kate Millett's *Sexual Politics,* Shulamith Firestone's *The Dialectic of Sex,* and Robin Morgan's anthology *Sisterhood is Powerful.* Women organized in a range of groups from the liberal National Organization for Women to the radical New York Redstockings took to the streets demanding their own equal rights and accompanied by their own anthem.[61] *Ms.* magazine began publication in 1972.

When she realized there was no song that expressed a positive feminist sense of self, Helen Reddy decided "I was going to have to write it myself."[62] Her 1972 "I Am Woman" soon became the anthem for the burgeoning women's movement. "I Am Woman" first appeared in a different arrangement on Reddy's first album and was used in the movie *Stand Up and Be Counted.* It was then expanded and rerecorded for release as a single. The song appeared on the charts briefly in 1972 and disappeared. When Reddy, pregnant with her son Jordan, began singing the song on television, American women responded. "I Am Woman" moved back onto the charts, eventually reaching number one and winning Reddy a Grammy for Best Female Performance. As she accepted the award, she thanked "God, because SHE makes everything possible."[63]

While black women like Shirley Chisholm and Audre Lorde were integral parts of the women's movement from its beginning, the movement's intense focus on gender in the context of American social hierarchies led to insensitivities to issues of race and social class. Black women often found themselves forced to choose between their race and their gender.[64] In feminist organizations, they were often marginalized because of race, and in the Black Power movement they were often marginalized because of gender. Nonetheless, these women developed their own tradition of protest music. In spirituals, the blues, the folk music of Odetta, and the rap of Queen Latifah (among many others), black women have described their unique position in a sexist and racist culture.

The majority of women who performed in the folk music revival were white, but guitarist and vocalist Odetta sang about black experiences. (Buffy Sainte-Marie, a Native American, was another of the folk revival's rare women of color.) Odetta began recording in the 1950s and achieved recognition in the 1960s when she released *My Eyes Have Seen* and *At Town Hall*. She appeared onstage at the March on Washington in 1963.

Beside Odetta that day was Bernice Johnson Reagon, who in 1973 founded Sweet Honey in the Rock, an *a cappella* ensemble of six black women still singing (and sign-interpreting) songs of protest. Reagon cofounded the Student Nonviolent Coordinating Committee's (SNCC) Freedom Singers during the Civil Rights Movement. The Freedom Singers' songs, recalls Reagon, "were a way of coming together, holding each other and proclaiming our determination as citizens to fight racism in this land of our birth."[65]

In the early 1970s Reagon became vocal director of the D.C. Black Repertory Company. A small group within the company decided to form Sweet Honey in the Rock. The group performed a wide range of historically black music—slave songs, gospel, blues, and jazz. Knowing this choice would put Sweet Honey outside conventional marketing categories, the group still refused to commercialize its repertoire. "I don't do music to scale Top 40 charts and neither does Sweet Honey, although there is no reason she, Sweet Honey, should not be there," Reagon explains.[66]

At first the group did not particularly identify with the women's movement, which seemed focused on the issues of middle-class white women. As she began to examine the experiences of the black women in her life, however, Reagon began to recognize the impact of gender on their experiences as black women. She especially remembers hearing the story of Joan (pronounced JoAnn) Little, a black inmate who had killed her jailer as he was raping her and then had managed to escape. The song Reagon wrote in response, "Joan Little," suggests that Joan is a member of every black family; she is a "sister," "mama," "lover," and "the woman who's going to marry your child." Reagon says that letting Joan Little into her consciousness and her music "meant that Sweet Honey would not test women at the door as to what we were carrying. We assumed that if you were grown, Black and female, you were carrying a load."[67]

In the late 1970s Reagon connected with the political lesbian movement.[68] Sweet Honey in the Rock collaborated on a Meg Christian record produced by Holly Near for Olivia Records and toured with Near and Amy Horowitz. Reagon says the coalition work was hard but worthwhile, as Sweet Honey had to continue to define themselves as black women within a predominantly white, middle-class coalition. Out of her experience with the radical women's movement, Reagon composed a song about women loving women. Despite their fears of losing their base of black audiences or being labeled lesbian themselves, the group decided that they would sing about every kind of oppression, including homophobia.[69]

The lesbian community itself created a wealth of music in the 1970s that would name the experiences and oppressions of lesbians. Singer-songwriters such as Holly Near, Cris Williamson, Meg Christian, and Tret Fure indeed gave birth to an entire genre of music that was generally gentle, lyrical, and completely woman-identified. We will explore what came to be known as "women's music" more fully in chapter 5.

Since the 1960s and 1970s, protest music has been a staple for many women singer-songwriters who have written about war, hunger, and poverty and have also paid specific attention to gendered issues such as sexual abuse, rape, domestic violence, and sexism within social institutions. Their testimony suggests that this music emerges not so much from a desire to write protest songs as from their own lives, inscribed though not contained by gender, race, social class, and sexual orientation. Tret Fure's parents both came from poor families. Her father grew up in a large farm family. Her mother's family immigrated from Italy, and her grandmother worked in a sweatshop when they arrived in the United States. Because of this family background, Tret says she writes a lot about poverty, hunger, and the plight of farmers. As Ani DiFranco explains, "It's not like I have an agenda in my music; it's just that to me, the world is political. Politics is music—is life! . . . I don't have this message that I want to convey musically. It's almost more subconscious. I'm telling my story; I'm writing songs about my life. Just like any other personal songwriter or rock musician, I'm a politicized person."[70]

As Odetta became the token black woman in the 1950s and 1960s who played acoustic rather than dance music, and as Joan Armatrading emerged in the 1970s, Tracy Chapman surfaced in the next decade.[71] At Tufts University in the mid-1980s, Tracy Chapman joined an African drum ensemble, developed her acoustic guitar skills, and began playing her music in Boston coffee houses. Early in her career she was compared to Joan Armatrading.[72] While Chapman respected Armatrading and liked her music, she did not think she wrote or sounded like her. Indeed, Chapman's sound was distinctive, and it is hardly difficult to distinguish these two remarkable and unique voices. Like Robin Renee, as a black woman Chapman has found that people have a hard time categorizing her music. Asked if she considered herself a folk singer, she replied, "I guess the answer's yes and no. I think what comes to people's minds is the Anglo-American tradition of the folk singer, and they don't even think about the black roots of folk music. So in that sense, no, I don't. My influences and my background are different. In some ways, it's a combination of the black and white folk traditions."[73]

Chapman's first album in 1988 went platinum, and she was called "folk music's new messiah."[74] This debut album eventually sold more than ten million copies worldwide and earned her three Grammies at the 1989 Awards. Performing "Give Me One Reason" at the 1997 Lilith Fair, according to Gerri Hirshey, Chapman was "the single act that roused the entire crowd."[75] Much of her appeal sprang from her politics. "I try to write about situations where you find the most conflict," she explains. "Those stories interest me the most. It's those gray, sticky, and uncomfortable situations where you find the best stories."[76] Certainly Chapman's experiences growing up in a poor black neighborhood in Cleveland provided stories that might illuminate American racism, sexism, greed, and violence during the Reagan years. Rather than being an exotic "other" or passive victim, as black women have often been characterized in this culture, Chapman positioned herself as a subject speaking her own experiences and truths. Emerging along with hip-hop culture that also spoke to the position of black people in the United States, Chapman continued to use the tradition of folk protest to call attention to many of the same social issues that animated rap lyrics.[77]

Growing up the daughter of a Southern Baptist preacher, Kate Campbell assumed she was supposed to be a contemporary Christian singer-songwriter. Campbell's songs, deeply personal and rooted in Southern history and religion, certainly deal with religious themes, although they are not exactly what she (or anyone else) would call Christian songs. So, she says, "that didn't go anywhere." Instead, she recalls that publishers told her, "You're really writing songs that are actually too socially conscious for the Christian market." They suggested she write songs that "could kind of be a love song to Jesus and kind of be a love song to a person, you know, an earthly person." She was uninspired by this formula for pop success among American evangelicals. "Even when I was a little girl, from the very beginning I wrote songs about people, but not love songs per se or worship songs per se. I wrote about things that bothered me, even when I was a little girl. You know, if I'd been listening to John Denver, I'd start writing about environmental issues."[78]

Many women musicians have carried their political activism beyond music. Tori Amos founded RAINN. In order to protect abortion rights and women's health clinics, L7 joined the Feminist Majority in organizing the first Rock for Choice concert, held on October 21, 1991, at the Palace in Los Angeles, and featuring Hole, Nirvana, and Sister Double Happiness. Since then, Rock for Choice has become a project of the Feminist Majority and raises money to help fund the organization's Campaign to Save Roe.[79] Concerts have featured such performers as Salt-n-Pepa, Liz Phair, Bikini Kill, Joan Osborne, Melissa Etheridge, Joan Jett, the Bangles, and Sarah McLachlan.

Jann Arden says half of what she does is to "just [be] out there trying to prop the world up. . . . I just, I feel responsible. How can I not?" In both musical and nonmusical ways, Jann has supported programs dealing with AIDS, cystic fibrosis, breast cancer, and hunger. "You do what you can," she explains, "but you get it back tenfold." She says she learned her social consciousness from her parents, whom she remembers gathering bags of clothes, dropping off contributions at food banks, and inviting people they barely knew to Christmas dinner. "It started at home. . . . They didn't have much, my folks. But they always had extra potatoes that they grew in the garden that they'd drop off to somebody."[80]

Emily Saliers, who remembers her parents being "sort of lefties," says her consciousness was shaped by growing up aware of the Vietnam War, the Black Panthers, and the presidential candidacy of Hubert Humphrey. "We were sort of taught to pay attention to all of that. And so I had that in me, you know, the seeds were planted." Amy Ray adds, "I think we weren't necessarily that politicized when we started, but we had a sense of activism. You know, doing things to give back because we both were brought up tithing and [were taught] the importance of tithing in the community." Emily points to early benefits for Greenpeace and a local shelter for women and children, while Amy dates their political "coming of age" from their involvement with the indigenous environmental movement. That spurred their gay activism, as well as their activism concerning many other social and political issues. Recently Emily, whose father is a Methodist minister, has begun to work within Christian churches to help church members extend their understanding of lesbian, gay, bisexual, and transgender issues, particularly around ordination. She began this work with some trepidation. Caught between churches that believe homosexuality a sin and friends who no longer will attend church, Emily has struggled to continue to engage with Christian churches. "I just try to come in as open and as honest as I can, not knowing what faith I am or even what I have to offer and just speaking from my heart about how I feel that gays and lesbians and bisexuals and transgendered people have to be ordained. They are loving and gifted members of the community, and the church has to come around because the church is wrong."[81]

Lilith Fair

As in church, so in the music industry. In 1997 Sarah McLachlan embarked on a three-year "girliepalooza" that would draw sold-out crowds.[82] Inspired by the mythical Lilith, McLachlan defied the male-focused music industry and proved that a multi-artist female music event could succeed artistically— and even make money.

Granted, the Michigan Womyn's Festival and similar events had brought women musicians together, but not in a tour format and not in venues that welcomed, and expected, mixed audiences (male and female, gay and straight—see chapter 5). Most promoters had assumed that two women on a touring bill would not be appealing, much less profitable. When McLachlan proposed Paula Cole as the opening act on her upcoming *Fumbling Toward Ecstasy* tour, Buffy Childerhose recounts, promoters balked. " 'Two women?' scoffed the promoters. 'Forget it. It'll never work.' Sarah angrily pushed for an explanation. 'Nobody wants to see two women in one night,' they declared. And the reason? 'Well,' they blustered, 'because that's the way it is.' "[83]

McLachlan persisted, and Cole did join her. Her refusal to give in to promoters of that tour grew into what came to be known as "Lilith Fair: A Celebration of Women in Music." In three years, 139 shows were produced and more than two million tickets were sold.[84] With one dollar from each ticket sold donated to charities that support women's health, education, shelter, and safety, the event made a profit *and* a social statement.[85]

At first, tour organizers were not interested when corporate sponsors wanted to get in on the act. But when corporations agreed to allow Lilith

Fair to choose which charities would receive their "cut," even more money for worthy causes was generated. Strict guidelines prohibited sponsorship by corporations that used child labor or animal testing.[86]

While some fans may have attended because of social politics, the musicians were the real attraction. The performers' roster rotated throughout the tour. That first year, any one show might have included Cassandra Wilson, Emmylou Harris, Fiona Apple, the Indigo Girls, Jewel, Joan Osborne, Lisa Loeb, Mary Chapin Carpenter, Meredith Brooks, Nina Persson, Paula Cole, Shawn Colvin, Sheryl Crow, Suzanne Vega, Tracy Bonham, Jill Sobule, Victoria Williams, Tracy Chapman, and, of course, Sarah McLachlan as the mainstay. One stage was not enough to hold these and other talented female voices, so producers set up a "B stage," then a "Village stage." As a result, local talent, young artists, and others just starting their music careers had an opportunity to be heard by thousands, to gain media exposure, and to learn from the "established" artists.

As with most all-female events, this traveling music festival engendered both praise and criticism. Some bemoaned the lack of diversity in the lineup that first year, one critic complaining, "Lilith Fair isn't a picture of solidarity so much as a picture of uniformity. McLachlan, the event's organizer, has chosen singer-songwriters in her own image: pretty, polite, folksy moderates with sensible hair and more melody than message."[87] Lilith's second-year lineup had a broader range of styles. McLachlan contended that there was no "sudden scramble for diversity," adding, "it's just that more people said yes this year," including Erykah Badu, Missy Elliot, Bonnie Raitt, Queen Latifah, Natalie Merchant, Me'shell Ndegéocello, and Sinéad O'Connor.[88] "I think music crosses barriers and boundaries," McLachlan contended. "If it's good, it's good. We're after good music."[89] Not surprisingly, some media voices couldn't resist Lilith Fair's easy target. Some contended that the women were "dissing" men, but as Jennifer Baumgardner and Amy Richards pointed out, "After all, an all-black tour of hip-hop musicians wouldn't feel obligated to assure people that they're not dissing whites."[90] When the American version of *Time* magazine put Jewel on the cover and portrayed Lilith Fair in a positive light, the mudslinging increased.[91] It should be noted that the Canadian issue of *Time* used McLachlan, born in Nova Scotia, on its cover. McLachlan was annoyed at the switcheroo, but she understood the cynicism of that editorial decision; Jewel's record label and *Time* magazine were both owned by Time Warner.[92] Many accused the tour organizers of turning a folk festival into a feminist manifesta. Others wanted a stronger feminist statement from Lilith. In a *Salon* magazine article entitled "Throwing Ovaries: The Second-Grade Sensibility of the

Pseudo-Feminist Lilith Fair," Sarah Vowell remarked, "I haven't read one thing about Lilith Fair that isn't complete puffery plastered with pseudo-feminist smiley-faces."[93] Responding to the criticism that she did not use the word "feminist" to describe herself, Sarah McLachlan said, "Absolutely I'm a feminist."[94]

The religious right's cultural radar picked up Lilith Fair. The ever-vigilant *National Liberty Journal,* which had warned toddlers' parents about the homosexual tendencies of the Teletubbies' purple, purse-toting Tinky Winky, now alerted the parents of teens to Lilith's insidious influence. Pointing to the rebellious mythical figure cast out from the Garden of Eden because she refused to submit to Adam, the article's author said, "Christian parents are advised to consider the Lilith legend should their children become interested in the concerts." After expanding on the various legends of Lilith, some claiming that she "took on the personification of the serpent" that tempted Adam, the author added, "This Lilith Fair alert is certain to draw more fire, but we are willing to take the heat in order to document the truth behind the benign appearance of this music festival." The author did recognize that the event supported the "worthy" Breast Cancer Fund; however, he also pointed out that some of the proceeds went to Planned Parenthood and that condoms were "dole[d] out" at all concerts on the tour.[95] If the article's intent was to warn parents, the author was a bit late. Lilith Fair concluded in August of the same summer the article was published.

These criticisms did not visibly daunt the artists during Lilith Fair's three-year run. Inviting and responding to parody of the festival, some participating artists intentionally exacerbated the stereotypes. As Ann Powers pointed out in her *New York Times* article, rock's tough queen, Chrissie Hynde of The Pretenders, even wore a tutu to poke fun at the feminine image of the event.[96] Often making light of hormones and ovaries, the artists spoke of camaraderie both onstage and backstage. The satirical newspaper the *Onion* had McLachlan saying, "This mass ovulation is a celebration of our fertility. It's a celebration of our sisterhood," and "By releasing these eggs, we recognize and honor our collective femininity."[97] In a more accurate interview before the 1999 tour, Me'shell Ndegéocello reported, "Lilith (Fair) is great, I did it last year and it's a very cushy tour, low maintenance, great people, great women, great catering and it's clean."[98] Calling herself the "den mother" of the tour, Bonnie Raitt joked that she was interested in testing out the theory of menstrual synchrony.[99] "I have to say, this is the highlight of the summer for me," Raitt commented of the 1998 tour. "This is one of a kind and long overdue. It's the best vibe I've ever seen backstage and onstage as well."[100]

Early in the first summer, some of the artists had been described as "guarded" and competitive.[101] McLachlan defended her colleagues, arguing that the tour had just begun, and it would take time to build a comfort level.[102] Behind-the-scenes footage from the 1997 tour revealed a special camaraderie. Lucy O'Brien points out, "There's Sheryl Crow in a backstage jam session with the Indigo Girls. Crow might have been the bigger star, but she is gracefully humble in the presence of Amy Ray's talent."[103] Of course, criticism persisted through the Fair's three-year run.

Audiences shared the performers' sentiments of community. Fans reported sensing a safety and security that they had not experienced at other concerts. Mosh pits and fights were absent, and one writer noted that "the mood was so easy and comfortable that it occurred to me: this is probably how boys feel at shows all the time."[104] Lilith Fair proved, Gerri Hirshey contended, that "there is a market for competent, thoughtful music performed in a kinder, gentler venue." She added, "No one seemed to miss the hurtling bodies and projectile vomiting of all those macho summerfests of yore."[105]

There was of course no way Lilith Fair could please everybody. Hirshey remembers a woman photographer at the 1999 fair complaining about multiple photo release forms and "astonishingly petty prohibitions" concerning individual artists.[106] Some reviewers, such as the vitriolic Sarah Vowell, simply had no use for the gentle prettiness, which she received as sentimental and thus perhaps inauthentic, of so much of the Lilith Fair music. Others simply could not get past the kind of fearful reaction engendered (so to speak) by women getting together on purpose to do things that primarily men had done before. But Lilith Fair, despite contemporary and subsequent backlash, served many purposes, among them an extended set of opportunities for networking among women artists. Jennifer Baumgardner and Amy Richards note that the Lilith Fair musicians made new professional connections with each other, touring or appearing on each others' albums.[107] Girls and young women who bought tickets got a glimpse of female camaraderie. If social learning theorist Albert Bandura's ideas on modeling are correct, many women were encouraged to pick up a guitar or a microphone. Bandura would say that through observational learning, individuals are more likely to pay attention to and mimic models most like themselves, especially if those models are prestigious and display competence. Of course, this could apply to Lisa Marie Presley carrying on the legacy of her father Elvis, to whom she bears a striking resemblance, but gender is also a powerful factor when it comes to modeling.[108] Watching Bonnie Raitt or Tracy Chapman model and be rewarded for mastery of a guitar likely had a profound influence on many impressionable young women at Lilith.

Whether insisting on an all-women traveling music festival or pro-testing social issues, many women in rock construct resistant identities through their songwriting. The songs give voice to the selves they are con-structing and the issues those selves deem significant. They connect with audiences of women who are relieved and thrilled to hear someone name their experiences publicly. While some women musicians may decry the term "women in rock," the saliency of gender in their experiences comes to life in their words. Certainly they write and perform songs with which men can identify, just as women have identified with men's songs for hundreds of years. Nonetheless, because they do so within a hierarchically gendered world, to write and sing those songs is to assert a resistant identity—whether it is one that embraces one's identity as a woman in rock or demands equal footing as simply a rock musician.

CHAPTER 4
THE GIRLS IN THE BAND

I remember the girls in my school, the pictures of the Beatles, and like, "Which one do you want to kiss?" And my immediate reaction: "Kiss? I want to do; I want to be like that."

—*Deborah Frost*

In middle school, New Yorker Deborah Frost could not find girls to start a band with. She got her best friend to go to *A Hard Day's Night* (1964) and talked her into forming a band. Deb was able to buy the sheet music for those Beatles songs, but by the time she had saved enough money to *almost* buy a small plastic drum at Corvette's, her friend had lost interest. This was a shame because her friend already had a guitar. "People really thought that this was bizarre," Deborah recalls about her passion to be a rock musician. "I could not find anybody interested, whereas every boy was starting a band." Playing those odds, she lassoed her younger brother and his friends into cooperating with her for a while, but they too drifted away. She ended up playing folk guitar, like so many baby boom girls, and also pursuing theatrical writing and acting, appearing in several off-Broadway plays before she went to college. When Joseph Papp read an early script and told her she was the voice of her generation, "I freaked out, and I never wrote another; you know, I was sixteen years old."[1]

Following her parents' dream to Harvard in 1971, she was derailed first by her fervor for rock music and more fundamentally by her father's death in a car accident as he was driving to Cambridge to visit her. Grief, guilt, and frustration finally drove her home to New York City, where she worked for a film company and continued combing the *Village Voice* ads looking for a band. She cannot believe, in retrospect, the situations she walked into for the sake of her dream. "I used to get in the car; I would drive to these places or out to Queens and go in somebody's basement. I remember the people who were playing, like guys in the basement of some flower shop. There were all of these weird people, and I had no idea where I was going or what I was doing." She and some singularly untalented musicians once got locked in a freight elevator in the middle of the night in their pursuit of a free practice space. "We never did do any rehearsing because the whole night was occupied with the police getting us out." Other disappointments and delays included interviewing potential bandmates who professed their love of Karen Carpenter. "I'd say, 'Karen Carpenter is not rock music. I want to play music like Led Zeppelin or the Rolling Stones.' . . . I was very clear; I wanted to play heavy, loud music."

At last Deborah found a band—the collection of musicians that became, briefly, Flaming Youth. This began a frenetic period of looking for venues (this was pre-CBGB Manhattan) and hanging out with people who were already making their names: John Bonham, Alice Cooper. She shared an apartment on East 10th Street with Allen Ginsberg and Peter Orlovsky. She recalls Patti Smith calling several times to meet Ginsberg—but she herself missed meeting Patti Smith because she chose to take a bath while her apartment mates were out at Smith's performances, rather than listen to poetry and miss the rare opportunity for decent water pressure.

Flaming Youth carried its own comic baggage. Elodie Lauten, the keyboard player, struggled with an organ Ginsberg had given the group. It had belonged to the Thugs, apparently, and they had trashed it. "There weren't that many keys that worked." Frost would ask Elodie to play a certain chord, and in heavily French-inflected English, the keyboardist would—seemingly—refuse. "I finally realized that she could not play this chord because the key did not exist or else the keys would just stand up like giving the finger. And they would just play themselves. So that determined the parameters of our music." Ginsberg got the group political gigs such as opening for Bella Abzug, whom Deb remembers announcing after one freezing outdoor performance, "I think my sisters are very groovy."

In 1973 Deb quit Flaming Youth, but not rock music. She became a rock critic, first for *Creem* and then for other publications. She remembers feeling like the Cameron Crowe stand-in in the movie *Almost Famous*, clutching his copy of *Creem* and believing that if he could write for that magazine, he could touch his dream. She feels now that she was naïve, like the young Crowe, not realizing that writing criticism would put her "on the other side of the fence." But she also learned she was good at it. When she returned to Harvard in 1974, she began working for the *Boston Phoenix,* a weekly arts tabloid. She did not give up on performance, though. Her rock mission became introducing her fellow students to good music, which she did by playing drums and bass in her undergraduate house at all hours of the night, turning up Bad Company on her stereo, and later becoming music director of the university radio station. Not all her friends appreciated her contributions. "You're going to be the reason I'm not Phi Beta Kappa," one classmate screamed at her.

The Opaque Ceiling

Deborah Frost came of age in a rock world that still matter-of-factly discounted women as performers just as businesses channeled women into secretarial positions and the "glass ceiling" was still unapologetically opaque.[2] She was an idealist, not uninterested in feminism but unconvinced that her gender determined how she participated in the world of rock music that commanded her passion. To her, rock represented a "freer" life, a rejection of the "bourgeois conventions" she had grown up with and "detested." She reinterpreted experiences that suggested that girls and boys were handed different tickets. "I was very naïve because it didn't occur to me that I could not do certain things. And people would say, 'Oh well, a girl can't do this.'"[3]

It was a confusing time. On the one hand, little had changed in women's day-to-day treatment in intimate relationships and public spheres. On the other hand, the 1960s saw the peak of the Civil Rights, Black Power, antiwar, and counterculture movements that generated a kind of camouflage of women's continuing repression for young girls eager to participate in the thrilling street politics of the time.[4] Loosened sexual mores supported by better birth control methods could be interpreted, however naïvely, as signaling more equal decision making between men and women. In fact these conditions did precipitate the collective disappointments that fueled a new movement.

The history of second-wave feminism is rife with narratives by women who attributed girlhood frustrations to their own deficits—stupidity, naïveté, fatness, uncool clothes, lack of know-how—or to bad luck and the idiosyncratic mean-spiritedness of the men they dealt with. "I was definitely second-class—a sort of 'Movement chick,'" recalls Annie Popkin of her days in the antiwar movement at Harvard. Feminist analysis became a way to reinterpret her feelings of inferiority. "My silence in political meetings, which I had attributed to some personality fault, I could now see as part of a system, in which men are at the center."[5] Andrea Dworkin abandoned the peace movement for the women's movement after sitting silently by while the men in one antiwar meeting "happily" discussed Marilyn Chambers, the pornography star, and what they would like to do to her in bed. "I noticed that the men did not notice that the women had suddenly become absent, at the table yes but not present, not verbal—there was a quiet resembling social or political death; in effect, the women were erased."[6]

Rock music was one of the contemporary realms that invited modern women to the door only to slam it in their faces. Psychedelic rock, carrying electric blues into a free-form "jamming" musical aesthetic, brought a couple of women to the front of the stage, but as vocalists rather than instrumentalists who also contributed vocals, the way men rockers more often fashioned themselves. At that time, few in the rock audience understood the aesthetic and technical demands of vocal styling as jazz and blues audiences had before them. Grace Slick of the Jefferson Airplane and Janis Joplin, originally of Big Brother and the Holding Company, created the San Francisco sound for national audiences as much as had other performers—but their popularity did not ensure a welcome to other women performers trying to break into rock.

Joplin Breaks

Janis Joplin's voice was remarkable, as her biographer Alice Echols makes clear, for its versatility. She began singing soprano in a church choir in Port Arthur, Texas, where she spent a miserable youth. Janis too got caught in the gap between what the culture seemed to promise and what was actually allowed. "I was one of the girls," she remembered, "who always wanted to do things that my mother said I couldn't because only boys get to do those things."[7] Yet when her mother insisted that she pass her secretarial tests before she ventured beyond Port Arthur, Janis complied.[8] Her first jaunt to California in 1961 ended with her bumming around in Venice and North Beach before she returned as the conquering bohemian to Port Arthur, to enroll in the local college once more.

While Joplin created her identity as a tough, wild, hard-drinking party girl, she also continued her musical career in fits and starts. She moved from sacred music to folk music, a natural journey for a white girl singer in the late fifties. She got jobs in her area of East Texas and later around Austin, where she moved to go to school in 1962. She quickly found the folk music crowd, coextensive with the group disaffected by the jock-and-Greek scene that dominated University of Texas social life. Initially shy about performing, she was thrust forward when a few friends accidentally discovered her astonishing voice. She had begun to sing in a "Bessie Smith" gravelly, bluesy voice, the seed of her signature sound, and she refused to revisit the pure choirgirl voice of her childhood. After she was "discovered," she used the burgeoning Austin folk scene to hone her chops and actually, as Echols contends, get quite serious about her music. She was never an instrumentalist and didn't even achieve much skill with the autoharp she sometimes used to accompany herself. But she worked on her vocal skills with studied intensity.[9] At Threadgill's bar outside Austin, she became the main attraction on Wednesday nights, when the students drove out with their guitars and banjos. The bar's owner became Janis's first benevolent patron, and she found room to grow as a performer. In January 1963 she moved to San Francisco, where her huge voice got her noticed. Yet it took another three years and another flight back to Port Arthur and Austin before the pieces fell into place. In 1966 she returned to San Francisco to audition for Big Brother and the Holding Company, the house band at the new Avalon Ballroom. Her voice and stage presence took over that band. *Cheap Thrills* went to number one in 1968; soon afterward, Joplin left Big Brother to form a new band, the Kozmic Blues Band, and then finally, months before her death in October 1970, the Full Tilt Boogie Band, assembled to back her on the album *Pearl*.

Biographers have searched for the victimizing force in Joplin's poignantly short life and career. Like Billie Holiday, she allowed her demons, wherever they originated, to overwhelm her great gift—and it is difficult to know, now, what was the cost exacted by the gift itself. Not black, not poor, but outspoken in a world where women were supposed to hold back, deemed "ugly" by a society in thrall to beauty magazine standards, sexually aggressive and experimental, and hugely talented, Janis Joplin never managed to organize her defenses (so weak) or her personality (so multifaceted) to build a trustworthy bridge from inside to the outside world. Historian Lucy O'Brien writes perceptively: "Joplin often said she wished she was black, not so much in a clumsy, naïve appropriation of black culture, but as a way to understand and reach something in herself, a depth of tensile feeling that was denied by her white prom-queen small-town upbringing."[10]

Just as many women in the 1960s and '70s were trying to create a new place for themselves in society, women musicians were also trying to create a new place for themselves in the band. While women had entered rock 'n' roll playing instruments and writing songs in their rooms, the core of the rock experience is being part of a band, and, in most ways, women were excluded from or marginalized within rock bands. Rock bands, like rock music, are gendered male; the collective American assumption is that being in a rock band is a male and masculine activity. To perform rock music, then, is to perform masculinity. The choice left for women is either to try to act like a man in a band, complete with swagger and aggression, or to become a caricature of femininity, which may lead to commercial success (as a reward for enacting gender scripts) but usually means leaving behind playing hard, driving rock 'n' roll. Brita Rae Borough, a guitarist in a rock band, says that people appreciate her playing more when they hear her on CD rather than live. She suggests this is because the way she looks when she plays guitar does not mimic expected masculine norms. People have suggested that she "headbang" or jump around onstage, but she explains, "I don't feel like banging my head when I play rock. I just don't have that level of aggression." She also tells the story of standing onstage with her hot pink electric guitar waiting to do a sound check when the sound man said to her, "So, when does the guitar player get here?" She was stunned. "The sound man thought I was, what, the girlfriend of the guitarist that plays a pink guitar?"[11]

Despite the obstacles, women have tried out for and found ways of being in the band. While some women have fronted male bands, as Joplin did, others have played in predominantly male bands, usually fronted by men. Some have formed all-women bands; others have become part of bands that have a gender balance or bands dominated by women. Especially talented vocalists have become headliners with their own bands whose players seem—justly or not—obscure and interchangeable; the band, in other words, serves as the backdrop to the vocalist. As we examine each of these ways that women relate to bands, we find (not surprisingly) that the serious business of the rock 'n' roll band is a gendered space in which women have had to negotiate the terrain between rock's male identification and their identity as rock musicians.

Boyfriends, Brothers, and the Boys in the Band

Many women we talked to came into their first band through a connection with a brother, boyfriend, or other male friend who saw through gender constraints to talent. Jill Sobule's older brother had a rock band in Denver that rehearsed in her family's basement, and Jill was always there, hankering to play guitar just like her big brother. At first, she notes, she wanted to play drums and got a drum set, but her parents convinced her "that the guitar is a much nicer instrument."[12] Animal picked up hand drums in high school when she started hanging out with some boys who had a garage band. The guys had some hand drums, and Animal started playing. "It was just like magic," she says. Of course, she and Bitch have gone on to stretch the notion of a band. Bitch explains, "Well, from the beginning, a lot of people were like, 'You guys just can't be a band with a violin and a drum or whatever.' I mean, not like we ever thought we were a band. We always thought we were performance artists." Animal stops her: "No, we thought we were a band."[13]

Paula Spiro's brother helped her select her first drum pad. In early adolescence, they both joined the drum and bugle corps. Girls were not allowed to play drums at that time, so Paula carried a flag and then a rifle in the color guard. Her brother would bring the other boys over to practice, and she would watch the boys play. When girls were at last allowed to play drums, Paula picked up a tenor drum for color guard competition. Her brother helped convince her mother that she was not "going to grow out of this," and so she bought Paula her first drum set in 1960, a Sears Red Sparkle set. The boys showed her one beat, and she joined her first band, Devil's Disciples. Despite her one beat, she recounts, she got a lot of support in the community because no other girls were playing drums in a band.

That changed when she moved to New York, where in 1969, "Girls just don't play drums. They watch boys play drums, but girls don't play drums." At that point, she started playing with all-women bands. Gratifyingly, these bands were under good management, and Spiro says she was able to make a very good living playing the clubs around New York. Of course, the band did not expect a record deal, and they did not play original music. "It wasn't even in our vocabulary to even be talking about being signed or getting any record deals. . . . We didn't play original music because we learned very early that you didn't get paid. So we played only cover material."[14]

Melissa Auf der Maur started her first band with a boyfriend and some other guys in town. The band only lasted for a year and did only about ten shows, but in one of those shows they opened for Smashing Pumpkins. Around 1990, Auf der Maur had met Billy Corgan, the band's lead singer, at a club. After she got her own band, she wrote Corgan: "Remember me? I met you at the show. And now I finally have my own band together and I see you have a big record, *Siamese Dream*, coming out, and I was hoping that my band, we've only played six shows, but I was hoping we could open up for your band." And Corgan said, "Yes."

Corgan became a significant friend and mentor for Melissa. After her band opened for Smashing Pumpkins, Corgan put his arm around Melissa and said, in a dream-come-true kind of moment, "Kid, you've got it. And I'm going to find a place for you one day. . . . One day you're going to be in my band." Seven years later, Corgan invited Melissa to join a Smashing Pumpkins tour.[15]

Both Scarlet Rivera and Paz Lenchantin got into bands by chance encounters. Scarlet met Bob Dylan walking down the street one day and became the first woman to play in one of Dylan's bands. When she was just eighteen, Paz walked into a bar one night and saw this "long-faced person, kind of morose, you know, feeling down." She went over to him and asked, "What's wrong? Why such a long face?" He explained, "I just lost a bass player, my guitar player, and my violin player in this band. And we were doing so well. . . . Do you happen to know any [players]?" Paz says her eyes shot wide open as she exclaimed, "I play." He did not seem to take her seriously, but later he called to schedule an audition. And she got the spot in the band.[16] Stacey Board says she got in her first band "because as a chick I could sing all the high stuff like Journey and Led Zeppelin."[17]

Lynn Frances Anderson pursued an opportunity to be in her first band. "There used to be a little mag, a little newspaper/magazine called *Portland Music Guide*. And in it there were contacts for all the bands in the Portland area. So I just opened it up, and I started calling people. I'm like, 'Hi, I'm a singer. I want to be in a band. Hi, I'm a singer. I want to be in a band.'" Then one day she went into a music store and started talking to some of the guys hanging around. They told her their band was looking for a lead singer. Lynn said, "Well, I'm a singer." They asked her to audition and she got into her first band, singing Top 40 songs. Her early interactions with the band were complicated because she didn't quite know how to come out to them. "It was kind of stressful because at first I didn't walk in and go, 'OK, I'm a lesbian, and I just want you to know.' . . . Once they figured it out, the heat was off." Lynn says she hated singing Top 40 in smoky bars. "I wanted to leave. But I thought, 'I have to do this. I have to do this. This is what I have to do to get over this so that I can go on.' . . . I've always known that my job in this lifetime is to be a musician and a singer and a songwriter. I've always known that. It's just taken me a long time to get brave enough to do it. And how the heck are you supposed to pay your bills?"[18]

Rose Polenzani reflected on both the need for and the dilemmas of male support. From family members to friends to music teachers to accompanists, men have affirmed Rose as a musician, and she has wanted and needed their support. Working for a Chicago record label, Rose found a songwriting mentor in Andrew Calhoun, the label's president. Just thinking she might play a song for him some day made her go over and over and over it because she was afraid he might not like it. She says it took a year and a half before he commented that he liked a song. "You know, it's not like he was rejecting me or anything, but he just never commented. And I didn't really know what he thought until one day when I sang 'Olga's Birthday,' and he said, 'Now that's a great song.' And I was like, 'Whew!' I was so relieved." So while Calhoun and many other men supported Rose's musical development, she says, they played a typical masculine role; they made her feel "like my work is valid because a guy says it's good." And it worked for her, she acknowledges, because, like most women, she is "set up for it."[19] And so while she gratefully credits these men with keeping her going in her career, she realizes that her need for male validation results from women being socialized to seek and depend upon male approval.

Not only do most women seek male approval, but, in the arena of rock 'n' roll, they do it in a context defined by male norms and standards. Good rock is male rock. And just as women are complicit in valorizing male approval, they may also accept male standards for acceptable or excellent musicianship. Several times in our interview with Rana Ross, who spoke eloquently about the constraints gender places on women musicians, she mentioned proudly that men came up to her after hearing her play and said, " 'Wow, Rana, you can hang with the guys.' " She even speculated that really good women players probably have higher levels of testosterone than other women. "You have to," she explained. "It's a boys club just like the rest of the world. And you gotta play in the boys club. And now I'm in the boys club. Well, how does somebody get in the boys club? You've got to be like a boy." Later, however, Rana talked about how rock also gives women a chance to be powerful in their own way.[20] Rose's desire for male approval and Rana's determination to hold her own with the guys indicate the difficult and conflicted position of women in rock. While challenging the norms of masculine discourse, they are also bound by them.

Being Me in a Big Way

In addition to getting into a band, women have to learn to perform in front of an audience.[21] Most of our informants started performing as children—in front of friends and family, at church, in school talent shows. Despite nerves and occasional blunders, they found themselves thrilled by the sheer joy of singing and playing for others. Along the way, they developed more finesse and professionalism, but most have maintained that initial exuberance at being in front of an audience. The majority of them have not constructed a stage persona that differs wildly from their own personalities, but they have paid attention to how they look and act onstage, and they have honed their performance skills to present a particular public image.

Because gender itself is a performance, part of the persona they perform is gender, and many women musicians are quite aware of that. Often, they choose to subvert traditional images of femininity in constructing their personae, making decisions that range from refusing to wear "gender-appropriate" clothing to exaggerating stereotypical female sexuality with short skirts, high heels, and fishnet stockings. Many play with gender-bending, dressing hypersexually while playing aggressively or presenting themselves androgynously.[22] Of course, not all women in music rebel against gender norms; in fact, many conform to these norms as a way to succeed in the music industry. (We will address issues of appearance in more depth in chapter 6.)

Many of the women we talked to told us that they first performed in front of family and friends, often during holiday celebrations or at school. Indigo Girl Amy Ray explains, "You play for Thanksgiving dinner. It's the first thing you do basically, like a talent show in your family or whatever. There's no other way to learn to play in front of people."[23]

Sarah Dash says she first sang in front of people in second or third grade. "I had to do a Thanksgiving song. And I remember, they told us, 'You cannot scratch your head or anything,' and my mother put all these heavy curls in my hair. And I wanted to scratch so bad, and finally I said, 'They told me not to scratch, but before I start to sing, I'm gonna scratch.' And then I sang the song, and people laughed. And I've been a clown ever since."[24] Leah Hinchcliff and Jill Gewirtz cite school talent shows in fourth grade as their first performances. Jill weighed in with "Kumbaya." [25]

Jann Arden never wanted to pursue music. She had secretly taught herself guitar, using the big orange binder her mother had gotten when she had taken guitar lessons from a local preacher. After she learned a few John Denver songs, she moved on to writing her own. Finally, she played one for a friend down the road. Then she started playing in Calgary in a Wednesday open-mic contest with a fifty-dollar prize for singer/songwriters. She would take a few friends with her, and she lost, she says, for months. "I just wanted to get up in front of people and play a little bit." Then one night, after about six months of doing the Wednesday night open mics, she won. "When they called my name, I just, I remember thinking, 'That can't be right. That can't be right.'" The next year, her classmates convinced her to sing at graduation. That was the first time her parents even knew she played guitar.[26]

Jonatha Brooke's first performances were actually in dance. At six, in London, she was taking her primary honors exam for the Royal Academy of Ballet. After working through her set of mandatory exercises, she was invited to improvise. "And so I, being the ugly American, went out, and I waddled around this little stage and quacked like Donald Duck. And I don't know how I did, but they gave me honors because I guess I had the ballet part down. They said, 'Very charming indeed.' That was my first performance, for these stodgy old ballet mistresses, British, very British ballet mistresses." Her first musical performance was at summer camp. "I sang a John Denver song, and it was 'Country Roads.' " From then on, she was hooked on performing. Like Amy Ray, she says that you only learn to perform by performing. "That's the hardest thing that you learn, and you can only learn it by doing it a million times and touring your butt off because at first it was so hard to figure out what do you say between songs? How do you address this audience? How do you bring them into your world? How do you communicate and give something of yourself besides your music?"[27]

Niki Lee, a Baltimore singer-songwriter, says that her "real training" for performance came from her years as a bartender. "You really learn a lot about being onstage from your position behind the bar. You end up being part school teacher, part sex symbol, and mostly an authoritarian with almost complete control." She has chosen several ways to relate to an audience; besides performing her individual songs, she has developed a one-woman show based on the writings of Dorothy Parker. On the one hand, she says, she would be "in heaven" if she could be in a studio all day. On the other hand, she loves performing, and getting that "high" from being in front of an audience. "For all the angst I've gone through to get onstage, I must really love it. No one would want to feel that sick about something they didn't love."[28]

Lynn Witting learns something new every time she does a live performance. "If it's what you love, you're only going to get better."[29] Feedback from friends certainly changed things for the Indigo Girls. Amy Ray says that she and Emily Saliers started out sitting down when they played. Then one of Amy's college friends bought her a guitar strap and said, "I think you need a guitar strap so you can stand up." Amy says she still has the friend and the strap. "That's when I started standing up." "That was pivotal," Emily adds. "It makes all the difference," Amy concurs. "I mean, if a lot of people want to sit down still, that's fine, but for me it was like, for both of us, we became" . . . "liberated," Emily finishes her sentence. "A standing band," Amy says. "We couldn't play the folk clubs any more because we stood up." Emily: "They hated us."[30]

Churches and bars are also common venues for first performances. Kate Campbell first sang in front of her church. She borrowed a friend's guitar, and she and her friend sang "Silent Night" for the congregation. Once a member of the church made a tape of her singing James Taylor's "Fire and

Rain." That was the first time she heard herself sing, and, she says, "I couldn't believe how I said, 'far' [that's "fire" with a thick Southern accent, for all you non-Southern readers]. I just didn't know I talked like that." Mortified though she was, she kept singing and added school talent shows to her venues. She began to sing her own compositions, which tended toward country-western. A science teacher tried to convince her parents to let him send her songs to a publisher, but her father, a Southern Baptist preacher, said, 'No.' After all, at that point, Campbell explains, "Country music was considered to be honky tonk. And there were certain places you sang country music."[31] A Baptist church was not one of them.

Lynn Frances Anderson's first appearance onstage at a club in Vancouver, Washington, was, in her words, "awful. I had been practicing with this band, which was not a very good band at all, but it was the first one I ever got into. And we started playing and some guy started, some drunk guy, and this always happens, started yelling 'Freebird.' I didn't even know what the song was. Like why is that guy yelling 'Freebird?' . . . Of course, the band, they laughed and they played a couple of bars of 'Freebird.' And I'm like, 'Oh, that's kind of familiar.' But it was so scary. I wanted to leave."[32]

Talent shows also seem to be a common launching pad for aspiring performers. Brenda Lee first performed at a school talent show that her first-grade sister had entered her in. And Brenda won. "I won the trophy for the school. Of course, the school got to keep the trophy for a year, and, whoever won it the next year, the trophy moved on to that school."[33] As recent immigrants from the Philippines, June and Jean Millington had a hard time adjusting to their new California junior high school. Music really saved them, Jean recalls. When she was in eighth grade and June in ninth, they performed one of June's first songs in the school talent show. People started to pay attention to them. The timing was great for them, she says, because of the folk revival and burgeoning interest in acoustic guitars. Because they played guitars, they started doing Peter, Paul, and Mary songs and other new folk standards. But then the Beatles hit, and folk music paled by comparison. The sisters decided to learn to play electric instruments. They persuaded their mother to help them (their father was dead-set against it; he wanted them to become "professionals"—doctor, nurse, that kind of thing), and she signed for them to buy a couple of instruments.[34]

The Shirelles chose to enter a talent show rather than take detention when a teacher scolded them for disrupting class. The girls decided they wanted to do an original song, and so one day they were sitting around an apartment babysitting and trying to come up with something. Finally one of the girls said, "Just pick a day of the week and make up something, a line." So Shirley Owens (now Alston Reeves) said, "So I met him on a Sunday." Then Micki Harris picked it up: "I missed him on a Monday." Doris Jackson chimed in: "I phoned him on a Tuesday." Beverly Lee added Wednesday, and they continued through the rest of the week. Shirley says, "Then we put a little melody to it and the hand claps and stuff. And that's what we sang at the school. But we also bought little outfits. We bought black taffeta skirts and white nylon blouses with, you know, like the kind of tuxedo front, you know, with the little pleats. I'll never forget. And we wore that with the little black pumps on stage at the high school." [35]

Leah Hinchcliff was not really aware that she had developed a stage persona until friends commented on the change that overcomes her when she moves from playing lead guitar or singing to playing bass. "I have this sort of attitude that I can't find any other time except for when I'm onstage and I have my bass in my hands. It's not like developing a stage persona. It's more like letting that part of myself be really present." "What part?" we asked. "Confidence, very, very confident. Kind of bad ass I think, because bass is kind of a bad ass instrument. And funky, and I think, I feel, I really feel like I'm myself then. So I'm very comfortable onstage. I feel very happy. Sometimes I just find myself smiling a lot. I think, 'I'm playing a sad song; maybe I shouldn't have this big grin on my face.' But it's hard to not smile. It's like you're doing this thing, and it's really moving."

Leah's very first performance certainly revealed her passion for music. She appeared onstage in first grade with a group of other kids singing, "Let's Go Fly a Kite" from Mary Poppins. "And I couldn't stop smiling. I was so happy that my face actually hurt. And I can remember going back to the room and telling my mom, 'I always want to do that, Mom. I always want to do that.'" [36]

Rana Ross took comfort in being behind an instrument when she first started performing. "There's a big difference between being, say, a lead Gloria Estefan, Britney Spears, Madonna, if you don't have an instrument in front of you. There is most definitely a feeling of 'I am secure behind this instrument; this is my safety, is my instrument.' And that's probably why I'm not a lead singer, because this instrument is what I need to be onstage. If this instrument was not on me, I probably couldn't be onstage." Rana said she did not get nervous any more when onstage. We asked her how she did feel. "Oooh. I feel really powerful when I'm onstage. . . . I've played with people who say, 'I go onstage and I become somebody else. You know, I put on a mask and I become somebody else.' I don't. I'm still Rana. I'm still me. I'm still who I am. I'm just given the opportunity to be me in a big way." [37]

The Front

Journalists Simon Reynolds and Joy Press suggest that women adopt four distinct though often overlapping strategies to construct themselves as rock musicians. The first simply imitates the male model: women enact the norms (toughness, aggression, rebellion) of masculinity. In the second strategy, women bring "femininity" to rock by positing a female strength (which may valorize normative constructions of femininity). The third, more postmodern strategy recognizes the performative nature of gender and relies on the construction of self-conscious and provisional identities that can be turned against the society that created them. The final strategy recognizes the painful tension that exists for women between assuming a feminine essence and performing a series of strategic identities, and it focuses on the process of negotiation between the two.[38]

In many ways, women who have fronted male bands illustrate this tension. On the one hand, women have probably found the greatest acceptance in rock as vocalists because singing is considered an appropriate activity for a woman. Nonetheless, those pioneering rock vocalists who wanted to sing hard, driving rock 'n' roll had only male models, and so often they likewise constructed themselves as tough, swaggering, macho rebels. And while they negotiated the space between acceptable female activities and the male genre of rock, their music often met with mixed responses.

Blondie, fronted by Deborah Harry, showed up in New York's CBGB in the mid-1970s with a sound that combined pop and punk and initially received little radio play. "[Our music] was pop that was very aggressive," explains Harry, "with a female front-person, and an aggressive female front-person had never really been done in pop. It was very difficult to be in that position at the time—it's hard to be a ground-breaker."[39]

One of the first and rare women to succeed as a front-person for a stadium rock band was Jefferson Airplane's Grace Slick, who emerged out of the 1960s Bay Area counterculture. Inspired by an early Jefferson Airplane concert (at the time the band was fronted by Signe Toly), Slick and her husband formed Great Society and recorded two albums for Columbia that were not released until after her success with Jefferson Airplane. When Toly left the band, the group approached Slick to join them, and she brought with her two songs she had performed with Great Society—"Somebody to Love," by brother-in-law Darby Slick, and her own "White Rabbit." The band's 1967 album with Slick, *Surrealistic Pillow,* immediately reached the Top 10. Slick had striking writing and vocal skills. "What we took for granted seems remarkable now," writes Ariel Swartley: "a fearless, authoritative, frankly female voice claiming rock & roll as a political force—arguing the case, even, and not just on paper. When Slick laid out her case, you could—if you weren't too fussy about a backbeat—dance to it."[40]

Chrissie Hynde of the Pretenders epitomizes the tough woman in rock. Her persona illustrates the tension between the masculine norms of rock and women's identity as rock musicians. Hynde's in-your-face vocals and aggressive guitar playing put her in a class with the most macho male rockers. And while Hynde is often held up as a model for women in rock, she distances herself from feminism, as Gillian Gaar notes, to the relief of many male critics and fans. Gaar points out the irony—the stereotype of a feminist is an angry, aggressive, masculine man-hater, which some could possibly see in Hynde's rough and tough demeanor. Gaar adds that when the Pretenders were gaining popularity, Helen Reddy ("hardly anyone's idea of a threatening personality") was the only mainstream musician openly identifying herself as a feminist.[41]

Rana Ross spoke to us of this tension. For women to get in the "boys' club" requires a lot of perseverance, she said. "It's lots of getting that armor around you and just knowing that you're powerful. You know? And I can't tell you how many times I've been called a bitch. . . . I am certainly a bitch when it comes to having my equipment onstage, having it right, having my tech do it right. It's not really a bitch. I just want it right. . . . If you're a guy you'd be demanding or perfectionist. So I'm a perfectionist too. So you just happen to be a woman perfectionist."[42]

Kitzie Stern says she did not enjoy fronting a male band. In fact, she started to learn an instrument so she wouldn't have to front any more. She was particularly uncomfortable dealing with audience members who heckled her and made offensive sexual remarks. Usually she was the only woman traveling with the band. "Sometimes the wives of the band members would come. That was rare. I was the only woman, and I wasn't connected to anybody in the band, although, God knows, they tried. I mean, you know, that's generally the case that the girl singer is involved with somebody in the band. And I just never wanted to do that because I figured if it didn't work out, then there goes my band and my source of income."[43]

Erin O'Hara, on the other hand, had a positive experience as the singer in her first band. When she was a student at SUNY-Albany, she and her roommates went into an ice cream shop where two young men were playing guitars. The guys said they were forming a band and they were looking for a singer. Helpfully, Erin's roommates told them, "Oh, she sings in the shower." Shortly afterward, Erin met with the guys, they wrote a song together, and that was the beginning of Mambo X, a band that played together for three years, opening for artists such as Michelle Shocked, 10,000 Maniacs, and Tom Tom Club. "It was wonderful!" Erin exclaims. [44]

The Singer

While artists like Hynde, Slick, and Harry have negotiated gender as vocalists in a band, other women vocalists have constructed their identities as solo artists for whom bands are accompaniment. As the main act, rather than part of the band, these women have a wider range of options for expressing gender, although their solo identities also leave them open for more pointed (and often caustic) critique. As is typical of women in other male-dominated professions, physical characteristics and personal relationships often seem more interesting to fans and critics than their work.

On one end of the spectrum, Pat Benatar assumed the persona of the tough woman rocker, but, as Gaar suggests, she was more palatable to United States audiences than Hynde because "her image was more conventionally feminine."[45] Benatar was also more commercially successful, with a steady stream of hits and Grammys. But the rock press quickly marginalized her musically for "pandering" to commercial tastes and focused on her as a sex symbol. "I used to think I could be real sexless onstage," she explains. "It doesn't work. You're a female, and it comes out no matter what you do." She also disliked the way her own record company played her up as a sex symbol. "I came back from the last tour and found out they'd made a cardboard cutout of me in my little tights. What has that got to do with anything?"[46]

Other vocalists seized on the performative power of their sexuality and strutted it across the stage, almost in a parody of the stereotypical sexiness expected of women. Cher, Madonna, Bette Midler, and Tina Turner have all demonstrated publicly their ability both to control and to flaunt their sexuality. Of course, as Lucy O'Brien suggests, the price they may have paid is that, while they are adored by their fans, both male and female, they are not really seen as serious rock stars.[47]

Certainly Cyndi Lauper understood her stage persona as performance, and she created an image of a thrift-shop-wardrobed, carefree, best girlfriend that celebrated female experience and friendship. Unlike many women performers, she did not distance herself from feminism, and her 1983 hit, "Girls Just Want to Have Fun," became a feminist anthem. In fact, *Ms.* magazine named her one of its "Women of the Year" for 1984, explaining, "If Helen Reddy's recording of 'I Am Woman' was about anger and a newfound collective pride, 'Girls Just Want to Have Fun' is about a newer, defiant joy and the celebration of our strength."[48] Ultimately, Lauper's appearance and wackiness worked against her. Elton John could wear boas and sequins and still be taken seriously and permitted room to re-create himself. But Cyndi Lauper found it hard to shake her early image and never again reached the level of success she had with *She's So Unusual.*

The Player

While the women out front grappled with their various presentations and representations, the women in the band, the instrumentalists, grappled with invisibility and marginalization within their own bands. Few women have ever been allowed entrée into the male rock band and certainly not on equal footing with the male players. Lamenting this inequality, Melissa Auf der Maur wonders how many times people can say, "You're pretty good for a girl."[49]

Carol Kaye was a pioneer in the late 1950s, usually the only woman playing with men. Following a short stint of touring and playing jazz and big-band music in nightclubs around Los Angeles, she moved into the studio to play for Sam Cooke, Richie Valens, and the Beach Boys, among others. Kaye says that a lot of women were playing, mostly jazz, in the '50s, "but you don't hear about them now. I think the rock 'n' roll era kind of stopped all that because women would [ordinarily play only] until they got married. See, because that was important back then to have a 'Mrs.' in front of your name, which is bull. . . . Anyway, my marriages didn't work out, so I had to keep playing. Take care of my kids."[50]

Maureen (Moe) Tucker was one of the first women to play in a predominantly male band. Her opportunity came when the Velvet Underground's original drummer quit. One of the band's members knew Tucker's brother. Initially the guitarist raised objections about having a "chick" in the band, but Tucker proved herself. When the band connected with Andy Warhol, he added vocalist Nico to the mix. Nico was the glamorous, mysterious European. Tucker, on the other hand, cared little for glamour. In fact, she was sometimes mistaken for a man because of her short hair and androgynous appearance.

Tucker left the band in 1969 to have her first child and, like Patti Smith, disappeared into the suburbs to have a family. This choice between music and family has often faced women artists, who, like their counterparts in other professional fields, are expected to be the primary caregivers within the family. Often when women rockers choose to have families, they must put their careers on hold or deal with the culturally induced guilt that follows women who leave their children at home while they work. When Deb

Frost finally reached her dream of a rock band, the Brain Surgeons, with her husband Albert Bouchard, she limited their touring so that their son could have a relatively normal school and home experience.[51] Chrissie Hynde chose to take her children on the road with her.

Tina Weymouth met David Byrne at The Rhode Island School of Design, where they and Weymouth's boyfriend Chris Frantz (whom she later married) were students. Byrne and Frantz were forming a band, which eventually became known as Talking Heads, and Weymouth and Frantz convinced Byrne to let Tina play bass for the group, despite Byrne's worries about having a woman in the band (he wasn't sure how it would be received, he says). When the band signed a record deal, Byrne made Weymouth audition for her place in the band again.

Weymouth did not want to be seen as a novelty and downplayed gender as much as possible, although she recognized sexism in the industry and her place as a role model for aspiring women rockers. Interestingly, because Weymouth did not focus on gender, the rock press often perceived her as asexual. Because she could not easily be placed into one of the stereotypes of women in rock, (male) rock journalists seemed left without a category into which to fit this competent, confident bass player who was neither a tough chick nor a sultry vixen. Rather than deal with the complexities of gender, sexuality, and identity, they preferred to sweep them aside, leaving an image, as one journalist described her, of "a kind of friendly Mother Superior."[52]

Byrne never really became comfortable with a woman in the band, taking credit for the band's creativity and marginalizing Weymouth. Eventually Weymouth and Frantz started their own band, Tom Tom Club, although they continued to play in Talking Heads until the group split in 1991.

Vicki Randle says that until she started working in women's music, she was almost always the only woman in the band, and because she played an instrument rather than being " 'just a vocalist,' " she was "a bit of an enigma to most of the guys." She explains, "There was always the initial test to pass. 'Can she play? Can she play as well as a man?' " But she adds, once she established that indeed she could "play as well as a man," she was "usually adopted as a honorary 'Cat.' " Because, however, the men in the band had no reference point for a female player, they either designated her as "prey" or "mom," or they treated her as one of the guys, subjecting her to sexist jokes and comments about other women. Once, when one of the guys in the band asked her to sew a button on his shirt, she explained that she was a musician and had never learned to sew. Eventually, though, the men came to accept her and, when they found out her salary was lower than theirs, they marched into the manager's office and demanded she be given the same salary.[53]

Scarlet Rivera had positive experiences as the first and only woman in Bob Dylan's band. "I really did feel like it was an important thing for me to be doing." Although she admits that initially other band members probably wondered what she was doing there, her introduction of the violin to rock 'n' roll received an enormous amount of good press. She recalls that much of the coverage characterized her as a "mysterious . . . gypsy" playing with "dark ominous fire and frenzy."[54] Leafing through *The Book of the Violin,* which someone gave her for Christmas, Scarlet was delighted to find she had earned a place in violin history, at least for that writer, who described Scarlet as playing with "dionysiac zest."[55]

For Scarlet, playing well behind singers relies mostly on developing a dynamic understanding between musicians and singers. She says she makes other performers happy when she plays with them because she doesn't "get in their way." On tour, band members traditionally spend time with the band, removed from the singer, who is often kept isolated from the group by a manager. When she toured with the Indigo Girls, however, the situation was very different. "They didn't act like stars," she explains. "They hung out with you, and they drank beers with you."[56]

Kate Schellenbach came into bands by way of New York's 1980s punk scene. When she was in high school, she and some friends went to a concert at CBGB. She suddenly realized that there was a whole other world of music being played in clubs where "you can be like two feet away from [the band]. . . . And it's not just like buying a ticket to go see a band at Madison Square Garden or something like that, which didn't appeal to me at all. So that was really my first introduction to a lot of music, and it's kind of when I started going out to see bands."

Part of the punk scene's appeal to Schellenbach was its inclusiveness. In the clubs, she saw young women playing drums, guitar, and bass. She says the punk scene became her "after-school hobby—seeing bands, going to record stores, finding new groups, listening to music, hanging out with friends, and everybody was like wanting to start to play instruments and be in bands together." About that time a friend of her mother's left a drum kit at their apartment and a neighbor from upstairs lent her a snare drum. "It's sort of like the gods rained drums down onto me and allowed me to play them," she explains. "And I'd just play along to records, records that I like that had some simple beat. And that's basically how I learned to play. And I was probably fourteen."

While hanging out in the punk club scene, Schellenbach met Michael Diamond, who was in a band called Young Aborigines. He asked Kate to play with them. The band eventually became the Beastie Boys. Initially the group was a safe, fun place for her. At the time, they were playing punk, reggae, hip-hop, and rap. The group began to focus more on playing rap and then hooked up with producer Rick Rubin. Schellenbach says Rubin was very sexist and his attitude rubbed off on the guys in the band. A lot of rap at that time was about posturing and bragging about sexual prowess. At first, the Beasties' raps in this bragging genre were self-consciously funny, but then, she says, the raps became serious, and, as the group became more well known, the guys in the band changed and began to enact the sexist scripts of male rock stardom. Uncomfortable with the change in music and attitude, Schellenbach left the band.[57]

In the early 1990s Schellenbach hooked up with some women friends she had known when she was a teenager. The two, Gabrielle Glaser and Jill Cunniff, were playing music and gave Kate a demo tape. They wanted to put together a band and invited Schellenbach and Vivian Trimble to join them. Together they became Luscious Jackson. Jill and Gabby gave one of their demo tapes to Beastie Boy Mike Diamond. The Beastie Boys were in the process of starting their own label, Grand Royal, and Diamond wanted to release the Luscious Jackson album. The independent label was soon signed over to Capitol Records, and so the band ended up working with a major recording company. We will talk more about the issues of the recording industry and independent labels in chapter 7.

All Women All the Time

Beginning in the 1960s a number of all-women bands had preceded Luscious Jackson. They often found it difficult to be taken seriously by fans and the music industry, who dismissed them as novelties or cast them as the diminutive "sister" to a male band. For these musicians, gender was foregrounded in a way that musicians in all-male bands never faced. Certainly, no one ever introduced the Rolling Stones as "an all-male band." Their designation as "all-female" moved these musicians' gender to the fore and overshadowed their music. While they may have escaped a great deal of sexism from within the band, larger cultural norms continued to grind the lenses through which they were seen and their music evaluated. Jean Millington says that when Fanny started on the road, the band always had to overcome the audience's initial skepticism. When male bands play, she explains, there is no prejudgment. The audience waits to hear how the band sounds. Fanny, though, had to overcome the assumption that because they were women they could not play well. Jean recounts an instance in England when the producer of the show took the women backstage to the dressing rooms. He pointed to one and said, "This is the dressing room for the girls." He pointed to another and said, "This is the dressing room for the band."[58] Vixen drummer Roxy Petrucci explained how, almost twenty years later, her band faced the same attitudes: "Everyone, and I seriously mean everyone, was waiting for us to make even one little mistake because no one believed that women could really rock."[59]

When Goldie and the Gingerbreads signed with Atlantic in the mid-1960s, they became the first all-woman band on a major label. Hearing them play in New York, Animals manager Michael Jeffries invited them to England, where they recorded "Can't You Hear My Heartbeat," which became a British Top 10. Unfortunately, the record was not released in the United States. When Jeffries got into a dispute with his business partner Mickie Most, who managed Herman's Hermits, Most gave the Hermits the song to record and release in the United States, where it climbed to number two on the charts. Despite their success in Europe (with two other British Top 10 singles), Goldie and the Gingerbreads never really made any money because their management misappropriated it. Although the women were exploited and promoted as a novelty, they did not seem to mind. They got to play, and they knew they were good at it.[60]

In 1969 Fanny became the first all-woman band to get a contract to record an entire album. Fanny began as the Svelts when June and Jean Millington formed a quartet with high school friends. The band went to Los Angeles in search of a record contract. One night when they were playing the Troubadour, record producer Richard Perry's secretary was in the audience. She called him and got the group an audition. Perry liked what he heard and signed them to Warner Brothers. The group changed its name to Fanny, which June insists was not because of its sexual connotations. "We felt it was a woman's spirit watching over us."[61] The record company, however, played up the sexual innuendo, distributing "Get Behind Fanny" bumper stickers and using photos of the group shot from behind. (In fact, that photo in its original context seems really rather *odd*, with a portion of June Millington's rear unmistakably gripped in Alice DeBuhr's hand.) June says the pressures on the group were tremendous. Management had great expectations that Fanny would be the next Beatles. For many people, June and Jean were the first women they saw playing electric guitar and bass. And the press treated the band only in terms of gender. Eventually the pressure became too great and, after four and a half years, the band broke up.

Inspired by Suzi Quatro, by age fifteen Joan Larkin had picked up a guitar, changed her name to Joan Jett, and put together her own band. Gillian Gaar notes that not surprisingly, sources vary as to the Runaways' origins and the amount of help Jett had from record producer Kim Fowley in forming the band; in any case the two met in 1975 and the Runaways emerged.[62] First Sandy West (Pesavento), a drummer since age nine, joined. She and Jett would be the last original members in the band when it dissolved. Sue Thomas, later known as Micki Steele of the Bangles, provided the vocals until she was replaced by Cherie Currie, whose twin sister Marie reportedly turned down the offer to sing. Jackie Fox (Fuchs) played bass, and Lita Ford, playing since age ten, added lead guitar. Currie and Fox left the band, Vicki Blue replaced Fox, and Jett became lead vocalist in 1977 following their Japan tour.

When the Runaways' first album was released in 1976, band members were unhappy that only Cherie Currie was on the cover. The band's relationship with Kim Fowley eroded. Their performances noisy and sexually provocative, the punk band had some success as a live act. But the press was often negative, and the majority of critics dismissed the band as an all-girl novelty act. The Runaways broke up in 1979. Deborah Frost comments, "Given that the overwhelming response of most of the Runaways' audience was, 'Hey, I can do that, too!,' they eventually sold many more guitars than records."[63] Reacting to criticism of their image, Joan Jett responded, "I think the Runaways were just too honest. Girls act like that—girls drink, girls smoke and girls swear. If it would have been an all-guy band no one would have given a shit."[64] While many debated the talent of the band, others agreed that they were "the most influential all-girl band to date."[65]

When the band separated, guitarist Lita Ford moved on to work on a solo career, collaborating with, among others, Sharon and Ozzy Osbourne. With a British influence and black leather, Joan Jett and her trademark "Ow!" broke through with the Blackhearts when "I Love Rock 'n' Roll" topped the charts in 1982. However, the success of that single did not protect her from negative reactions by male crowds. While performing in Italy and Spain to an all-male audience, Jett remembers, "I was covered in spit, and it was hanging off of me." She adds, "I cried every night because I didn't understand why they hated me so much." When Jett finally asked them, they responded, "'Girls playing rock & roll—you shouldn't be doing this.'"[66] But she persisted and many women rockers claim her as an inspiration.

The same year that Joan Jett had her biggest hit, the Go-Go's had the first number one album by an all-female band. *Beauty and the Beat* included "We Got the Beat," one of the catchiest, most irresistible singles in pop rock.

Originally a product of the punk scene in the late 1970s, the Go-Go's came out of the punk scene, worked on their music, and transformed themselves into pop stars. Gillian Gaar points out that unlike the B-52's and Blondie, groups that had done the same, the Go-Go's were the first all-female band to realize such commercial success. With Elissa Bello (eventually replaced by Gina Schock) on drums, Margot Olaverra (eventually replaced by Kathy Valentine) on bass, Jane Wiedlin and Charlotte Caffey on guitar, and Belinda Carlisle as lead singer, the group quickly dispelled the myth that an all-female band was not saleable.[67] Caffey said, "There had been Fanny and there had been the Runaways, but I guess 'cause we formed our own band, wrote all our own material, and played all the instruments, maybe they thought it would never work."[68]

The majority of us think of the Go-Go's visually as latter-day Supremes or, more accurately, Shangri-Las, posing in identical outfits and looking like a small gang of best girlfriends. Admittedly, their carefree and fun-loving photographic personae did not match their private lives. "We weren't happy. Everyone in the band wanted to do something else," Carlisle said.[69] "I got tired of being cute, bubbly, and effervescent all day."[70] Additional stresses included the drugs of the eighties, the pressures of success, and worldwide touring.

Playing in an all-woman band is no paradise of female sweetness and light. Tensions exist, as in any band, and problems arise. There is something, however, unique and special about playing with other women. Leah Hinchcliff sums it up: "We obviously have experiences together that men can never have. They're not women, so they've not been oppressed; well, some of them have, but not in the same way. Just fundamentally, no one has ever gone up to a guy and said, 'Wow, you're pretty good for a guy.'"[71]

In the Mix

A few bands in rock history have achieved a gender balance in the mix of musicians. Particularly successful examples of this blend are Fleetwood Mac and Heart. In each of these bands, the women were strong and truly integrated into the identity of the band. (In the case of Heart, the women eventually took over the band's identity.) And in both, sexual tensions among band members created disruptions along the way.

Fleetwood Mac reincarnated itself a number of times, and made a lot of terrific music, before taking the form Americans knew best in the mid-1970s. Stevie Nicks, joining the group in 1975, had a look and a voice that worked for a frontwoman. With wide eyes, flying blond hair, and flowing capes, she mesmerized audiences. Mysterious and enchanting, she had what Ann Powers describes as a voice that sounded like "she wasn't quite human, a creature from the deep."[72] Her distinctive soprano that cracked occasionally, coupled with the soulfulness of often-underrated Christine McVie (who predated Nicks as one of the group's writers and singers), produced a sound that appealed to post-teen rock lovers. Christine's husband John McVie, Mick Fleetwood, and Lindsey Buckingham completed the band that sold more than twenty million copies of 1977's *Rumours* within two years. Also known for their ever-evolving love triangles, the band has sold more than a hundred million albums worldwide. They gained additional recognition when their hit "Don't Stop Thinking about Tomorrow" was used in Bill Clinton's 1992 campaign for the White House, and they played at his Inaugural Gala. A decade later, the group has enjoyed a resurgence in popularity with their album *Say You Will,* released in April 2003.

When the Beatles came to America, young teens Ann and Nancy Wilson wanted to buy guitars and be as much like Paul, George, John, and Ringo as possible. In addition to the guitar, Ann learned to play flute and keyboard, while Nancy mastered several instruments, most notably guitar. Recruiting and teaching girlfriends to play, the Wilsons formed several bands, performing in schools, churches, and homes. From the late 1970s on, these women were known largely as a sister act, and they struggled to be seen as simply two members of their mixed-gender band, Heart, whose non-Wilson, male component had come together before Ann and then Nancy joined. Image mattered, and the Wilsons sometimes answered questions about their band roles defensively: "We don't try to be like men and we don't go in for the heavy feminine bit either."[73] The cover of their widely acclaimed 1976 album, *Dreamboat Annie,* which featured the two back-to-back with a red heart between them, enlarged their defensiveness. Ann complained that the cover was deceptive and implied that the buyer was in store for "cute, pink, lacy music," and their hard-driving music was anything but. Twenty-three years later, in a plenary session with Ann Wilson at the first Rockrgrl Conference in Seattle, woman after woman testified to *Dreamboat Annie's* seminal influence on their rock aspirations—no apologies needed, in retrospect. But at the time, the constant media focus on the sisters strained the group. "It's hard for any male to be in a band where the focal points are females who automatically get all the attention," said Nancy.[74] Because the two were romantically involved with the Fisher brothers—Roger, one of the band's guitarists, and Mike, their road manager—jealousies and politics sometimes got heavy.

Not wanting to exacerbate the gender issues in the band, Ann and

Nancy tiptoed around the feminist movement, at least during the 1970s. In 1977 Ann complained that she hated "being asked what it's like to be a woman in the rock business."[75] However, in the 1980s, the Wilson sisters started taking a more head-on approach to questions about women in rock. Selling more than thirty million records since the late 1970s with hits such as "Crazy on You," "Magic Man," and "Barracuda," Ann and Nancy Wilson have had a profound influence on rock.[76] They are still rocking, with a new tour and new music in the summer of 2003. Over the decades the nature of the band has become clear—the unvarying heart of Heart is indeed the Wilson sisters, whose talent now attracts an impressive backing band.[77]

Women on Top

In another group of bands, while men participate in the group, women definitely rule. The Breeders and Hole moved in a different direction from Fleetwood Mac and Heart. Guitarist/vocalist/songwriter Kim Deal, formerly of the Pixies, talked her twin sister, Kelley, into joining her band before Kelley even knew how to play. In 1989 Kim and her friend Tanya Donelly of the Throwing Muses cofounded the Breeders, a coed band that made its way onto college charts, fronted by Kim's voice that sounded "like a Girl Scout with a pack-and-a-half habit."[78]

Following their acclaimed 1990 album, *Pod,* their 1993 single "Cannonball" gave the Breeders "stadium status."[79] The men in the group were not tokens; they also surely helped deflect some of the special scrutiny accorded earlier groups. As Lucy O'Brien points out, "The attraction of mixed gender is that when it works at its fullest, a woman is paradoxically freer to be herself: attention is less on the 'novelty' tag," unlike the experience of the Runaways.[80] "Everyone that works with us—the monitor guy, manager, record company—doesn't talk about how we're girls," Kim Deal said. She complained that the only time the question came up was during interviews. Like Ann Wilson in 1977, more than a decade and a half later Deal obviously hated gender-related questions. "Evidently, talking to journalists, we aren't allowed to have a person's thoughts—we're only allowed to have a woman's thoughts."[81]

Kim Deal's candor can be seen in another woman in a mixed-gender band. Known for outspokenness, spunk, intelligence, tragedy, good acting (at least in *The People vs. Larry Flynt*), misbehavior, and metamorphosis, Courtney Love has been called "the most controversial woman in the history of rock."[82] After playing with Babes in Toyland and Faith No More, she met guitarist Eric Erlandson in 1989 after placing an ad for a band in a Los

Angeles newspaper. Bassist Jill Emery (replaced by Kristen Pfaff) and drummer Caroline Rue (replaced by Patty Schemel) completed the band that would become Hole.[83] In 1991 they released their hard-core punk debut album, *Pretty on the Inside*. The album found an international cult following, especially among the young feminist movement known as "riot grrls."[84] Hole's 1994 *Live Through This* "featured primal guitar riffs and high-IQ lyrics by Courtney Love," according to *Time* writers Farley and McLaughlin.[85] The fact that Love's husband, Nirvana's Kurt Cobain, committed suicide just before the album's release linked Love and her band—with their own sound and their own career—more tightly to the now over-the-top Nirvana cult. More tragedy struck the band when bassist Kristen Pfaff died of a drug overdose shortly after the release of the album. (She was replaced by Melissa Auf Der Maur.)

Following the release of *Live Through This,* though some riot grrls still claimed Hole and Love as influential, others responded to the album with animosity, upset that the group had compromised its artistic integrity by producing a commercially appealing product.[86] Many riot grrls were dismayed that Love had left her punk roots for the pop world, that her voice was more melodic as opposed to her earlier raging screams. This prompted the slogan at a 1996 riot grrl convention, "Grrl Love, Not Courtney Love."[87] In 1997 Love responded that she was glad she ignored those who were "trying to oppress me and not allow my natural instinct for pop to emerge."[88]

Hole became largely inactive after their 1998 album, *Celebrity Skin,* when Love moved on to pursue an acting career. From slugging Bikini Kill's Kathleen Hanna at Lollapalooza in 1995 and journalist Belissa Cohen at a fashion show in 1998, to dropping her dress at a video shoot in 1999 and being arrested for verbally abusing the cabin crew on a transatlantic flight in 2003, Love is never at a loss for spontaneity and drama. Despite the tragedy, controversy, and criticism Courtney Love has faced, her band has become one of the most successful bands fronted by a woman.

Equal Opportunity Punk

Definitions of the word "punk" are hardly flattering. With an etymology dating back to the sixteenth century, the word has been used to mean "a prostitute," "nonsense or foolishness," and "a young, inexperienced person," including a petty gangster, a hoodlum, a ruffian, or a youth used as a homosexual partner.[89] The word also refers to a combustible material often used to start fireworks. Punk music, possibly incorporating many of these references and originating in the early 1970s in Britain, typically carries a connotation of alienation and antiestablishment social discontent. The music is often "in-your-face" offensive. Many female punk musicians would take this a step further in an attempt to dismantle the established image of femininity.

Female British punkers Poly Styrene, Siouxie Sioux, the Slits, and the Raincoats believed that they could do anything the guys were doing, and they did. The explosion these women created in the mid-1970s had largely died out by the late 1980s. "But," Joy Press points out, "it was that first wave of girl punks, with their angst-venting screams and gouged-out guitars, who provided today's female performers with something that men take for granted: a legacy."[90] They would prefigure 1990s riot grrl bands such as Bikini Kill and crossover bands such as Sleater-Kinney. If, however unjustly, "women's music" connoted female stereotypes of softness and sensitivity, punk and riot grrl bands changed that, giving women a chance to be abrasive and offensive. Evelyn McDonnell adds that punk "allowed women to be nasty, aggressive, vitriolic, and outraged, to howl and roar and raise a ruckus," and to use bad language, as Tipper Gore feared in the late 1980s.[91]

In 1992 a *Newsweek* article entitled "Revolution, Girl Style" described the riot grrls "as a support network of activist 'girls' from 14 to 25 who are loosely linked together by a few punk bands, weekly discussion groups, pen pal friendships and more than 50 homemade fanzines."[92] This was the year before Lorena Bobbitt's justified anger over "domestic rape" got the best of her (or more accurately her husband's member) and the year after Kathleen Hanna formed Bikini Kill, a three-woman, one-man band, with bassist Kathi Wilcox, drummer Tobi Vail, and guitarist Billy Karren. While Hanna denies founding the movement, her consciousness-raising about personal experiences of oppression and sexual abuse certainly captures what riot grrls are about.

Bikini Kill's concert behavior extended their confrontational lyrics. Hanna would interrupt shows to get guys to stop harassing women, and try to relegate men to the back of the mosh pits to ensure the safety of the women dancing up front. ("This proved about as effective as leafleting Attila," Gerri Hirshey notes.)[93] Many were puzzled by the band's seeming inconsistency of message and presentation. The women in the band "started out by paying for their instruments through stripping, and early shows had them peeling off to their bra tops."[94] Sometimes topless with "slut" written across her stomach in black marker, Hanna's irony and sarcasm were lost on some members of her audiences. Once when a guy sprayed her in the face with a mouthful of beer, she said she doubted that Tommy Tutone would have to contend with such behavior.[95] Her treatment at that show bears a striking similarity to the indignities Joan Jett suffered in Spain and Italy, described earlier. The association does not end there; Jett produced and performed on one of the group's singles, "Rebel Girl," and cowrote with Kathleen Hanna. On 1994's *Pure and Simple* by Joan Jett and the Blackhearts, Hanna received vocal and songwriting credits.

In 1999, having moved away from the riot grrl scene when it got too "defensive" and self-destructive as a movement, Hanna formed "the very fun, and very feminist" band, Le Tigre, with Johanna Fateman and Sadie Benning (who was replaced by J. D. Samson). [96] In her new group, Hanna continues to sing about women's issues: domestic violence, exploitation, reproductive choice. Unlike much riot grrl music or indie music in general, Le Tigre's gets the audience dancing; it is "a funky mèlange that's like the girl-rap-funk trio of Luscious Jackson crossed with Kate Millett." [97]

Named after a road near Olympia, Washington, the Pacific Northwest trio Sleater-Kinney avoids the riot grrl label, but claims the influence of groups such as Kim Gordon's Sonic Youth. [98] After six albums, these women have gained critical acclaim for their intelligent musicianship. Drummer Janet Weiss, replacing Lora Macfarlane, joined singer/guitarists Corin Tucker (formerly of Heavens to Betsy) and Carrie Brownstein (formerly of Excuse 17) after the release of their first album in 1995. "Simultaneously girly and tough," the trio combines the personal and the political, and can move from banging, clanging, hardcore sounds "toward audible tenderness and plea-sure." [99] In an article at CNN.com, Donna Freydkin described the group following the release of their more introspective 1999 album, *The Hot Rock*. "The trio straddles the line between the grubby aesthetic of Bikini Kill and the polished California punk of Hole. Just imagine, perhaps, what might have been if the Go Go's hadn't gone so totally cutesy MTV." [100] Charles R. Cross of *Rolling Stone* recently called Sleater-Kinney "the best indie-rock band of the last ten years" and possibly "the brainiest band in rock." [101] Referring to journalists' claims that the trio is "the world's greatest rock-'n'-roll band," *Time* called the band "worthy of discussion in a Women in Modern Media seminar." [102] Perhaps the praise would have been more of a compliment had it not been gender specific.

While neo-punk bands such as Bikini Kill, Le Tigre, and Sleater-Kinney may not be considered mainstream, the latter appeared on Late Night with Conan O'Brien in October 2002. Appearances by these female indie groups on major television networks are rare, but with a keen enough eye, America can get a nightly glimpse of women rockers on late-night television. Even David Letterman and Jay Leno have responded to the times by adding a woman to each of their bands. Guitarist Felicia Collins provides a female presence in the CBS Orchestra on Letterman's show, and percussionist Vicki Randle, the only female member of the *Tonight Show* band, warms up audiences.

Unlike the punkers and riot grrls who are, with few exceptions, white, Collins and Randle are black. As Robin Renee mentioned in chapter 2, constructing an identity as a black woman rock musician is especially difficult. For these performers, the shape of their gender identities is racialized in a way white women's is not. Because whiteness is normative in American culture, white women are not generally marked by their racial category; black women are. So, in addition to the constraints placed upon women by virtue of their gender, black women who play rock music face racialized gendered constraints. In other words, the fact of their race is not simply additive; rather it shapes the ways black women experience gender. As Robin Renée suggests, black women who play rock often face opposition from members of the black community who suggest they have sold out to white music, and from the predominantly white record industry that believes there is no market for music by black women rock 'n' rollers.[103] Those black women who do construct an identity as rock musicians recognize both the roots of rock (which are most certainly black) and their own right to play the music they love.

Finding a Place

The girls in the band are still trying to find their place in rock 'n' roll. Certainly there has been progress over the past fifty years. Rana Ross was named Los Angeles bassist of the year, the Go-Go's got back together to do a successful album and tour, and the Rock 'n' Roll Camp for Girls became a private nonprofit, bought a Portland building, and finished its third annual camp in June 2003. A second rock camp for girls had its first season in the summer of 2003 at the Institute for Musical Arts in Northampton, Massachusetts (see chapter 8 for more on the IMA). Yet it only takes perusing a few issues of *Rolling Stone* and *Spin* to figure out that the band is still a male domain, at least in the minds of these purveyors of pop culture. But as they have all along, women continue to ignore criticism and create strategies to lay claim to their right to play rock 'n' roll.

By making a place for themselves in the band, women have furthered the construction of their identities as rock musicians in the face of rock's continuing masculine discourse. For many of the early players, this identity was centered on proving they had their chops together. They thought that if they just played well enough, they would belong in the band. Of course, despite their musical skill, the culture still gendered them female and, hence, outsiders in the rock 'n' roll band. Some, then, developed strategies to minimize gender; others played and acted "like the boys." Some played like the boys, but still maintained feminine and even hypersexualized appearances. In recent years, others have developed strategic identities that allow them to toy with gender as a direct challenge to the masculinism of rock.

By maintaining their right to play in a band, women have constructed a resistant identity that asserts their confidence in the face of cultural forces insisting on women's essential inferiority as rock musicians. By their actions, women have maintained that they can play with or without men and they can make rock music that is both musically excellent and widely appealing. The myriad ways women have chosen to be in bands reflect the complexities and difficulties of constructing identities within the masculine domain of the band. In the next chapter, we explore how the construction of identity as a rock musician is further complicated when women identify as lesbian, bisexual, or queer.

CHAPTER 5

IMAGINE MY SURPRISE!
THE WOMEN'S MUSIC MOVEMENT

A movement requires passion, audacity and action—a Women's Music movement requires women inspired into action by other women through and in music. Folded into that is a chosen commitment to serve a community, a vision and a belief system.

—Margie Adam, "Thoughts on Women's Music"

Deb Frost knew she could be in a rock band because of Fanny. In 1970, as far as she knew, there were two girl rock bands, Birtha and Fanny, and she was particularly taken with Fanny. She played their music at every opportunity, and often based friendships and even a dating relationship on a shared appreciation of the group who represented everything she wanted to be doing.[1]

Thirty years later, Deb introduced us to June Millington at the Rockrgrl conference in Seattle. We knew June best through a well-worn solo album, *Running*; in a subsequent interview we learned more about her years with Fanny and her multifaceted behind-the-scenes service to women's music. How had she made the transition from mainstream rock to the far more obscure women's music world? we asked her. She laughed. "I fell apart."

The journey from one musical world to another, though neither obvious nor direct, seems to her in retrospect "very simple. It was taken care of for me." She had a nervous breakdown. Though she knew she was a lesbian at age twenty—in fact "everybody" knew—"you didn't talk about it." The pressures of touring, recording, coping with success, maintaining success, and maintaining a certain image in the boy-defined rock world became overwhelming. "Instead of carrying it all, I just fell apart."

June hooked up with Cris Williamson after a time of rest and renewal in Woodstock, New York, that community of folk musicians and the counterculture. She played on Cris's *Changer and the Changed* (1975)—the contact was made through Jackie Robinson, June's friend and the bass player already contracted for the album. "[Cris] had been a fan of mine, which I didn't know. And I didn't know who she was." June agreed to go on tour with Cris because some other opportunities didn't pan out. She expected the tour to be boring; far from boring, the tour revealed "this whole other life and this whole other energy."

Coming from the rock and roll "circus," June Millington helped Williamson cope with the emotional impositions of the star status that Cris enjoyed in the lesbian community after *Changer*. Still, it took June quite a while to plug into the meanings of this music for their audiences. June saw her own musical role as getting the groove, so she barely listened to Cris's lyrics or her larger musical message. "I think it was probably a decade before I even understood what she was singing about." She remembers sitting on Cris's porch in Oregon, as they were preparing to record *Strange Paradise,* and enthusiastically quoting a piece of graffiti that she had just seen in a women's room in Arkansas. "[Cris] looked at me, and she said, 'June, that's me. Those are my lyrics.' She loved it."[2]

If any demographic group casts a fainter shadow over the history of popular music than women, it is *lesbian* women. Leafing through the most authoritative encyclopedia of rock, the *Rolling Stone Encyclopedia of Rock & Roll,* it is a discouraging task to locate lesbian artists. Starting with those with the greatest name recognition in lesbian communities, we can take Cris Williamson, a founding Olivia Records artist whose *The Changer and the Changed* found a spot on hundreds of thousands of women's record shelves in the 1970s. Whoops! Not there! A flash in the pan? Seventeen albums over thirty years (counting conservatively). Williamson can rock out, but her sound is often mellow ("like honey dripped on a cello," as her friend and collaborator Bonnie Raitt describes her voice).[3] Let's check for a more "plugged-in" artist. Fanny, not identified as a "lesbian" band, achieves mention in the *Rolling Stone* volume, but electrified and electrifying June Millington on her own does not merit inclusion. Holly Near, Tret Fure, Alix Dobkin, Linda Tillery, the Chicago and New Haven Women's Liberation Bands, Meg Christian, Teresa Trull, Ferron: no, no, no, no, no/no, no, no, no. And this in a volume claiming to have erred on the "permissive" side of inclusion.[4] Talk about flying under the radar.

Probably even earlier than Maxine Feldman's single "Angry Atthis" of 1969, uncloseted lesbians were performing and recording love songs without the usual pronoun switch, as well as protest songs, often cast as comic commentary, that quickly became classics in lesbian communities.[5] Sue Fink and some friends in Los Angeles wrote "Leaping Lesbians," a song made famous by Meg Christian, who recorded it and made it a concert staple.[6] Christian's own rueful "Ode to a Gym Teacher" spoke for many former schoolgirls furtively seeking a love object for a young heart that did not quite fit in. Christian's album *I Know You Know* (1974), a collection of musically sophisticated songs composed and performed by a soft-spoken southerner with a warm sense of humor, was the first full-length album produced by Olivia Records, founded in 1973 in Washington, D.C.[7] Legend has it that Meg's radio interview with Cris Williamson following a 1972 concert struck the spark. Shortly after Williamson commented that a women's record company would be a good idea, Christian, Judy Dlugacz, and a handful of other women sat down and sketched out their plan for a music collective in which women managed all art, production, and business. Christian's successful debut album was followed the next year by her new friend Cris Williamson's *The Changer and the Changed,* Cris's fourth album but her first with the fledgling Olivia. *The Changer* was an unanticipated success, selling over 60,000 copies its first year and reaching 250,000 in sales over its now thirty-year life span. (It would be difficult to find a lesbian in the forty-five-to-seventy demographic who was not affected by *The Changer.*)

"Hand-carried," writes L. Margaret Pomeroy, "is just how the music of Williamson, and other independent artists, has been distributed—in the lobby of concert halls, through the mail, in small women-owned bookstores."[8] Olivia created a distribution network of women's bookstores and other woman-identified businesses and outlets, bypassing frustration at the hands of mainstream distributors and retailers who carelessly or deliberately ignored the new women's albums or relegated them indiscriminately to "Folk—Other." (This still happens. One has to be a resourceful detective to find women's music albums without resorting to the Internet or specialty catalogues.) Not just Olivia Records, but also Holly Near's Redwood Records and the products of other small labels such as Alix Dobkin's and Kay Gardner's Women's Wax Works, Pleiades, and Galaxia were shared from household to household.

In chapter 7 we will discuss the upsurge of independent, "DIY" labels; but while the feminist labels of the 1970s and 1980s anticipated many aspects of today's homegrown companies, more than just technological changes differentiate Olivia from the indies of the new century.[9] The commercial history of women's music might aptly stand in for the ethnography of modern lesbian communities more generally. Lesbian social life in post-Freudian America followed the contours of an underground political or social movement. While many lesbians continued to find satisfying social relations in the women's networks of neighborhood, church, Girl Scouts, camp, and college, others were chastened by the increasingly militant drumbeat of sexual and social conformity. To speak freely of one's feelings, desires, life—that took a special place, often hidden, even though women's organizations and institutions normally drew little notice from a male-dominated, male-obsessed social order. Since World War I, bars had filled that role. Dark, small, out-of-the-way, sometimes hazardous to get to, and often controlled by the same local forces that controlled gambling, drugs, prostitution, and illicit liquor traffic, these places could be thrilling but were hard to find, encouraged alcohol and tobacco abuse, and carried the risk of police raids with dire personal and political consequences for the women "busted." For women who sought to avoid the bar culture, random local sites—coffee shops, restaurants, gyms, boardinghouses and YWCAs, bookstores— increasingly offered alternatives, quite by accident, but such places were potentially fraught with the same hazards of being overheard or observed by hostile or overly curious bystanders.[10]

By contrast, musician Sue Fink has observed, "in women's music we have basically an audience of women, each one wanting to be at an event where women somehow are performing and speaking to *her,* and she gets to be in her community and have a night out in the company of other women, without necessarily going to a bar."[11] All the in-group flags of lesbian identity—the pink triangles, the rainbow bumper stickers, pins, and earrings, the explicit T-shirts—wave proudly at the women's concerts. Despite the illusion of safety and the feeling of comfort in numbers—as at a tribal gathering—there is always the sense that things could still somehow "go wrong," and that outside the walls waits a hostile or uncomprehending world. There is no completely safe place. At the Olivia tenth anniversary concert at Carnegie Hall, Meg Christian sang the wistful John Calvi lyric:

> I'm thinking about the ones who aren't here
> And won't be coming in late
> Home all alone
> And the family
> And won't be coming out tonight
> Wish I could know all the lovers and friends

Kept from gathering
I think of you now, the ways you could go
We're all of us refugees.

The festivals launched in the mid-1970s brought the women's music experience to a fever pitch. Women producers, sometimes first-time producers, in Sacramento, San Diego, Missouri, Illinois, Michigan, and Boston (and surely a few not named here) began creating a festival culture: a wraparound experience of music, art, workshops, networking, talking, hanging out, sleeping in tents or dormitories, and struggling to find common ground. The festivals became lightning rods of conflict, compromise, and evolution in lesbian communities. They also became the training grounds of many women performers, as well as women organizers, producers, emcees, sound engineers, security coordinators, chefs, entrepreneurs, and mediators.

For women who are not festivalgoers, the festivals' conflicts may sometimes seem most significant, as Bonnie Morris has commented.[12] Political fights over access, over free speech (from musical S&M references to what merchandise would be allowed on the grounds), over meat, over who is and is not a woman (transsexual individuals and boy children have been excluded or sequestered at Michigan and Campfest, for example), over appropriate leadership styles in a feminist organization, and over who would receive profits have made headlines and earned some festivals a notoriety that has occasionally overshadowed their simpler achievement of creating a safe, creatively charged meeting place for thousands of lesbians.

"You have to understand what it was like in 1976," says Karen Dodson, a festival veteran interviewed by *Lesbian News*. "It was lezzie fever. It was an incredible upswelling of grassroots energy: you could put one lavender flier up in a city of 3 million and 500 women would find out about it."[13] The Michigan Womyn's Music Festival began that year as a weekend of music and camping for a fee of twenty dollars at the gate. From an attendance of 2,000 and a profit—this was quite an achievement—of four hundred dollars, Michigan has grown into the mother of festivals, with an attendance of 8,000, several stages, "40 performances, hundreds of workshops, a film festival and the crafts of 150 artisans," as the organizers describe the festival in 2003.[14] Lisa and Kristie Vogel, who have produced the festival from its beginnings, wrote in 1982 of the evolutionary struggle from collective to company, and from a shoestring to solvency. Today the festival owns land, a 650-acre site in Michigan—a permanent home for the summer gathering.[15]

Reports of internal conflicts have also, true to form in the histories of subordinated social groups, overshadowed analyses of obstacles and hostile conditions imposed from outside. The festivals' initially ragged production values were gradually overcome by women engineers who had to seize their training where they could. Boden Sandstrom of Woman Sound remembers trying to apprentice in production at the male-run sound companies around Washington, D.C. "Nobody had any time for me, and it was very frustrating. I tried to get hired, to get some experience, to figure out what to rent. I would end up at gigs with systems that didn't work or were missing parts because men would just throw me out the door with this stuff. Finally, this one company, National Sound, . . . whose owners were really unusual guys, kind of took me under their wing."[16] A handful of women blasted through the barriers to doing their own engineering. Consequently, the women's music festivals, and women's music concerts more generally, are the one place where the audience will as a rule *not* see men either as engineers or in the band. (By contrast, all three of the annual "Women Rock! Girls & Guitars" concerts on the Lifetime television network, programmed as benefits for breast cancer research, have been engineered by men, and have featured male musicians playing drums, bass, lead guitar, and keyboards, leaving the women stars to "front" the band.)

Percussionist Vicki Randle objects to the moniker "women's music" as encoded language that means music by and for lesbians. How is it supposed to be a declaration of pride and strength, she asks, "when it dare not even speak its own name?" Rather, she says, the term underscores lesbians' internalized homophobia.[17] In addition, as its originators tried to define a "female-oriented" music, they excluded lesbians who did not play acoustic instruments and soft types of music. She also notes the intrinsic racism of this definition—the primary proponents of this music were white, and essentially the definition excluded the kinds of music played by many lesbians of color. "This was supposed to be a step in the direction of musical freedom for women, and yet women who had already broken through the stereotypes by playing electric bass, guitar, keyboards, horns, trap drums, playing loud dance music and rock, experimental jazz, were initially being told that their music was not affirming to women. . . . Fortunately, this particular set of constraints didn't last long. The definition of 'Women's Music' began to be based on primary lyrical content, rather than musical form."[18]

Linda Tillery agrees that in the early days of women's music she felt alone as a black woman until she met Olivia's Mary Watkins, with whom she could "sit down and have a conversation about hymns and spirituals."[19] These experiences again highlight the difficulty of constructing an identity as a musician in which all of the intersecting facets of one's being are welcomed and acknowledged. In this instance, because women's music was so focused on lesbian identity, many of the movement's (white) leaders came more slowly to the shaping of lesbian identity by race.[20]

Like most musicians, women's musicians have had to forge their own careers. The difference for them is the boundaries around acceptable and accepting venues. Heather Bishop, a pioneering women's musician from Canada, has described her own struggles to make a living. Performing since the 1970s, she ventured into any space that would have her. Unlike many lesbian musicians, she decided at the outset that she needed to be "out." At the Regina Folk Festival in the mid-1970s, she recalls performing a "lesbian" song written by her friend Connie Kaldor. "I thought I would try it on the home-town crowd; that would make it or break it." To her surprise, she got a standing ovation. She continued to place lesbian music in her folk performances, generally putting the numbers about three-fourths of the way through the show. That way, the audience "would have to go home wondering how it could be that they really liked this person who was standing up there saying she was one of those horrible critters."

Like the majority of open lesbians, she has not found that her outspokenness—and its generally good reception—has made coming out in a performance any easier. "It's *still* hard." At the Canadian folk festivals, she was often "real lonely." Men would avoid her, probably because she was known as both a feminist and a lesbian, and often women would avoid her, too, perhaps not wanting to be tainted by association. Sylvia Tyson, of Ian and Sylvia, was friendly and helpful; there were several others. In the United States, women's musicians did not play the mainstream folk festivals, whereas in Canada they had nowhere else to play. After feminism began making inroads into alternative culture, some U.S. folk musicians coming to Canada for the festivals appreciated the chance to play with the "big name" lesbian-identified musicians. "I can remember having a talk with Meg Christian and Tom Paxton at a festival one time, and him saying how much he appreciated women's music, what a great thing it was. So in Canada he got that chance," Bishop commented, "to play with me."[21]

This musical segregation is the most volatile and least tractable issue for "women's music" performers. As Bishop's experiences suggest, mainstream musical culture has excluded lesbian performers as well as lesbian experience. Girls searching for them-"selves" in popular music have always had to make do with love songs with crossover potential, such as ones sung by an "I" to a "you." On the other side, since the festivals' inception, straight women have found themselves in a tiny and sometimes uncomfortable minority at these "women's music" events, while for political and social comfort reasons, men are usually excluded. (Even at Lilith Fair, far from a "women's music" scene, "liberal" male attendees bemoaned the relatively low proportion of women audience members available for heterosexual approaches.)[22]

Several influential women's musicians came to women's music as refugees from a rock scene that offered them initial success and then imposed its own glass ceiling. June Millington and Tret Fure both played in rock bands, Millington in Fanny and Fure in mixed-gender bands, before they became session musicians, engineers, and artists with Olivia. Tret Fure had started to work as a recording engineer in Los Angeles in the mid-1970s, after she and her brother had cut their performing teeth in coffeehouses around their hometown of Marquette, Michigan. She engineered a number of punk and new wave bands and became intrigued with the electric guitar as a different medium from her acoustic instrument. "The way I learned was by putting together a punk band and just playing." Influenced by Andy Summers ("much more of a pretty but tough sound of muted strings and melodic lines as opposed to something that would be more heavy metal"), she developed her own style. She met June Millington and was hanging out with the Fanny band members. They introduced her to Spencer Davis, and she auditioned for his group. "I could play a lot of twelve-string slide, and I could play a lot of Leadbelly-style music at that time. That's what he was doing. So he took me on as his guitar player, and then I went on to do *Mousetrap* [the album] with him as a sideman, or a sidewoman." Though their trio disbanded after that album, Fure got management through her relationship with Davis. She began to encounter the familiar roadblocks to women musicians' success. "Every label had a woman, and that was how it was. . . . 'We have a girl. We don't need more than one.'" MCA finally signed her; six months later her A&R people were fired and she was dropped. The label literally melted down her product from that period, both master and copies, to save money.

Another time, Fure went to a Los Angeles audition for a Bay Area band, hit it off with the leader, and moved to San Francisco to take the job. "When I got up there, the rest of the band members did not want a chick in their band. So I have moved everything, and I got fired immediately. . . . It really hurt my feelings. I never had encountered something like that"—except in the studio, she amends. "Every time I had a new client, I had to prove[myself]." Often it became obvious that the client had booked with "Tret," an imagined man, when the client showed up at the studio ready to record but bewildered by the engineer's apparent gender change. "So it meant that I had to work twice as hard as anyone else to prove that I knew what I was doing. But I never lost a client once I got in the studio with them. I never lost a client, because I was good at what I did. . . . But it was a struggle, and it was a struggle I hated."

Even with her extensive successful history working with men in bands and in the studio, Tret found working with women musicians "a breeze" by comparison. "The camaraderie was so much easier." In 1981 Tret engineered Cris Williamson's children's album, *Lumiere,* and then Williamson's next five albums. The working relationship became personal as well as musical, and the couple began touring, writing, and recording together, producing three albums and beginning a fourth before parting in 2000. Tret credits Cris with helping her develop her vocal powers so that she could emerge from her often supporting musical role. "I would be more concerned about making sure the band was in time, was happy, and my guitar parts were right, than concentrating on my voice." Tret also formed a working relationship with June Millington that is now thirty years old. "I love producing with her because we pretty much read each other's minds. You know, we can talk the same talk. . . . And that's really rare."[23]

When few other singers dared to openly claim the lesbian label, Holly Near was taking lesbian music to a wide audience. Often a "lifeline" for many who were coming out, Near's songs brought solace to women who felt alone and in danger of being found out. "Lesbians in the military mentioned Holly's name as a code word while trying to find each other amidst the hostility of the barracks." When others were silent, she raised a "lone voice at folk festivals, peace rallies and Hollywood fund-raisers, not only daring to say the word, but often getting large crowds of people to sing '. . . We are gay and straight together, singing for our lives.' "[24] Founded in 1972, for more than two decades her Redwood Records label provided a vehicle for politically conscious artists around the world and became a major force in alternative music.

Since the 1997 release of *With a Song in My Heart,* she said "I get letters in particular from lesbian couples who say they put this record on and they light some candles and they dance to these songs and they sing along."[25] In 2000 Near "celebrated the feminist and lesbian movements" with her *Simply Love: The Women's Music Collection.*[26] However, neither the music nor the life of this entertainer and activist is easily categorized. She told us, "I live with a man now but as far as the world is concerned I am a dyke. I still sing lesbian songs along with songs that challenge capitalism and racism, narrow and short range thinking."[27] Pointing to the transformative power of Holly Near's music, Nancy S. Love says " 'Women's music' not only provides metaphors for democracy, but also exemplifies its practice."[28] As Near expressed her own take on music, "Whenever new ideas emerge, songs soon follow and before long the songs are leading."[29]

The work of Canadian artist Ferron has a similar transformative power. Described as a "literate, sly lyricist" and "a big, tender woman" who "dodged self-righteousness and eluded type," Ferron says that music was "one of the sweet things in life" throughout her difficult childhood.[30] When we asked the Indigo Girls about their musical role models, both Emily Saliers and Amy Ray mentioned Ferron. "Ferron was really important because she was from this women's scene that I could not relate to as well sometimes. And it was this one writer that came out of it that I was like, I can relate to that. And she's being written up in *Rolling Stone* and she's being paid attention to, and it means 'you can do it,' " recalled Amy. Emily said that she sometimes felt debilitated when she compared herself to artists like Ferron who have the ability to "turn a phrase real well."[31] Ferron's masterful lyrics are often narratives of life's difficulties. "It seems to me that you can get tenderness and all your ideas across with music, and it's very healing," explained Ferron. Still, she seems bemused by the appeal of her early music. "I don't know what life is made of. . . . I was just trying to tell somebody what was going on. And you know and I waked up and realized I was on the stage."

Modesty shines through in Ferron's lyrics as well as her assessment of her early career. "What happened was someone asked me to play somewhere else, and I went. And then there was the 8th Street Coffee House. It was a women's coffee house. . . . And I also was shoveling gravel and driving a taxi. And they asked me to play again. . . . It was just a little thirty-seat room, and then after a while there [were] sixty-seven people coming. [Management] didn't know what to do. Then we had two shows, and then it was lined up around the block. And so then I went over to the Soft Rock Café, which was a three hundred seater or something, and said, 'I'd like to play here. I need a bigger room.' And they said, 'Well, you can play and pass the hat.' " She was shocked at the response. "So when I went there to play, we passed the hat. I can remember I made $864, which was like astonishing to me because I think maybe I was making fifty bucks at the other place when I first started. Then I was so nervous about that money I tried to give half of it away to a friend of mine."[32]

Categorizing Ferron's music has always been next to impossible. While reviewer Lori Medigovich noted that her 1996 *Still Riot* has "hints of folk, rock, jazz, country and zydeco," Ferron told us that initially her music was called "women's music."[33] "It was in a bin, you know, usually in some corner of a store. . . . I mean in some stores I'm still registered under 'women's music.' . . . I understand the politics of it. But I think sometimes by naming and claiming that way, we put ourselves in a small box."

After fourteen years on an independent label, Ferron signed with Warner Brothers. "Because I was a lesbian, I think they thought I wanted to sell lesbianism," she recalls. "And I didn't. And in fact when I went with Warner Brothers after all these years, they tried to sell me to the gay community. I mean it was hilarious. It's like they didn't understand that I already had that because I am that."[34] Warner Brothers may have been pitching to what they perceived as a lucrative market. About the same time, in 1995, *Billboard* reported that gays and lesbians purchased "eight times as many cassettes and CDs as the average consumer." The same article noted the prevalence of stories about the gay and lesbian music scene "in *Rolling Stone* and *Spin,* on CNN and MTV," and reported that a documentary about the gay music revolution was being produced.[35] Holly Near commented somewhat ruefully about the maturation of women's music, "What was a movement has become a market now."[36]

Just as the movement and the market evolved, so did Ferron. As she moved from one season of life to the next, Ferron brought her audience along. In her teens and twenties, she says she could "name what's stupid and painful and also say, 'Guess what? It's not even gonna last as long as this song is.' " In midlife now, she finds writing is a bit more difficult. "You know, because really, what's everybody thinking about. You know, breast cancer. . . . Like it's a whole different ballgame, mortgages, did I make the right choice, my life's half over, have I lived it? And these are just kind of Sunday morning musings, you know? They're not really something you want to write a song about."

Each of her CDs carries a social message. The focus of her 1982 *Testimony* "was really the women's movement," she says. In *Shadows on a Dime* (1989), "what became apparent to me is that the political is personal." Of *Driver* (1994), written in the early years of parenting a daughter, she says, "There's a stillness to it. . . . Imagine that we have enough. Imagine that we are enough." *Phantom Center* (1995) reflected Ferron's despair at the cynical brutality of American politics: "Where is the eye of kindness? Where is that center? And who's saying what it is? And who's deciding what's good?"[37] In *Still Riot* (1996), she examined "the meaning of unabashed love, the excruciating pain of desperate heartache and the wonder of how interconnected and interdependent we are."[38] In all of her music, Ferron gives poetic voice to what so many women experience but have difficulty articulating.

"By accepting the view that Women's Music is only a historical artifact, we may be backlashing ourselves. I suggest there is no expiration date on the women's liberation movement, on Women's Music or on the women's community," comments Margie Adam.[39] "Festivals, lesbian feminism, and women's music are all far from dead in America," writes festival historian Bonnie Morris. "But they are supported and sustained in no small measure by women age 35 and older, which, in a youth-focused market, is the same thing as being dead."[40] Though the women's music pioneers still make beautiful music, a new phase in the mingling of rock and lesbian sexuality was ushered in partly by the very success of women's music.

Yes, She Is . . . Isn't She?

While the artists who perform women's music have always been out of the closet (and therefore generally marginalized or invisible in mainstream rock), other lesbian performers have hidden or downplayed their sexuality—at least until they have achieved some modicum of mainstream success, to the chagrin of lesbian fans just waiting for them to come out. (The grapevine thrives among subdominant populations.) Of course, coming out is risky business, particularly in an industry built on assumptions of heterosexuality and female sexual availability.[41] Many lesbian performers have adopted a strategy of androgyny. They do not set up gendered markers in their songs, which address the lover in the second person. They don't present as really "butchy" and they don't come across "girly" either. Sociologist Arlene Stein muses about this strategy: "Are 'androgynous' women performers cowering to a homophobic industry, enacting a musical form of passing? Or are they pushing the limits of what is possible and, along with it, lesbian visibility?"[42]

In another essay, Stein argues that these artists' ambiguous identities may have reflected their resistance to identity politics, insisting on the priority of their art and the complexity of their identities. She says that as a strategy, artists' sexual ambiguity allowed them to reach both a mainstream audience and the lesbian subculture. But this strategy relied on the lesbian audience's ability to read the subtext of performance. "Young lesbians could finally see images in the mainstream that closely resembled them, but since lesbianism was still unspoken and since the vast majority lacked the necessary knowledge to cue into these codes, the heterosexual norm remained, for the most part, unchallenged."[43]

By the early 1990s both k.d. lang and Melissa Etheridge had achieved mainstream success, and both came out, very publicly. Of course, while lesbian fans on the whole cheered the announcements, many wondered if these revelations might end the performers' mainstream careers. In fact, in both their cases as well as in the case of Elton John, one of rock's handful of superstars, that did *not* happen. Howie Klein of Reprise Records suggested in a 2000 interview, "k.d. and Elton were both pioneers. They proved a point that coming out doesn't necessarily have a cataclysmic effect, that it's safe" (although "safe" may be a bit overstated).[44]

k.d. lang was the first to come out publicly. While she felt that her lesbianism was "more or less hiding in plain sight," she worried that publicly acknowledging her sexuality might harm her rural Canadian mother, who had to put up with harassing mail and phone calls after lang condemned meat-eating in an ad campaign for People for the Ethical Treatment of Animals (PETA). When lang finally did come out, it was a "totally positive" experience. "The really, really big thing I experienced this year was the intimacy between me and the audience, not just because of the number of women, although that is part of it," she said. "It's that I feel comfortable knowing that they came there knowing." In a poignant expression of the fearful fantasies of this "invisible minority," she clarifies: "That I don't have to worry that if they finally figured it out, they would get up and leave."[45] lang's manager, however, contends that her career has suffered because of her sexuality. "She was guided to be a lesbian poster child, and it would have been more important to emphasize her art rather than her sexuality."[46]

Certainly coming out is still perilous. Focus on a performer's sexuality may overshadow her music. If a woman performer has a repertoire and a persona that *is* largely heterosexually identified (unlike those of lang and Etheridge), the revelation of her lesbianism would change her career. Also, the lesbian community often expects gay celebrities to be spokespersons and champions of lesbian causes.[47] One queer theorist suggests that lesbians are "starved" for representation in popular culture and long for a lesbian musician to be the "Perfect Star." Of course, she continues, insisting someone be the Perfect Star is not fair, "but this need stems from the grim fact that lesbians are still a terribly oppressed minority. The ironic mechanisms of oppression work simultaneously to instill an intense desire for lesbian visibility while maintaining a need to vigorously criticize the very woman who is visibly and audibly lesbian."[48] In 1991 one lesbian writer lamented, "Millions of queers in this country . . . are aching to see a mainstream performer stand up and say, 'Yes, I am!' "[49]

Like k.d. lang, Melissa Etheridge never doubted her identity as a lesbian, but, following the advice of her manager and record label, she kept her sexuality obscured within her music. After growing up in Kansas, Melissa dropped out of Boston's Berklee College of Music and at twenty-one headed to Los Angeles to become a rock star. She remembers that she played as an equal, and was treated as an equal, as a young woman in guy bands. Out of sync with the '80s heavy metal scene, she ended up playing in local lesbian bars, where she says she was "nurtured" and found a "following."[50] She got her big break when a woman gave her demo to Bill Leopold, who came to a bar to hear her and subsequently became her manager. A few years later, Leopold brought Chris Blackwell of Island Records to hear Etheridge perform at a bar in Long Beach. He heard only a little before deciding to sign her. Leopold and Blackwell knew of her sexual orientation, and their response can be constructed in a number of ways; though they did not show her the closet, they asked her not to "flag-wave," whatever that might mean.[51] Her first album won a Grammy nomination for Best Rock Vocal Performance, Female (she lost to Tina Turner), and the album went gold.

Throughout her career, Melissa's social life revolved around the gay scene in Los Angeles, but she had not come out publicly. Though she realized that some day she would, she had not really made any plans to do so in 1993, when after Clinton's election she attended the first gay and lesbian inaugural ball, sponsored by the Human Rights Campaign, the National Gay and Lesbian Task Force, and the Gay and Lesbian Victory Fund. She says she was at the ball with her friend k.d. lang, who had recently had a good coming-out experience. Various celebrities were invited to speak to the gathering, and, when k.d. lang's turn came around, she told the group that coming out was the greatest thing she had ever done. The applause was raucous, and then she invited Melissa to the microphone. "I went 'Cool, OK,'" Melissa told *Rolling Stone*'s Rich Cohen. "You know: 'Gosh, it's great to be here, and, you know, I just . . . I'm really proud to say I've been a lesbian all my life'" (no flag-waving there). She walked away from the podium and said to then-partner Julie Cypher, "I think I just came out." The next day, she says, "It was in the *New York Post*: 'Butch rocker Melissa Etheridge comes out.'"[52] "I knew that I really couldn't go on in my career having this vagueness, saying 'my lover, they . . . ,' using all the non-gender specific answers," she told *The Advocate*. "It was really getting kind of annoying. And I was being misquoted. Sometimes [a story] would have me saying, 'Well, my boyfriend . . .'"[53] When asked how coming out has changed how she performs before an audience, Etheridge responded: "I can now do all the classic '70s songs that I love. Springsteen songs like 'Thunder Road,' you know: 'Screen door slams. Mary's dress waves.' I mean, now I can sing that. The classic rock songs were written about women, and I always felt I couldn't do them because it would make people feel awkward. But now people are in on it and appreciate it. I do 'Maggie May.' People love it."[54]

While Indigo Girls Amy Ray and Emily Saliers were out of the closet from the beginning of their careers, they did not at first make public state-

Wanda Jackson.
(Courtesy of Wanda
Jackson Enterprises,
Inc.)

Carol Kaye recording in 1974. (Courtesy of Carol Kaye and *Down Beat* magazine.)

Brenda Lee, "Little Miss
Dynamite." (Courtesy of
Brenda Lee Productions.)

Mary Wilson. (Cour-
tesy of J. D. Schwartz
& Associates.)

Left, Martha Reeves. (Courtesy of Ideal Entertainment Group.) *Right*, Sarah Dash. (Courtesy of Sarah Dash. Photo by Steve Lindsey.)

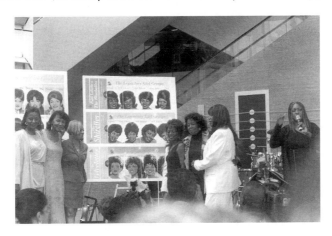

Members of the legendary girl groups gather at the Rock and Roll Hall of Fame and Museum in Cleveland, Ohio, in August 2002. The occasion was the unveiling of postage stamps minted by the Caribbean nations of Nevis, St. Vincent, and the Commonwealth of Dominica and the African nations of Ghana and Liberia to honor the girl groups. (From the authors' collection.)

The Crystals, one of several groups of women who were successful at Motown Records, sing at Cleveland's Fat Fish Blue in August 2002. (From the authors' collection.)

The Cookies reunite in August 2002 to honor the girl groups of the 1960s. (From the authors' collection.)

June Millington. (Courtesy of June Millington. Photo by Toni Armstrong Jr.)

Jean Millington (right) with June Millington. (Courtesy of Fabulous Records.)

Janis Ian. (Courtesy of Janis Ian. Photo by John Scarpatti.)

Scarlet Rivera. (Courtesy of Scarlet Rivera.)

Deborah Frost and the Brain Surgeons. (Courtesy of Deborah Frost. Photo by Bruce Johnson.)

Holly Near. (Courtesy of
Holly Near & Company.
Photo by Lisa Johnson.)

Tret Fure. (Courtesy of Tret
Fure. Photo by Irene Young.)

Above, Paula Spiro sponsors a female drummers workshop in New York City. (Courtesy of Paula Spiro. Photo by Dianne Athey.) *Below,* Indigo Girls. (Courtesy of Indigo Girls. Photo by Frank Ockenfels.)

Kate Schellenbach. (Courtesy of Kate Schellenbach.)

Jill Sobule. (Courtesy of Jill Sobule. Photo by Marc Joseph.)

Lynn Frances Anderson. (Courtesy of Lynn Frances Anderson. Photo by Joni Kabana.)

Above, Jann Arden. (Photo by Raeanne Holoboff, courtesy of Insomniac Press.) *Right,* Leah Hinchcliff. (Courtesy of Leah Hinchcliff. Photo by Linda Carlson.)

Above, Emily White. (Courtesy of Emily White.) *Below,* Michelle Malone. (Courtesy of Michelle Malone. Photo by S. Shope.)

Kate Campbell. (Courtesy of Large River Music and Kate Campbell. Photo by Michael Wilson.)

Robin Renée. (Courtesy of Robin Renée. Photo by Paris L. Gray.)

Jonatha Brooke. (Courtesy of Universal Music Group.)

Melissa Auf der Maur. (Courtesy of Melissa Auf der Maur. Photo by Lisa Johnson.)

Rana Ross. (Courtesy of John Ross. Photo by Russell Baer.)

Erin O'Hara. (Courtesy of Erin O'Hara. Photo by Bryan Cole.)

Niki Lee. (Courtesy of Niki Lee.)

Above left, Madeline Puckette. (Courtesy of Madeline Puckette. Photo by Margaret Puckette.) *Above right,* Rose Polenzani. (Courtesy of Daemon Records.) *Below,* Magdalen Hsu-Li. (Courtesy of Chickpop Records.)

Bitch and Animal. (Courtesy of Righteous Babe Records. Photo by Mr. Means.)

Ellen Rosner. (Courtesy of Ellen Rosner.)

ments about their sexuality because they did not want their lesbianism to distract from their music. While Ray answered press questions about her sexuality openly, Saliers was a bit more reluctant. "I've always thought of myself as a very private person," she told *Out* magazine, "and I'd be that way whether I was straight or gay. I object to sexuality becoming a focus. I just basically did not want to be thought of as first of all gay and then secondly as an Indigo Girl, so that the music was always secondary. [But] I finally decided that it is important—for the cause and for understanding—to come out publicly."[55]

From the beginning, the duo's lesbian fans formed the core of their audience, although the group refused to play shows that banned men from the audience. Ray explains, "I can see a place for separatism in history, especially in the growth of the gay movement, but I thought that was defeating the purpose of what my music is about."[56] Still, the two performers have been very involved in gay activism, including playing at the 1993 gay rights march on Washington. In 1998 three high schools in Tennessee and South Carolina cancelled free concerts by the Indigo Girls because of their sexuality. The school principals' decisions set off a storm of protest and national attention. In characteristic Indigo Girls manner, Emily responded: "It hurts my feelings, but I understand prejudice and where hate comes from. I know that it is in the world and it's not just directed towards gay people, but it's directed towards lots of groups of people."[57] Rather than allowing homophobic principals and parents to have the last word, Ray and Saliers rescheduled the concerts at different venues (still free to students and low-cost to parents). As mentioned in chapter 3, Saliers has recently begun working with churches to create more understanding and acceptance of gay and lesbian people.

While Lynn Frances Anderson has been an out lesbian performer her entire career, only recently did she really realize the importance of her lesbian and gay fan base in building an audience. "We're talking about growing an audience, and one of the best ways I've been able to start to expand it is by going home, going to my own people, going to the gay community and saying, 'I am here. This is what I've got to offer. If you like it, please come along. If you don't, please don't talk badly about me.'" Lynn says she asked herself who her target market is, to whom her music appeals. "The first thing is the gay audience, the second thing is women, the third thing is the folk or singer/songwriter. And so if I look at it in a very businesslike way, the smartest thing to do is to go to where there is the highest possibility of acceptance. And gay fans tend to be really loyal. I mean, we support each other. And it's because we support each other that we can be successful."[58] And so

Lynn submitted her promotional materials and was selected to perform in two of the largest gay pride events in the country—those of San Francisco and Atlanta.

Similarly, Bitch and Animal recognized the importance of connecting with the queer community.[59] Bitch says that because of "dyke solidarity," they can "call up dyke clubs and say, 'Hey, we're a dyke band from New York.' And it's like, 'Oh, cool!'" She says that when they went to London, they played a queer venue. "Nobody knew of us there, but we were like queer, and they were queer. And they let us come! So there is something to that, you know."[60]

Contested Identities

While many women performers and fans comfortably identify themselves as lesbian, in reality, categories of sexual identity are often quite fluid and contested.[61] What, for example, exactly is a lesbian?[62] A woman whose sexual/affectional orientation is exclusively toward other women? A woman whose primary sexual/affectional orientation is toward women? A woman who identifies herself as lesbian as a political commitment while maintaining sexual relationships with men? Lesbian feminist Adrienne Rich has suggested a "lesbian continuum" on which all women can identify as lesbian depending on the level of their woman-identified experience—those "forms of primary intensity between and among women, including the sharing of a rich inner life, the bonding against male tyranny, the giving and receiving of practical and political support."[63]

While the contestation of sexual identity may be less problematic among women who self-identify as lesbian, the identities of those who refuse to fit neatly within the boundaries of either lesbian or heterosexual identity seem to create a great deal of disruption among fans and the larger culture. Bisexuality, in particular, seems to evoke especially harsh responses from both lesbian and heterosexual audiences.[64] Bisexual singer/songwriter and bassist Me'Shell Ndegeocello, who is in a relationship with a woman, received a great deal of criticism for her 1993 *Plantation Lullabies*, which contains cuts that celebrate sexual relationships with black men. A segment of the lesbian community accused her of selling out, and *The Advocate* (a gay and lesbian magazine) alleged that she was like every other closeted gay musician, claiming to be gay but singing about men. Her response? "I'm bisexual, and how could you negate my life? Just 'cause I'm not waving your flag."[65] One song on her 1996 *Peace Beyond Passion,* she said, deals with her own homophobia and self-hatred. "Leviticus: Faggot" drew sharp criticism for its critique of religious hypocrisy and use of the word "faggot," and, even though the song's message is anti-homophobic, some radio and video programs refused to air it. The message was apparently in too complicated a package—or else both the misheard message and the *real* message were unacceptable. "I got nominated for an MTV award for a video I never saw played," Ndegeocello said ruefully.[66]

Ani DiFranco has also struggled with acceptance of her refusal to be easily categorized. She says, "It's funny. Often love—the politicization of love—is so claustrophobic for people on any side of the equation. In the dyke community, your love affair is a political statement; you can't avoid the politics. But sometimes it's like everyone forgets the real purpose of being with this other person." She says that she's had pressure from both sides—"Hey, stake a flag, right here—where are you going to be?" But, she explains, "It's not something I can choose. I don't experience love or sex as sleeping with a woman or a man. It's the person."[67] Even the way Ani has constructed her appearance has been an issue. She says her early look of shaved head and big boots came about as a way to distance herself from her teenage years when she had long hair, looked very feminine, and received much male sexual attention. She says that the "young chick" vibe was not conducive to her work, and so she changed her look and the environment of her performances. But, she says, after many years of that, "it's like, OK, I want hair to play with. Or, oooh, that's a pretty dress. And I remember the first time that I started walking out onstage in a dress and hearing young women screaming, 'Sellout!' "[68]

While Ani uses the word "bisexual" in response to an interviewer's question about what she calls herself, she says that she really prefers the word "queer."[69] She says "queer" is "an open-ended word. It means, like, the kind of love I experience is not the kind of love that's on TV."[70] "Queer" also seems to be the word of choice for a whole generation of young radical musicians whose sexuality challenges the heterosexual/homosexual binary. Queer identity emerged in the late 1980s and, previously, in the early 1970s with the activism of politically radical groups like act up and Queer Nation.[71] Queer identity rejects essentialist categories of heterosexual/homosexual and insists on an understanding of sexuality that embraces fluidity, ambivalence, and shifting boundaries.[72] Queer identity also recognizes the intersections and interactions of gender, race, and social class with sexuality.[73] Kaia Wilson, lead singer of the Butchies, for example, says she is not concerned with assimilating in mainstream society. "That focus I don't really feel solidarity with. The white, middle class values. The world is really focused on consumerism. . . . We want to do good things in the world. To do good things you have to involve yourself in politics."[74]

Wilson says the Butchies deliberately reach out to the queer community. "People need to hear and see representations of others who are more like them," she says. Of course, she admits, their politics keep them marginalized in the press and in music. "Our out politics hold us back. That is a fact."[75] In fact, because she felt there was not a record company that could really represent her work, Wilson and her girlfriend Tammy Rae Carland started Mr. Lady Records, a label founded to promote queer musicians and filmmakers.

Combining queer politics and punk music led to a musical subculture often described as "queercore" (queer + hardcore). Michael DuPlessis and Kathleen Chapman developed an elaborate analysis of "queercore" in 1997; one of the most helpful aspects of their definition, perhaps, involves what queercore is *not*. Like queer politics, queercore shuns the more traditional institutions of gay and lesbian identity—GLAAD, NGLTF, Gay Pride marches, and even the Michigan Womyn's Music Festival.[76] Queercore intentionally challenges traditional boundaries and paradigms with its raw, radical, in-your-face style of music and politics. Queercore musician and Tribe 8 singer Lynn Breedlove, for example, offers this advice to aspiring queer bands: "Get in their face! Be OUT OUT OUT! Be who you are. . . . I think the more the mainstream, straights and gays alike, hear queer music, the more they're going to start to accept that we exist and that we're o.k. and that we are not the enemy and we're not evil and we're not monsters. We're just people."[77] Cultural theorist Robert DeChaine explains, "As much as queercore resonates with the punk rock aesthetic, it is also informed by issues of queer identity and the tensions which a queer politics brings to traditional lesbian and gay subjectivities. Queercore is not just about the music—it is about the lives and values of the people who participate in it."[78]

Two stories from our research process may prove illustrative of these generational differences. Mina and Susan learned of Bitch and Animal through June Millington and arranged an interview with them at a coffee shop in Manhattan. The two middle-aged academicians arrived early and got a table. Having only emailed the musicians legally known as Bitch and Animal, and seen their pictures on the Web, the interviewers were not quite sure how to recognize their subjects—especially in the heart of Greenwich Village. At last, Susan said to Mina, "So what are we going to do? Walk up to two women and say, 'Excuse me. Are you Bitch and Animal?' " As they sat at the table pondering their dilemma, two young women came into the coffee shop. "I think that's them," Susan whispered to Mina. "They sort of look like the women on the Web site." At last, at Susan's prodding, Mina approached the two women and turned the tables. "Are you looking for a couple of . . . ?" Luckily, the right academics found the right artists that day.

The interview was delightful, and Mina and Susan promised to catch the show that night at CBGB. Later that day, they enthusiastically discussed which university or church venue in their own town would best showcase these talented, engaging artists. That night, as Bitch and Animal began their show with a recitation of their "Pussy Manifesto," the wandering professors realized that their Oregon town might not be ready for this duo.

Tisa saw the band later when they came south in the fall of 2002. She arrived about an hour before the show, and the line of young women, some in neckties and Doc Martens with many sporting buzz cuts, already circled the building. As the forty-something, conservatively dressed college professor approached the line, two young women caressing each other asked politely, "Ma'am, are you lost? May we help you?" "I'm here for the concert," she replied. "Are you aware of who's playing?" they asked. "Yes, I'm actually here because we're writing a book on women and rock music." "No way! Far out! Cool!" they responded. When the doors finally opened and the show began, the room was filled with eager fans, none over the age of thirty except Tisa.

First to perform were the Butchies, a three-woman band dressed in black pants, white shirts, and black neckties. This energetic trio, who often perform with Amy Ray of the Indigo Girls, produced a punk, garage-rock sound received with gusto by ecstatic fans who danced like popcorn in front of the stage. Mixing humor and politics, Kaia Wilson (guitar/vocals), Melissa York (drums), and Alison Martlew (bass/vocals) promoted gender equity and spoke out against hate crimes in their lyrics. *Billboard* has said that their music "borrows as much from Led Zeppelin as it does from the Sex Pistols."[79] They named themselves the Butchies, Kaia explains, "because people certainly recognize it as queer and know that they can come to one of our shows and be in a safe space."[80]

Next up were Bitch and Animal. Their deliberate, rhythmic tapestry of sound is not easily categorized, a combination of funk, rap, pop, spoken word, and even a little hoedown country. Knowing that *Eternally Hard,* their 2001 album from Ani DiFranco's Righteous Babe label, carried explicitly feminist, in-your-face lyrics, Tisa thought she was prepared for the show. She knew from their Web site that the shorter, mohawked Animal played djembe, other African drums, and ukulele while the taller, fountain-haired, classically-trained Bitch played violin, bass, and also ukulele. These mid- to late-twenties women were raunchy, irreverent, political, and hilarious. Quickly recognizing "Sparkly Queen Areola," an ode to the breast part that most states have deemed illegal to expose, many in the crowd sang along. Even the few men in the audience seemed quite amused by this chant. Sick of her genitalia being used as an insult, Bitch recited her Manifesto, putting a positive spin on the popular pejorative slang word for "vagina."[81] Commenting on her "Pussy Manifesto," the *Los Angeles Times* explained that "the body-part references are often broadsides at stereotypes in these tales of sexual and social politics. There is a lesbian sensibility at work, with a humor and underlying vulnerability that is almost always universal."[82]

While rock 'n' roll has always been sexy and sexual, that sexuality has normatively been constructed as heterosexual and male. For women musicians, particularly those who do not identify as heterosexual, negotiating the terrain of rock 'n' roll has meant confronting rock's masculinist and heterosexist norms. From women's music to queercore, women performers have insisted on the rightful place of their sexualities. Despite differences in musical and personal styles, by asserting their right to name their desires and speak their realities, these artists have furthered a politic that demands acceptance and equality across genders and sexualities.

CHAPTER 6

WHO'S THAT GIRL? WOMEN AND IMAGE IN ROCK 'N' ROLL

When the band was setting up for a showcase arranged for label executives who were visiting from London, I noticed someone pointing to a monitor directly in front of me and telling a technician to move it "so the pigs can see her legs."

—*Margot Mifflin, "The Fallacy of Feminism in Rock"*

When Susan first saw Lynn Frances Anderson perform at a little coffee shop on a funky street in Portland, Oregon, in 1994, she never would have guessed Lynn had ever fronted Top 40 bands. Accompanied only by an acoustic guitar, Lynn's powerful voice took the audience on a journey through bluesy songs reminiscent of Bonnie Raitt and Stevie Nicks, with an occasional dash of James Brown. She was dressed simply, her long dark hair moving hypnotically as she swayed to her music. Her music too complicated for commercial radio and her image definitely her own, Lynn exuded determination to set her own path in the music world, but, as she told us in 2001, she was not always able to be herself as she tried to break into music.

Lynn recalls that when she started singing in bands in the 1980s, "there was definitely a role that the woman's supposed to play in the band. You know, you're supposed to be the pretty front girl. . . . I auditioned for a band that the guy, all he did was look at me. And then he had decided before I even sang whether or not he wanted me in the band—which was not. I wasn't the shape of girl he wanted." She adds that her role as "pretty front girl" was complicated by being a lesbian. "I'm a singer, but I'm supposed to look like a stereotypical straight girl in order to front a band." So, she says, in the 1980s she had big hair and wore tall shoes and glittery, shiny clothes.

Lynn still wants to look "feminine" onstage, but now, she says, "wearing girlie clothes" is part of her persona, and that she would never come out in a T-shirt and jeans. Why not? we asked. "Would you ever imagine seeing Stevie Nicks walk out in a T-shirt and jeans? Part of her persona is how she's dressed." Whereas men can wear "whatever," she argues, women tend to be more self-conscious about creating an image through clothes. She uses her own image to extend her musical impact. "When I imagine what is the persona of Lynn Frances Anderson, . . . I have to do a process of elimination: OK, I'm not wearing leather. OK. That doesn't work for me. And I don't really have the grunge thing going on. And what do I want people to get from what I have to offer? And a lot of that is a softness, and a lot of that is acceptance. And that's a lot of what my music is about."[1]

Issues of beauty, fashion, and appearance pervade the conscious and unconscious struggles of most women in cultures that value women primarily for the way they look. Sociologist Rose Weitz argues that attractiveness "serves as an indirect form of power, by increasing women's odds of obtaining the protection of powerful men—at least so long as the women's attractiveness lasts."[2] And issues of appearance are heightened for musicians whose performance requires that they be looked at. While appearance has been a central theme for women since the beginnings of rock 'n' roll (remember the Motown charm school?), the advent of MTV gave a new spin to the looks of performers, who up to then had primarily been voices on the radio and, occasionally, concert artists. No longer was being an outstanding musician enough. Now women performers' physical beauty would be packaged and marketed in new ways, to an audience of people multitasking in their living rooms or idly glancing at a bar TV rather than attending a live event or paging through a magazine. "Now, the most famous faces in music were right there next to the Ping-Pong table and the bean-bag chair in your paneled suburban basement, singing away while you and your friends drank Dr. Pepper, ate Doritos, talked about the scuzzball teacher who gave you a D in chemistry."[3] Being a rock star also meant being a video star.

Like Lynn Frances Anderson, many women musicians have managed an ambivalent relationship to "looksism." Little girls, and more little boys than will admit it, grow through a dress-up phase that for Western females often feeds directly into the capitalist shopping culture. Dressing up is about appropriating power to shape others' responses. Dressing up is about experimenting with one's identity. It is about being onstage. For Lynn as for other women, it can be just plain fun to stun an audience with a shiny costume.

By the time Wanda Jackson, who has been called America's first female rock and roll singer, appeared on the Grand Ole Opry in the 1950s, she was already designing her own clothes and her mother was making them. She didn't like what the country girls were wearing: "boots and full skirts and hats." Wanda told us, "I just couldn't see myself in those things, so I started designing the tight skirts and the silkier fringe and the straps and the rhinestones and the long earrings and high heels. I wanted to get a little glamour or sex appeal in it." At the Grand Ole Opry, dressed in one of her new designs and waiting to go on, she suffered a humiliation that clearly still stings. "I was backstage and had my guitar on and everything. And Ernest Tubbs . . . came back and said, 'Are you Wanda Jackson?' I said, 'Yes sir.' He said, 'Well, you better get ready; you're on next.' 'I *am* ready,' " she told him. "He said, 'Well, no, you can't go on the stage of the Opry like that.' I said, 'What, what do you mean?' " Laughing, she explained to us, "I thought something had ripped or torn. He said, 'Oh well, honey, you can't go on the stage of the Grand Ole Opry with bare shoulders.' I said, 'My goodness, you know, it's the only thing I brought.' He said, 'Well, you're up next, and if you don't cover up, we can't use you.' "

Fortunately, she did have something in the dressing room, a new, nice leather jacket with long fringe on the arms. Wanda adds, "It was pretty, but my heart was just broken, and I was mad, and when I get mad I'm the type that starts crying. It was all I could do to sing." After her performance she told her father, "That's the last time I'll sing on that stage." True to her word, she told us laughing, "I did sing on that stage again, but it was on a different program. I sang on the new Opry stage. I did go back, but not under those circumstances. The rules of the Grand Ole Opry, that was fine," she insists; "it was family, it was country, but the problem was, I didn't know it ahead of time. No one informed me. They didn't bother to look at a picture of me and see what I was wearing. That's what hurt and made my experience so unpleasant." Daring to challenge the rules and create her own "sexier" image, the young Wanda ran up against rigid notions of professional demeanor and a "woman's place" in the world of the Grand Old Opry.

Encouraged by her friend Elvis Presley, Jackson moved from country music toward rockabilly. That move began with a slow evolution in dress. She remembers, "When I first started changing, mother started making these outfits. We still would have . . . a soft suede fringe [and] I put a rhinestone on the end of each one, and a scoop neck and no sleeves, and fringe then on the skirt." She suffered the full skirts and cowgirl boots just as long as she could, but then rebelled. Her mother made her a copy of the dress that Marilyn Monroe wore in *The Seven Year Itch* (1955). "I had to have the high heels, and long earrings, full hair."[4]

"Women's hair is central to their social position," Rose Weitz contends. Drawing from a series of interviews with forty-four women and other research on the subject, Weitz concludes that many women use their hair to seek power by wearing it in ways that reflect conventional norms of attractiveness. "There is widespread agreement that conventionally attractive hair gives women power, or at least makes them feel powerful."[5] Other women use their hairstyles to challenge conventional norms, whether it is black women sporting dreadlocks or lesbians wearing butch cuts. Even in acts of hirsute resistance, Weitz reasonably concludes, "these strategies unintentionally lend support to those who equate women's bodies with their identities."[6] For women rock musicians, this tension is palpable. Musical talent aside, to a great degree, their success depends on how audiences receive the way they look.

A certain "look" was certainly crucial for Shirley Alston Reeves, who remembers a Bermuda concert as she was breaking out as a solo artist in the mid-1970s. Fighting her nerves, she hired a band and worked on the music; but without the other Shirelles, she plunged into a musical identity crisis. "So I said, 'If I can't do it with song, I'm gonna do it with outfit.' . . . I had a cape, a white chiffon cape made with white ostrich feathers around the hood, a big hood with feathers around the face, and it was down to the floor. And I had a white gown on; it went around my neck. I was, I don't know, I had a bit of a shape too." She laughs. She remembers the rhinestone bodice of that gown. "When the spotlight hit it, I mean, it was like glittering in people's faces. It was just beautiful." And then, in that moment of excitement, she forgot the words to her song. Playing with the audience's enthusiasm and adulation, Shirley worked the crowd like Pearl Bailey, shaking hands and greeting her fans until she gathered her wits. The evening was a huge success.[7]

Appearance has drawn the thickest of boundaries around female identity and, by extension, female behavior. Throughout the post–World War II era (to consider just the period coincident with rock music), girls have faced a lose-lose situation. If you were not born "pretty," you could always try to make yourself "pretty." But if you tried too hard, you could be labeled cheap or, in this era of debased pseudo-Freudianism, narcissistic. Baby boomers remember draconian dress codes—like curfews, more draconian for girls than for boys—that governed their clothing choices for school, church, visiting grandparents, even leaving the house to do an errand "downtown." Enforced skirt-wearing ensured that girls would not climb to the upper rungs of the playground jungle gym without risking being thought of as sexually provocative—at eight years old. Most colleges and universities did not give up their dress codes for women until the last years of the 1960s.

As a young girl, Indigo Girl Emily Saliers rebelled against the dress code, even when it came to "church attire." It helped that she had a complicit mother. She recalls, "Very early on I dressed and acted the way I wanted to. I wanted a boy doll instead of a girl doll. I wanted to wear pants instead of a dress on Easter, so my mom made me Easter pants, you know? I mean I just never really considered gender until later when I got out in the world and [realized] what women were up against. But early on I didn't."[8]

The Indigo Girls' other half, Amy Ray, experienced similar gender issues in her identity formation. She remembers, "I mean the way I considered gender was that the people that I was emulating were all men, and I thought of myself when I was little, you know, like ten and eleven playing guitar in front of the mirror, I was a boy, you know, and never considered myself a girl at that age. I mean, I just didn't. I identified in a certain way." However, her mother made her wear dresses often, which Amy says was fine. She adds, "But I think in a way that was pre-puberty, and there's a lot of that that goes on I think in anybody because you identify with who's got the power, probably. You know, you're like, I want to be able to do that so that's what I am." Even though she had really strong sisters, Ray says, "As soon as things start shifting and you kind of get into high school and your identity starts to be a struggle and you don't have the freedom that you thought you had and, you know, your parents have brought you up that you can do anything. But all of a sudden, well, maybe you can't do anything," she remembers, echoing the research on the deflation of girls' self-esteem at puberty by Mary Pipher, Carol Gilligan, Peggy Orenstein, and many others.[9] "And even your parents change when you go through puberty because they start feeling like . . . maybe we should not have you mow the lawn, you know, on the weekends . . . because they're starting to think that they're developing you the wrong way when they see the way people are treating you in high school. I know my parents went through that because they didn't care that I was a tomboy until I started getting abused for it." At that point her parents responded, "I think we need to work on the wearing dresses thing."[10]

Observing the double standard placed on appropriate attire, Holly Near told us she refused to succumb to social pressure. "I think fashion is often a good simple barometer for social discomforts. I used to be amazed how women were expected to dress up more than men. So, there I would be wondering what to wear. I used to say to myself, 'What would Jackson Browne wear?' and I would put on a nice pair of jeans and a jacket and I would be fine."[11]

Thin and Unblemished at All Costs

Along with the dictates regarding clothing were the much more damaging essentialist rules about body discipline.[12] To reach adolescence was to enter a new relationship with one's body: formerly a thing to move and sense with (for those children fortunate enough not to be unduly interfered with), the body was now a burden, a war zone, an accessory, an enemy.[13] "Fatty," as Ann Wilson recalls the ubiquitous taunt, the surefire cruelty. Desiring ectomorphic body types, girls starved, purged, puked, corseted, draped, closeted, and cut themselves as self-punishment for their "fatty"-ness.[14] By the 1960s the family medicine cabinet had become one more drug stop. Girls did not need to go to the street corner or the girls room to get laxatives, emetics, Darvon, Midol, or Listerine, as well as whatever mothers were taking for whatever ailed *them*. American supermarkets overflowed with colorful packages of reconstituted items with which young women could fool themselves that they were eating very little, indeed. A chocolate bar for lunch—how efficient. Then there were always cigarettes to cut the appetite and enhance the "cool" look.

During this same decade, the Ronettes accentuated their ectomorphic frames with form-fitting gowns. They were thin and their female fans yearned to be. When Gerri Hirshey asked Ronnie Spector what adoring teens in the sixties wanted to know from her, her response was indicative of these girls' obsession with food and body image. " 'It was the weirdest thing,' she said. 'They wanted to know what we ate.' "[15]

Dinah Washington, Karen Carpenter, and Cass Elliott died of the pre-MTV emphasis on slenderness, dieting their bodies into system failure. Karen Carpenter's doctor put her on a water diet in 1967. She lost twenty pounds and gained one more authoritative voice telling her that it was better to be thin than well-nourished.[16] In 1983, at the age of thirty-three, she died from the.effects of anorexia nervosa. A few years later Kim Gordon, of Sonic Youth, wrote "Tunic (Song for Karen)." "I wanted to put Karen Carpenter up in heaven playing drums and being happy," she told *Rolling Stone* several years later. "At what point," she asks, "do girls start getting their sense of self-worth and [need to please] people, and why don't they have anything else?"[17] In 1963, two decades before Carpenter's death, Dinah Washington, remembered best for her 1959 hit "What a Diff'rence a Day Makes," died from a combination of diet pills and alcohol at the age of thirty-nine. "At their deaths, both women weighed about seventy-five pounds."[18] Cass "Don't Call Me Mama Anymore" Elliott died at thirty of a heart attack brought on by her many diets' ravages of her body.[19]

When Belinda Carlisle gained twenty pounds, she hated it when people commented, " 'Uh oh, she's been hitting too many deli trays.' "[20] Janet Jackson, teased about her shapely rear by her "buttless wonder" brother Michael, fought to claim "mastery over her career and her body," writes Gerri Hirshey. Her brother is not the only family member to change images; Janet morphed from a 1986 "slightly chunky dancer in 'Control' " to a "hollow-cheeked" Michael look-alike in their "Scream" video nearly a decade later.[21] By the turn of the century, she could even be described as "cut" and "buff," but how much damage had those early taunts done? As a kid in the late 1950s, Janis Joplin hated her looks because everyone else made fun of her for succumbing to adolescence. "At fourteen Janis started to put on weight and her face began breaking out in what her sister calls 'a never-ending series of painful bright red pimples.' Janis's acne was so bad," writes her biographer Alice Echols, "her mother took her to a local dermatologist, who applied dry ice to the worst outbreaks—one of several ineffective treatments at the time—and blamed Janis when her skin failed to clear up."[22] Then as now, huge segments of the medical profession colluded with the culture's "professional" requirements of its female pop stars—and young women in general. Janis Ian captured the teen angst of so many "ugly duckling girls" like Joplin, who wished in vain for those "clear-skinned smiles," in her 1975 song "At Seventeen."

Even today, could a female larger than a size ten with less than perfect skin become the American Idol on Fox network's popular television show?[23] Judge Simon Cowell's requirements for the American Idol certainly involve a weight bias, at least for the women. He drew criticism in February 2003 when he told American Idol contestant and Bette Midler look-alike Vanessa Olivarez, "This isn't going to make me very popular, but I'm going to say it. I would say, 'Vanessa, you have a great personality, a great voice . . . and need to lose a few pounds.' "[24] Vanessa's compliant response was: "I think he wants to see who can take it and who can't. In this business it's important to be able to take constructive criticism without becoming overwhelmed. . . . I am going to take his advice and lose a few pounds." She added, "Simon, be ready for me because I'm going to be a thin, little hottie!"[25] This twenty-one-year-old woman's experience reminded us of Jann Arden's story, although the punch line is rather different. "I had a guy say to me, one of the record company execs, he said, 'You know, you're thirty-five pounds away from superstardom in this country.' And I never rebutted it. I didn't say anything. I went to my hotel room, and I remember calling my mom and sort of telling her the story. And there was a long pause on the line, and she said, 'Well, why didn't you tell him that you didn't want to gain any more weight?' "[26]

Perhaps if Aretha Franklin–like Frenchie Davis, the plus-sized early front-runner in 2003, had become the American Idol before executives booted her off the show when they discovered her topless photographs on a Web site, a new model might have emerged for adolescent girls. Instead, in June 2003 that round's American Idol was crowned: Ruben Studdard, 300-pound crooner, with a voice of liquid gold in an outsized container that did *not* doom this male contestant's chances at stardom, American style.

During adolescence, if not before, kids, especially girls, will develop the classic "imaginary audience." Believing she is constantly onstage, she becomes self-conscious, thinking everyone is watching her, that everyone believes she is obese or sees the pimple that she discovered with horror this morning.[27] Walking down the corridors of the mall, she cannot avoid floor-to-ceiling images of slender Gap models or Britney Spears–like mannequins displaying well-toned abs. It may be impossible for her to pass by a mirror or a shiny show window without stealing a glance.[28] She may be the biggest fan in her own audience, or she may detest what she sees. If the girl thinks she is unattractive, fat, or gawky, she may develop a coping mechanism whereby she controls her audience's first impression of her. A shaved head, purple hair, out-of-style glasses, or wildly ill-fitting clothes may serve to call attention to an aspect of her appearance over which she has total control. She can then meet derogatory comments about her appearance with, "I choose to dress this way," or "Yeah, I think it's cool." If she thinks she is attractive, she may do everything possible to accentuate her best traits. Of course, some girls, no matter how conventionally attractive, may decide to buck social expectation. We will focus on women performers who take this stance later in this chapter.

Many adolescents eventually lose their imaginary audience, but obsession with public image persists for some into adulthood. One item on David Elkind's Imaginary Audience Scale asks if you discover a grease spot on your clothes, do you go on to the party or return home?[29] How might the answer change if the audience is no longer imaginary? Many performers would not think of going onstage with a dab of hummus on their lapel, instead changing their entire wardrobe. But others might hurriedly wipe it off and proceed with their performance, maybe even intentionally drawing attention to the stain.

Stage Persona

A stain on their public persona was not acceptable to The Shirelles. Shirley Alston Reeves recalls a time when The Shirelles were on one of Dick Clark's Caravan of Stars tours. She recalls, "When he announced us he would say the same thing almost every night about us. He'd always talk about how fast we could get dressed. He says, 'I'm telling you,' he says, 'We could pull into town . . . [a]nd if nobody else is ready, those Shirelles are always ready to go on.' He said, 'I can count on them.' He says, 'So ladies and gentlemen, the fastest dressing girl group in show business, The Shirelles!' They're playing our ramp, our intro, and he's looking by the curtain. He's got his hand like this. Nothing. We didn't come out. So he's standing there. He's like, 'Now, you know nobody's going to play a trick on Dick Clark!' So he says it again. He says, 'Maybe they didn't hear me, ladies and gentlemen. The Shirelles!' Nothing." Micki's zipper had popped and the whole dress gaped open. "Now we're not one not to be uniform. We were not going out there with anything mismatched on. She wasn't going to wear one thing and we wear something different. We all took all of our clothes back off." Not one but four new dresses had to be ironed. "We're on the floor with a towel and an iron. And he just kept doing it. And they were playing the music, and the audience was dying laughing."[30] Image mattered to The Shirelles.

Many women in the music profession will spend hours selecting their wardrobes and being sculpted by a makeup artist (or surgeon), while some concentrate more on a true "self" appearing. Tina Turner enjoys the makeup process. "Yes, there is something calming about putting myself together to face people onstage. We love makeup. It's just girls playing."[31] Not all artists take as much pleasure or put as much stock in that process. Holly Near sees her stage persona differently. "Theatricality has always been a part of my performance work. But not like being different characters or wearing different costumes. Rather I project my 'self.' Interestingly, this is not an easy thing to do."[32] Janis Ian has a knack for being onstage, but when asked how her stage persona developed, she said, "You know, I don't know that there is a persona per se. My partner says there is. She says that she can always tell when I'm turning into Janis Ian. But I'm not real aware of it unless I consciously stop and think about it. I think it's more that when I was studying with Stella Adler, I figured out that a great part of my job as a performer was to only bring the best of myself onstage, not bring the dross, not bring the business that people weren't paying for. So I've worked on making sure that that's the part of me that appears."[33]

As we mentioned earlier, the stage personas of Bitch and Animal are so true to who they believe they are that they legally changed their names to reflect these selves. Animal says the names came to her one day as she was lying on a futon in a loft, staring at the ceiling. "I was thinking of archetypal sorts of images of who we were. And it was, like, Bitch and Animal. And it hit me." Initially Bitch wasn't so excited. "We had words," Animal explains dryly. But soon Bitch too was sold on the name and the image. Animal says it made sense to her on many levels. "I mean, so much of what we were doing just naturally was about finding our own voices and being able to be who we wanted to be without anyone's criticism. . . . I've always been told I was too loud. I was too crazy, too wild. You know, and it was like OK, yeah, I'm an animal. And that's who I am. And there's nothing wrong with that. And I am a woman, you know. And to own the word and to own being a bitch. So many times women are just called 'bitch' because they're speaking their minds. . . . It kept getting stronger and stronger how important it was for us to own those names and identities. And it just keeps getting clearer to me, and we really just had adopted it into our lives. I mean, that's who we are."[34]

Being so true to her authentic identity has not been so easy for Tina Turner, who commented to Gerri Hirshey in the thirtieth anniversary issue of *Rolling Stone* on women and rock, "Before, it was raunchy Tina, legs open, her red lips, her long hair. Wild! They just thought I was just another of those raunchy singers, 'cause no one knew the other side. Only people very close to me knew." Putting on makeup may be relaxing for her, but projecting an image that was far from her "self" was not easy to live with. She confessed, "So I never liked [being thought of that way], but I thought, 'Well, that's what you've done, Tina.' "[35] What Tina did to herself onstage was exacerbated by her television appearances, for better or for worse. Television's impact on women in rock, their success and their demise, cannot be overstated.

Television Exposure before MTV

In 1956 Brenda Lee appeared as a guest star on Red Foley's national television show, *Ozark Jubilee,* singing "Jambalaya." That appearance led to a booking on the *Perry Como Show* in the late 1950s while she was still a teenager. As mentioned in chapter 2, her producer Owen Bradley protected her youth and innocence and did not allow her to be sexually objectified. Even though she was in her teens, Brenda often appeared on television in black patent leather "Mary Janes" with white turned-down socks and wore a crinoline petticoat that made her Shirley Temple–style dresses stand out. (This different, "little-girl" idealization certainly bears analysis, but not necessarily in the context of this discussion.)[36]

Ike Turner was not as protective of Anna Mae Bullock's youth and innocence, even though she was still a teenager when they began working together. Ike was after an image, and when Anna Mae was seventeen or eighteen, Ike dressed her in "really grown-up clothes": sequined dresses, long gloves, costume jewelry, "bare back shoes and the stockings with the seam in the back."[37] Changing her name to Tina was a part of the package. But this eventual diva had an early image problem when she was dying to get onstage at a club in East St. Louis in 1956. "I was always this kind of very skinny girl, and I didn't look the part, so I was never called."[38] When the microphone was finally passed to her and she got onstage with Ike, he knew he had a hit. By the time Tina Turner appeared on American Bandstand in 1960, image was crucial. Tina didn't just sing a song; she acted it, and you need more than radio for that. The camera loved her, and in the mid-sixties she appeared on *Shindig* and *Where the Action Is,* on *The Ed Sullivan Show* in 1970, and *The Tonight Show* in 1981.[39]

The image Tina portrayed onstage or in front of the camera did not accurately reflect her offstage life. "I've always been very spiritual, but my image—in terms of my work—was very far from that." When people realized after a *60 Minutes* segment that chanting and spirituality were an important part of her life, she says, "everybody went, '*What?*' " However, she understood their reaction: "That's what people see. They have no way of knowing anything else."[40] Even in 1997 David Letterman introduced her on his show as "having the best legs on the planet."[41] While the compliment was kind, Tina Turner is much more than the terrific set of "Proud Mary" legs that the camera caught regularly.

Of course, the dilemma of appearance and image for earlier black women performers was compounded by the marketing designed to make them appeal to white audiences. As feminist theorist Patricia Hill Collins suggests, dominant understandings of black women's sexuality have been constructed within the framework of white male power, "othering" and reinforcing the objectification of black women's bodies.[42] As mentioned in chapter 2, appearing "good," proper, and nonthreatening was an important strategy of acceptance for the 1960s African American girl groups. These young women dealt with white fears of black female sexuality by downplaying overt sexuality and constructing stage identities that targeted the projected tastes and mores of white audiences.

With Motown since 1961, Mary Wilson, Diana Ross, and Florence Ballard were often referred to as "the 'no-hit' Supremes" within the company.[43] The miracle of television would change that. Appearing regularly on *The Ed Sullivan Show* from 1964 until the end of the decade, The Supremes caught the American public's eye in their uniform sequined gowns and perfect hairdos along with their subtle, choreographed dance steps and arm gestures. Also gracing shows such as *Hullabaloo, Shindig, American Bandstand, The Hollywood Palace, Soul Train,* and *The Tonight Show,* this group projected a conservative, polished image that sold albums and pleased crowds. Mary Wilson told us that owners of the record company also used their "presence." "In fact, we were used a lot. And I think that's the way a lot of women were used in those days. . . . We were like ambassadors. So we were used to go to the record companies to sell the product, to even sell Motown. . . . So in that way I guess it was good because it helped us, but we definitely were ambassadors."[44] Their "look" was crucial to Motown and to the group's popularity, and television certainly contributed to this trio's success in the 1960s.

In addition to the shows mentioned earlier, The Supremes also performed on *The Sonny and Cher Comedy Hour.* Premiering in 1971, this variety show featured a constantly bickering couple who sang pop music, performed comedy sketches, and always ended with "I Got You Babe." Sometimes including their daughter Chastity, this groovy family was the closest thing to the Osbournes that America would see in the 1970s. While Sonny was adorable and sweet, Cher may have been the real reason folks tuned in. His fur vests were no match for the raven-haired, exotic contralto, whose husky voice dominated the wacky show. With a wild array of wardrobe options, Cher bared her midriff in a way that most had never seen. Each episode left the television audience asking, "What will she wear next?"

Guests on *The Sonny and Cher Comedy Hour* included LaBelle in 1975, but not until the group had undergone a major transformation from the 1960s girl group, Patti LaBelle and the Blue Belles. An earlier appearance on *American Bandstand* signaled a first change in appearance. Sarah Dash told us, "They transformed us with this show [*Bandstand*] because they like chopped off our hair, put on this makeup. My father was looking at the TV going, 'Where is my daughter?' "[45] Then Cindy Birdsong left the group in 1967 to replace the Supremes' Florence Ballard, leaving Sarah Dash, Patti LaBelle, and Nona Hendryx. Later in this chapter, we will look at how this trio became LaBelle.

Set to a 1960s sound track, the nostalgic NBC show *American Dreams* (2002) brought *American Bandstand* back into the living rooms of baby boomers. Struggling with issues from race to sex role stereotypes, the Philadelphia family featured in each episode evolved along with the music of the era. Using original footage from Dick Clark's show interspersed with images of contemporary stars dressed as sixties teen idols, the show reintroduced a wide variety of acts, from The Shirelles to Dusty Springfield.

MTV: Visual Overload

In 1981 Kim Carnes's "Bette Davis Eyes," Blondie's "The Tide Is High," Olivia Newton-John's "Physical," Dolly Parton's "9 to 5," and Juice Newton's "Queen of Hearts" were *Billboard*'s Top Hits by females. That same year, television shows *Knot's Landing, Hill Street Blues,* and *Dallas* shared the airwaves with music videos from a rookie cable network. With the advent of MTV, image became everything, at least in the eyes of the music industry. At first, video budgets were modest, with emphasis placed on quick-cut editing, images changing every two to three seconds. Early music videos with women artists were fairly innocuous, almost innocent. Cyndi Lauper and the other girls just wanted to have fun. But when the tide began to turn, even teenage girls wanting to "make it" found themselves succumbing to the pressure to sell sex. Perplexed by their drive, Jann Arden told us, "They'll do whatever they can to get to where they're going." She expressed disgust over "sixteen-, seventeen-, eighteen-year-old women and these sexual wacko images that they're presenting," adding bluntly, "They look like hookers." She predicts that eventually these women will wake up and say, " 'Um, that's not what I ever wanted to be. That's not even real.' So I watch it, and it's so interesting just to see it unravel. Thinking, well, you need better direction."[46]

Modest budgets evolved into million-dollar productions, and with increased slickness came a more pernicious image. In *Where the Girls Are: Growing Up Female with the Mass Media,* Susan Douglas says, "The MTV that initially brought us Culture Club, 'Beat It,' and Cyndi Lauper switched, under the influence of market research, to one of the most relentless showcases of misogyny in America."[47] In her analysis of the gender politics of MTV, author Lisa A. Lewis suggests the "M" in MTV stands for "male."[48] She says that when MTV's blatant commercialism came into conflict with rock's ideology of rebellion and authenticity, MTV turned to rock's implied white male adolescent "ideology" to assure audiences that the channel was true to rock's roots. Black artists were excluded from MTV play, and women were positioned as adolescent male sexual fantasies or "obsessive" fans "uninterested in musical artistry."[49]

Cultural critic Joan Morgan argues that when viewers protested against degrading images unsuitable for young viewers, MTV cleaned up its act to some extent. But when VIACOM bought BET (Black Entertainment Television), it allowed programming that it would not have allowed on MTV. "Evidently it wasn't acceptable to air near-pornographic images for the young, largely White audience of MTV, but it was fine to dump them on the young, largely Black BET audience."[50] Morgan recounts an incident when she was speaking at the University of Massachusetts. "I can't watch rap videos anymore," a young, black woman in the audience lamented, her frustration resonating with the rest of the crowd. Morgan suggests that five years earlier the discussion would have been different. There would have been some criticism of rap videos' sexism, but the conversation would also have engendered lively debate about "freedom of speech, Latifah's Afro-femme regality versus the punanny politics of Lil' Kim, and the deliciously guilty pleasure of discarding feminist principles for a few hours of booty-shaking hedonistic abandon." Now, Morgan writes, young black women simply feel "degradation" when they watch rap videos. "The average rap video," she argues, "taps into just about every insecurity and erroneous belief about sensuality related to Black women."[51]

Lisa A. Lewis contends, however, that the misogyny of music television may ultimately undermine its own sexism by making it so blatantly visible. She claims that MTV's exclusion of women from its assumed audience and its use of degrading images of women actually ended up highlighting women's social inferiority. Women then waged what Lewis calls a "cultural struggle" against MTV. By *appropriating* and redefining the symbols used in music videos, women artists created videos that addressed issues relevant to women, and their commercial success underlined the identification of female fans with these women musicians.[52] Similarly, feminist critic Robin Roberts argues that women can appropriate the music video genre in order to assert a "a vibrant and inviting female sexuality—a sexuality clearly pleasurable to the performer and under the performer's control."[53]

Calculated Evolution: Avoiding Parody

"Performers often project caricatures of themselves," argues Holly Near.[54] She herself looks for professional "evolution." Lucy O'Brien contends that Stevie Nicks, whose voice was central in Fleetwood Mac's selling more than 100 million albums, got stuck in her own distinctive look, with her trademark streaming hair and ethereal dresses. From her 1970s tenure with Fleetwood Mac through her 1980s solo career, her image was unmistakable and consistent. In the early 1990s Nicks even became the subject of theme nights for drag queens at a New York gay club, Jackie 60. "She had become a parody of her former self," argues O'Brien.[55] Likewise, Joan Jett's look became too predictable, and even she recognized it: "That heavy makeup, black-hair thing, I was becoming a parody of myself."[56]

Although a few male rockers such as Alice Cooper, Marilyn Manson, and Kiss, have indubitably become parodies of themselves, they have largely escaped the critical scrutiny these women faced. Typically, a male artist's "look" is not as central to his performance, although some would say Elvis's was, especially when he began to add pounds to the image his fans wanted to immortalize. No doubt Michael Jackson had his share of attention, especially in early 2003 with Martin Bashir's documentary, but no one ever accused Jackson of being too predictable, at least in terms of appearance. While Queen, Kiss, Elton John, and Boy George were derided for their androgyny, they did not have to avoid parody. The Rolling Stones' persona has not evolved significantly over the past thirty years, but no one seems to care. Journalists do not seem particularly concerned about what Justin Timberlake is wearing to the Grammy Awards, much less how he dresses for a performance. But in the music industry, if women do not evolve, if they do not continually change their images, they may find themselves slipping in the charts if not absent from them altogether.

Eventually, Joan Jett's early dark look, influenced by Liza Minnelli, gave way to a softer, peroxided buzz cut, a far cry from the parody.[57] The black leather was still evident, but the hair saw a drastic change, much more than, say, even Michael Bolton's. Patti LaBelle and the Blue Belles also underwent similar visual transformation while shortening their name to LaBelle. However, this change was not to avoid parody. Sarah Dash explained their trademark silver "space" outfits of the mid-1970s: "Well, when you're in a group, you kind of think group oriented. And you do what's best for the group, . . . all wearing the same thing, wearing the same color. And then we decided, you know, in changing our image from Patti LaBelle and the Blue Belles to LaBelle that we would be one of the same but different entities."[58] Later, though, LaBelle tried something new. Looking back on their switch to individual costumes, Sarah Dash reflected in 1990: "Why do black women all have to look alike because they're singing together? I'm not putting that down," she hastened to add, "but we wanted to change the whole image and the whole mentality of how black women were supposed to represent themselves in this industry."[59] However, this change did not come without criticism. "When we decided that we weren't going to wear the same gowns anymore, the same hairdo," Dash told us, "we were laughed at, picked at. But we kept going because we knew that we had to make a difference in the way females were accepted in the industry." In doing so, Dash says, "as black females, we influenced other female groups and other male groups as well."[60]

Their 1974 hit "Lady Marmalade," along with their image transformation, helped pave the way for groups such En Vogue and Destiny's Child.

While Cherilyn LaPierre was never a member of a girl group, appearance has always been a huge issue for her. When someone stole a "beaded, braided, teal and black" wig during her concert at the Richmond Coliseum in February 2003, she filed a report with the Richmond police. What was the big deal? The wig was valued at over $8,000 and matched a Hindu outfit that was integral to her show.[61] From those early 1970s days on *The Sonny and Cher Comedy Hour* until her 2003 Living Proof Tour, a rich career including lauded film portrayals of a wide range of characters, Cher is seemingly ageless in appearance. Lucy O'Brien captures Cher's approach to image: "Allegedly nipped and tucked more drastically than Michael Jackson, Cher adheres to the American Dream of reinvention of self: 'Getting old does not have to mean getting obsolete.' "[62] How does Cher compare to Cherilyn? O'Brien says Cherilyn the woman would prefer to appear "on stage in sweatpants and a T-shirt singing songs by Bonnie Raitt and Bob Seger."[63] Regarding the stolen wig, Cher did get it back, in poor condition. She was willing to take a global perspective on her loss; in the scope of world affairs at that moment, she commented, "It's nothing."[64] The United States would invade Iraq the same month.

As much as any performer, Madonna has avoided becoming a parody, constantly reinventing herself, often manipulating the media. Her steady evolution, physically and musically, continues to work for her. She has gone from the Marilyn Monroe look to one resembling Alanis Morissette, and she is surely not finished. In 1997 Gerri Hirshey commented, "Madonna would writhe before she walked on MTV," adding, "In 1984, her video for 'Lucky Star' was a study in bare-tummy floor exercises."[65] One of the most memorable moments in rock history, her performance of the title track from *Like a Virgin* at the inaugural MTV Music Video Awards left a lasting image with viewers. Clad in a lace wedding dress, Madonna snaked sexually across the stage floor of Radio City Music Hall. Along the way the Material Girl found religion, henna-painted hands, and parted-down-the-middle dark tresses with her 1989 *Like a Prayer*. With *Bedtime Stories* in 1994, her heavily mascaraed eyes and flaming red lips were framed in a short, bleached-blonde 'do. By the time she was the elegant, coiffured Evita in 1996, many outside the pop world recognized her talent and well-trained voice. Now a mother, in her more spiritually focused 1998 technopop *Ray of Light*, she had toned down the explicit, in-your-face sexuality, but the sensual was still there, hot as ever, with well-defined triceps and cut post-baby abs. Seeing her play acoustic guitar on David Letterman's show in 2000 to introduce *Music* was a surprise to many. The queen of pop had evolved into an urban cowgirl. Is her constant metamorphosis contrived? It would seem so, and Madonna has been taking that to the bank for more than two decades. For Madonna, change has been a good thing.

Motherhood brought a more profound change. In 1997 she told Gerri Hirshey, "Ever since my daughter was born, I feel the fleetingness of time. And I don't want to waste it on getting the perfect lip color."[66] Her daughter Lourdes no doubt has been reckoning with a different world than her mother did as a young girl. Before Madonna's mother's death in the mid-1960s when Madonna was only six, "Mrs. Ciccone had taught her girls that it was sinful for girls to have pants that zipped up the front."[67] That double standard would be reflected in Madonna's response to a question regarding male and female images. In a "very looks conscious" industry, she said, men are still given much more freedom than women.[68] Like Tina Turner, Madonna believes that her visual representation is "only 1 percent of what I am. And what everybody is." She says that constantly turning herself into something different is "just not as much fun as it used to be."[69] Perhaps she does not need to do that any more.

The connotations and images evoked by the name "Madonna" are not what they were twenty years ago, and the matured icon now defends young stars like Britney Spears who are constantly scrutinized by the press. While television was one vehicle for her success, Madonna shields her children from it. In 1999 she told Larry King that her daughter did not watch television because she did not want her to get addicted to it.[70] Again in 2002 she told King that her son and daughter were not allowed to watch television but instead they got information by reading books, listening to their parents, and having friends. When King asked her why television would be harmful, she responded, "Because there's a lot of junk on TV."[71] While her evolving persona is part of the reason for her mammoth success, Madonna would now prefer to have attention focused on her music rather than her looks.

Courtney Love's media-savvy makeover from goth, disheveled punker to respectable, sophisticated movie star disappointed many in the riot grrl movement. As Kylie Murphy points out, lipbrushes, rhinoplasty, and Versace gowns did not fit their idea of what their poster girl should look like.[72] Other alternative rockers now referred to Love as a Girly Grrl, lumping her with Gwen Stefani and Shirley Manson. Defending her move toward pop, Love would say the instinct was natural and that she "departed completely from playing into the idea that I have to sound crappy to do what I want."[73] Making no apology for her transformation in appearance, when asked how she could rock in a Versace gown, Love responded, "Well, easy—let me show you."[74] Glamour was not a new idea for Love. Even as a girl in the 1970s, she wondered why participants at the women's movement marches her mother attended did not wear heels.[75] Not being allowed to wear "girlie" clothes as a child, and suffering the usual indignities of adolescence—facial breakouts and weight gain—in a culture intolerant of female cosmetic imperfections may have added to her youthful focus on appearance.[76]

Love, a self-professed feminist, sees herself as androgynous but never butch, describing the latter as "an emulation of a masculine form." Desiring to be as feminine, elegant, and graceful as she wants, she sees no reason to look male, as she perceives the butch stance. Neither does her in-your-face "sexual rage" come from anything masculine. Believing clothing should be dictated by preference, Love says a woman should wear what she wants, regardless of size or body type. "If you're beautiful, it helps. If you're not, it hurts a little. But who cares," she told *Rolling Stone* in 1997.[77] However, she did care enough that she said, "Fat is the nastiest thing you can call somebody."[78] When Love melted away forty pounds for her role in *The People vs. Larry Flynt,* she did not want young girls to see her as anorexic model but rather an actor fitting a part.[79]

Pointing to Susan Bordo's work on the relationship between a woman's sculpted, muscular body and social class, Kylie Murphy says the well-toned body speaks of discipline and achievement in our culture that focuses on meritocracy.[80] Love wanted that look. Spending hours in the gym honing her lower body and abs with the help of Hollywood personal trainer Valerie Waters, the now elegant Love stepped onto the red carpet at the 1997 Academy Awards.[81] Arguing that "Love's make-over, from punk rocker to movie star, highlights the contentious place that discourses of beauty and authenticity have within feminism," Murphy scrutinizes the association of cosmetics and clothes with power for women. Dress and makeup, for many, support identity construction, with some of these identities wielding more power than others. "Knowledge about clothes and cosmetics does provide women with social power. A well-groomed surface has the ability to grant women the discursive power of authority."[82] Courtney Love capitalized on this cultural truth, for better or worse, argues Murphy. For decades mainstream artists have either intentionally or inadvertently capitulated to this notion, to the chagrin of many alternative rockers.

After the well-publicized makeover, perhaps Courtney Love yearned for those alternative years. By 2000 she had reverted to a less than demure look with a shredded black frock for the Golden Globe Awards and a sheer, panty-revealing dress with obviously missing bra for the Oscars. Ridiculing

Love's outfit worn to a Manhattan fund-raiser in 2001, a *People* cover story likened it to a Hefty bag.[83]

The Anti-Image Look

With the pressure to conform to a fashion image, many artists have adopted an intentional anti-image look.[84] As mentioned in chapter 2, many of them do not care about or seek the power that a certain image may bring. Speaking of the newer artists, Jann Arden says, "They're sort of throwing a finger up at how women are supposed to be perceived."[85] Even before those artists stepped onto the stage, singer-songwriter Joan Armatrading defied conventional mores regarding appropriate attire for female performers. In the mid-1980s, video producers would ignore this brilliant veteran's look, simple, androgynous, "dressed in a crisp white shirt and black jeans," not to mention the red canvas sneakers.[86] As mentioned earlier in this chapter, Holly Near uses Jackson Browne as her wardrobe standard. Cyndi Lauper "dressed in glorious Goodwill Technicolor" with vari-colored, vari-cropped hair.[87] Annie Lennox says she started bending gender with her "mannish clothes" and short hair done in various 'do's reminiscent of twenties chic in order "to detract from what people had come to expect from women singers," adding "I simply [wanted] to get away from wearing cutesy-pie miniskirts and tacky cutaway pushups."[88]

In the mid-1990s Lisa Loeb looked like a librarian, wearing retro black-rimmed glasses before they were cool, many seeing them as geeky at the time. Tracy Chapman's dreadlocks and comfortable clothes proved "that dressing down, or dressing 'asexual,' does not mean commercial death."[89] Her collection of Grammy awards can attest to that.

Kim Gordon, who has been involved with "alternative" groups such as Sonic Youth and anti-image bands such as Bikini Kill, reacts strongly to façades that some artists use. "The Spice Girls—they're masquerading as little girls. It's repulsive." Asked what she thought of the emphasis that rock puts on youth and beauty, she responded, "I think everyone likes eye candy—you just don't want to be it." Her bands have not been commercial bands making commercial music, possibly because they did not "want to have to deal with that much baggage that surrounds all the creativity."[90]

Joan Osborne believes she is not conventionally attractive, and finds that her music, rather than any conformity to external standards of appearance, empowers her and draws an audience. "People can realize that not everyone has to look a certain way to be beautiful."[91] As described in chapter 5, with Bitch's wild mane of hair and Animal's Mohawk, the group's look is as wacky and creative as their music, and the Butchies with their coveralls or neckties deliberately thumb their noses not only at society's expectation of performers but of women in general. Of course, refusing to look the socially expected part can exact a price. Bitch tells the story of their first gig. When they walked into the café where they were to play, it was "pretty obvious" they were "not from there. We were getting all this shade from all the girls there." After the duo performed, however, the atmosphere changed. "People were like being really nice to us. And we've always been annoyed about that, like people wouldn't just assume that we're beautiful, wonderful human beings, you know, before like we've proven ourselves."[92]

Being cruelly nominated by a fraternity for "Ugliest Man on Campus" at the University of Texas in 1963 probably did not help Janis Joplin's self-image. She defied appearance conventions as she defied so many other social rules—wistfully and ambivalently. Those feather boas became one of the trademarks of her all-too-brief stage career. What would MTV have done for (or to) her? Like Tracy Chapman and so many others, Joplin's talent, not her (un)conventional look, boosted record sales. We could argue, of course, that both artists created a unique presence inseparable from their art and their popularity.

Because appearance is such an important part of the gendered script for women, women rockers are constrained, penalized, or rewarded based on their approximations of culturally appropriate standards of beauty, in a way male rockers are not. At every turn, these women are judged by what they wear, how much they weigh, and how their hair is styled, rather than by the quality of their music. Employing a variety of strategies—from meeting cultural expectations to defying them—they nonetheless persist in their determination to make rock music.

CHAPTER 7

THE BUSINESS

Even on this last record—because I produced it—many people in the press wanted to know whether I was a control freak. Throughout history, male artists have produced themselves and been really held up for that in a really respectful way. And I'm approached as being a control freak.

—*Sheryl Crow, in* Rolling Stone *(1997)*

When I first met the people at Capitol Records, a woman who worked their press mentioned that a guy I was going to meet at a radio station liked cute women—and maybe I could change my clothes, and if he pawed me not to worry about it. I was aghast. I felt like someone was trying to fuck me after a handshake.

—*Liz Phair, in* Rolling Stone *(1997)*

Scarlet Rivera has had no illusions about the music industry since she figured out what happened to her on that Thanksgiving Day when a company executive invited her to dinner with his family. He followed up the feast by having Rivera sign away a hundred percent of her own publishing for the next two years. "I didn't expect to be screwed on Thanksgiving Day. It's family; it's warm. You know, he was like a father figure on that day to me." Alas, history is replete with stories of such father figures. "I really deplore anybody who does that, who knows better, and who does that to a young artist." She gave us several more stories of exploited musicians, including the young artist dropped from a label Friday night before her Monday departure on her first major tour, to promote the planned release of her first CD. Scarlet and the other band members "had our tickets in hand, the bookings, the hotels, the stage plan." Why?, we asked. "They had a bigger artist." The company said they would take the half-million-dollar loss rather than spend any more on the artist who had fallen from favor.[1] Our informants have told us innumerable stories of bad experiences with the music industry—in particular, recording companies. We have heard a few positive stories as well: of artists well treated, recognized for their talent and originality, and respected through the evolution of a career.

For instance, when we asked Brenda Lee if being female in the male-dominated industry brought her any disrespect, she said, "Not with me. I'm sure it did with a lot of people. I was under the management of my manager Dub Albritten from the time I was about eleven years old. And he just was one of those kind of guys that, he had a vision for me and he worked towards that end."[2] Regarding headlining, she says, "I did some package shows before I got with Dub. But most of my shows I always headlined, which was unheard of for women to do back then. But that was Dub's deal. You know, he wanted me to headline my own shows." With all of her positive experiences, she did have to re-record some of her songs in order to release her own music. She explains, "The reason I did my CD is I can't get my masters back from MCA, and the reason is because they sell so well. So, I had the rights by my contract to go in and re-record those, and that's what I did."[3]

Janis Ian earned respect in the music industry early on, not only for her talent but also for her assertiveness. When we asked her to describe her work with producer George "Shadow" Morton, she laughed and told a wild story about her introduction into the music business. "I was hanging around with the Reverend Gary Davis, who was an old blues singer, and his wife took a liking to me. And he had a show one night at the Gas Light Cafe, and she convinced the owner to put me on for a couple of songs. And when I finished, this guy literally ran up to me and said, 'Kid, I'm going to make you a star.' And I laughed and said, 'Yeah, right!' "

The next day an attorney led her by the hand up to Shadow Morton's office. "Shadow was going through one of his periodic 'I hate this business; I'm quitting the music industry' phases." Walled off by his newspaper, he ignored the young singer, but Janis started singing anyway. "I think I was getting more and more irritated that Shadow hadn't looked at me and hadn't responded in any way. So apparently I set fire to his newspaper and left."[4] Morton recalls, "My newspaper is on fire! The damn thing is burning up in my hands, in my lap! I'm jumping around, stamping it out." When he caught up to her at the elevator and asked her what in the world she was doing, he recalls her saying, "Nobody reads a newspaper when I sing!" Shadow explains, "I had respect. Nobody ever demanded my attention like that! Talk about moxie!"[5] He asked her back to the office. "Go on; sing me something." She sang the eight or ten songs she had written.[6] "Society's Child" struck him.[7] "We'll cut that one," he said. "What are you doing next week?" Revolutionary for 1967 and risky for any record label, the song told of a young white girl in love with a black man. Verve/Forecast eventually released the song after it was pitched to all twenty-two New York record labels. Ian says Verve took it "because they were probably supposed to be a tax loss for MGM. I don't think anybody expected it to be a hit."[8]

In the majority of cases, the positives about dealing with the "biz" are shaded by negatives, however. Perhaps part of the difficulty women face in the music business is that, while they are struggling to construct an identity as rock musician within rock's masculine norms, they also need to see themselves as businesswomen. Yet business is another realm characterized by masculine discourse, and women have long been discouraged from entering it. On the whole, women have not been taught to be business-savvy, and they have not been expected to construct an identity as a businessperson. Thus, for many of our informants, engagement with the record industry has often meant disappointment, neglect, and exploitation.

To put that statement in a larger context, few artists, female *or* male, have been well treated by music industry entities, if "well treated" means attention to the artist's unique career development, respect for her own sense of artistic integrity, and solicitude toward her personal bottom line (in the financial sense). It is not hard to perceive *how* this happens, American capitalism being what it is, but somewhat more difficult to perceive *why* it keeps happening. With the major labels in disarray as we enter the twenty-first century, what has emerged among the young and mid-career artists we have interviewed—and many more sounding off in outlets as diverse as *Rolling Stone* and *Performing Songwriter*—is a strong preference for "indie" status over being signed to a major label. The leakage is spelling trouble for the labels, which have been inclined through mid-2003 to blame their woes on consumers grabbing free music illegally on the World Wide Web rather than paying for CDs in the big chain outlets.

But don't most artists long to "make it" by being courted by a big label? Maybe so, if we go by the surfeit of performing wannabes competing for slots on *Star Search, American Idol, Making the Band,* and *Nashville Star,* all "reality" television shows documenting the "discovery" and coronation of the newest rising star. Like the deathless *Miss America* "pageant," these spectacles are popular among audiences for a number of reasons: like soap operas, they offer ongoing suspenseful narratives of hometown heroes and narcissistic villains vying for fame and fortune; they allow viewers to bask in the humiliation of talentless contestants and enjoy the gratuitous cruelty of "judges" such as Simon Cowell, mentioned in chapter 6, who bring back all the repressed pain of hapless children chastised by Dickensian teachers and coaches. These shows also drive home the relentless standardization of popular culture and its icons. The range of acceptable personalities, stage personae, musical styles, and body types was different in 2003 than it was in 1950, but just as narrow. But contestants are not only popular among audiences; there are many extremely talented individuals struggling not just for their moment in the sun but also for that nearly unreachable star, the solid gold career. These shows also spotlight the major labels' newest bid for attention, since Kelly Clarkson and Ruben Studdard, the first two winners, are signed with RCA, and Buddy Jewell, the new Nashville Star, brings out his first album with Sony Music Nashville.

James Dickerson, a close observer of trends in the American music industry, points out that, in the latter half of the twentieth century, popular music became particularly "masculinized." Men had always commanded higher compensation, controlled the vast majority of band and orchestra positions, and held the purse strings, but women *sang*. The trend toward men fronting the bands as well as dominating them began with the crooners of the 1940s. Elvis Presley may have been unique, but he was also influential, and in the mid-1950s he inaugurated the era of male pop stars and male-driven rock and roll. Although women scored 30 percent of the Top 20 hits between 1955 and 1959, that percentage would drop through the next two decades. "In truth, the freewheeling 1960s and 1970s proved to be disastrous decades for women, giving them their lowest numbers of the century."[9] Of course the issue was not just numbers of women but the quality of their musical contribution and the degree to which they controlled their own careers. Janis Ian has written of the 1960s, "Forget about seeing female role models playing guitar, bass, or drums in a band. . . . If you grew up a female musician or writer in that time, you were male-identified. You had no choice. Female artists such as Nina Simone, who played piano on her recordings and onstage, created the arrangements, and wrote a good portion of her material, were rare and under-valued. And they certainly weren't on the charts."[10]

Not surprisingly, behind the scenes women fared slightly better in pockets of the industry. Marion Keisker at Sun Records, Vivian Carter at Vee Jay, Estelle Axton at Stax, and Marian Leighton Levy at Rounder Records made their marks in the small-label arena, though each of these owners and producers faced gender-related challenges.[11] Songwriters Carole King, Cynthia Weil, and Ellie Greenwich thrived in the Brill Building milieu of turning out hits for big-name artists. And though in many ways she was an exception, Carol Kaye played guitar and bass on hundreds of pop music hits produced in Los Angeles studios through the 1960s, giving as good as she got in the sexualized banter of session musicians.

Kaye believes she succeeded in the studio by being good at what she did and doing it like the men—actually, better than the men. While she was grappling with domestic violence at home, she kept her family together by bringing in good money from session work, at the same time changing the nature of electric bass playing. "There was so much call for my work that if they couldn't get me, then they'd ask the guy to get the Carol Kaye sound and feel." Kaye grew up in Everett, Washington, with musician parents who moved the family to the California shipyards during World War II, then broke up shortly afterward. Living with her mother, Carol worked for a living from the age of nine, when she started cleaning apartments to help make ends meet. Her family's commitment to music persisted, and Carol was allowed to buy a used guitar for ten dollars, saved pennies at a time. She showed so much talent that her guitar teacher offered her lessons for free. Three months after she started taking guitar lessons, she began making her living playing jazz gigs. By the age of nineteen she had married a bassist and was playing on the road with Henry Busse's band.[12]

Carol remembers black musicians being more receptive to a woman player than whites were. She also recalls individual women jazz musicians in the fifties, obscured by stereotypes denying their presence, but there none-theless, peering out from the band photos in jazz singers' houses. "There was a bias against the women back then." After making her mark as a jazz guitarist, in her early twenties Carol took an opening as a studio player and, as a colleague had warned her, she never looked back. "When you get in the studio, there's a real craft. There's a real art to . . . making a hit happen. . . . What the background players do, there's a real art to that, and I got in love with that." In 1963 a fellow musician failed to show up to play the Fender bass, and Kaye took over. Sick of playing rock and roll guitar, and tired of carrying six different instruments to each session, she found the bass more creative and more efficient. She heard the bass in a new way. "I could play, and there was nobody that could touch me."[13] She worked with Henry Mancini, Ray Charles, Motown artists, the Beach Boys, and Sonny and Cher. She did television and movie work with Quincy Jones and many others. We heard her on "Wichita Lineman" and the "Mission Impossible" theme. She played on the soundtracks of *The Thomas Crown Affair* and *In the Heat of the Night.* Altogether, she has logged ten thousand studio sessions.

"They all thought of me as one of the guys," she remembers. "And if they didn't, I'd outswear them." The key to her longevity, she insists, was professionalism. "You've really got to have your chops together because that's what speaks." She made friends with the men by sharing a code of conduct and by siding with them, quietly, against the producers' fumbling. "You know, we'd kid. We'd get a little crotchety from not enough sleep or something, and we'd rag on each other back and forth and then just bust out laughing because it was us against them in the booth because they didn't know what the heck they wanted a lot of the time."[14]

There is no gainsaying Carol Kaye's professional success, or her musical contributions. Although she doesn't frame it this way, she tells the story, ruefully, in bits and pieces, of a home life more typical of persistent gender inequality: variously victimized by indifference, indolence, brutality, one husband who was "a little bit mean to my kids," another who was mean to her. A single parent, in fact, for most of her children's lives, she could pull down $75,000 a year, great money in the hot years of the mid-1960s, taking care of her kids, her mother, and the live-in helper she needed to make her career happen.

Melissa Auf der Maur, another bass player, also learned about the financial benefits of session playing. Having toured as part of Smashing Pumpkins and been a regular member of Hole, she found she made more money as a session player with the former than a "permanent creative member" of the latter. "I was pretty much screwed in terms of the financial agreements I made." The romance of quitting the day job at Kinko's and staying in four-star hotels on tour is attractive, she admits. But as she plans to release her own solo album on a friend's label, she gives us a lesson in recording finance. "If I were to sell ten thousand copies on that label, I would make the equivalent of what I would make . . . selling two million copies on a major label. So forget [the major label]. I will never go that route again."[15]

The disincentives are not just financial, Auf der Maur reminds us. "Ultimately it's about your relationship to yourself, that you don't want to feel like you're like marketing yourself as a caricature of yourself and like selling this little piece that's only a little part of you, but selling it as if it's your whole life and your whole everything."[16] The label decides who the artist is; what the artist should look like; what the singles should be; and how long the artist will continue to be involved with the label. In a 2002 interview with Bill deMain, Aimee Mann outlined her history with the big record labels—sadder than most, but not atypical. After the third 'Til Tuesday album did not do as well as the first two, Epic held her hostage to her contract for five more years. Subsequently, Imago released her first solo album, then lost their distribution deal. The next label, Geffen, disappeared into Seagram, as did *I'm With Stupid,* Mann's new album. *Bachelor No. 2* was underappreciated at Interscope, and she entered a long but ultimately successful fight to get her master recordings back.[17]

In another interview, she detailed some of her problems with the label. The personnel kept changing—a constant theme in discussions of the record companies—and each set of label reps wanted a different sound, depending on what was big and definitely linked to their expectations of 'Til Tuesday's sound, based on *previous* recordings. "I realized that once you make a record that does well, you're expected to repeat just that exactly over and over. I thought that was counter to what being a good musician is. I think you're supposed to keep growing and getting better." After 'Til Tuesday laid down tracks for their second album, new label people came in fresh from working on Heart's comeback. "They had these big ballads and big hits and they wanted us to sound like Heart. We were just like, 'That's not appropriate at all.'"[18]

Declaring Independence

After her misadventures among the labels, Mann's solo career got back on track with Paul Thomas Anderson's decision to feature her music in his film *Magnolia,* and she created her own label, SuperEgo, which released her acclaimed album *Lost in Space.* Echoing Melissa Auf der Maur's journey, Mann observes, "I had to get to the point where I would rather have sold records out of the back of a van than stay on a major label." She lances the major label "myth" that "they have all this power and they can promote your record in a really big way, and you can reach an audience you can never reach on your own. Which of course is true," she observes, "but only if they *do* that." If they don't, the artist languishes.[19]

Like Mann, Melissa Ferrick wonders at the one-sidedness of the artist's relationship with the big record labels. She signed a seven-record deal with Atlantic in 1991 after opening on a tour with the British artist Morrissey. "I didn't realize when I signed that it was seven records if *they* wanted to make seven. That it was in *their* hands to decide whether or not they wanted to continue making records with me." She cut two of the seven albums and found herself persona non grata at the label because she had not scored a "hit." Her Atlantic A&R man, who was in favor because he also had the Hootie and the Blowfish account, offered to get the label to keep her on as a favor to him, at the same time advising her to get out. Atlantic dropped her in 1995, and from December 23 of that year until December 23 of 1996, "I pretty much did absolutely nothing but drink." After she lost everything— her money, her girlfriend, and her apartment—she got sober and realized that she had let her contract with Atlantic define her. "What I really lost was *me,* in that I realized that my existence had depended on the stamp of Atlantic records." She then went to What Are Records, a small label out of Denver, and cut three albums. After that, she established her own label. "I really think that if you're an artist that sells less than 50,000 records, there's just absolutely no reason to sign with anyone." She and three associates run the whole show by Internet out of Provincetown, Massachusetts. "I incorporated the company online, we have a fax machine and three computers, and we do all of our T-shirts and our hats and our poster and our Website— everything is done on the Internet."[20]

Erin O'Hara had the same kind of revelation partway through a similar seven-record deal with Arista Records. Her discomfort with the pressures at the label was compounded by her discomfort with the overly cozy behaviors of the A&R person assigned to her. "It just felt so sticky, you know, it just felt like, God, this doesn't feel good at all. I know it's supposed to feel good, and I know it looks good on paper, and I know it sounds good, like 'scoring a major label deal,' but it wasn't fostering my own growth in the way I knew I needed to grow." Without a manager, burdened by an attorney she didn't really trust, Erin lost faith in her career at Arista. "It just got caught up in this . . . negative space, you know, politics, and so then after a while I just realized it wasn't really gonna happen there." She made one record, which languished in a vault after she asked to be released from her contract. "I got to a point where I felt like there was a fork in the road, and I could go down one branch and maybe have some commercial success . . . sort of by good behavior, by like filling a role . . . but I felt like if I did that, I would really lose my soul. You know, it felt like one of those deals with the devil kind of things." On a diva-oriented label, as she saw Arista at the time, Erin could get molded and take direction, or she could take the risk of an independent career and make a break. Like Melissa Ferrick, only perhaps less self-destructively, after leaving Arista, Erin also left music altogether, for about a year. When a filmmaker approached her about scoring a short film, she found herself back in the world. The film won best score at the NYU Graduate Film Festival. That success "kick-started me back into playing guitar and writing songs and doing shows."[21]

"I'll be very excited when this record deal is over," Amy Ray commented in January 2003 about the Indigo Girls' contract with Epic Records.

"I would never sign again with a major label, because I feel like it's run its course. Major labels right now are pretty obsolete for artists like us."[22] She harbors no animosity toward Epic; some of their employees are friends, and they have done favors for Ray's own label, Daemon Records, when the Indigo Girls have been on tour. But she believes that Epic doesn't know what to do with the Indigo Girls, and consequently, the label does nothing. "They never did anything for the last few records. They do the basics— publicity and such—but they don't do marketing campaigns or street teams or posters—the creative stuff we used to do, and they used to do, that doesn't even cost anything." She has concluded that "alternative" politics and the "mainstream" market do not mix well. "[Epic] are burned out on us. We're women, we're gay, we're more political—it's so far out of the realm of what they deal with now."[23]

Why did the Indigo Girls first sign with Epic, if they could see the disadvantages from the start? As Ray tells it, the decision was practical. "I felt like, this is my choice: I can either sign to a major and have these re-sources and have my own indie label and put out five records a year by other people. Or I can talk Emily into staying independent and we spend all of our time on our own career, and we won't ever get to do anything else with anybody else." Reasoned out that way, and given her own dreams of creat-ing a label, "the choice was obvious."[24]

Ray's difficulties with balancing financial, logistical, and artistic con-cerns led to the birth of a unique label. Since 1990 she has created an enor-mous fund of goodwill among her artists by behaving in ways that are clearly different from the majors. "Daemon Records is different from the majority of record labels, primarily due to the intimate relationship between the bands and the employees of the label," write members of the band Nineteen Forty-Five. Paul Melancon also underlines the attention Daemon gives to the fit between artist and label. His first conversation with Amy and Daemon man-ager Andrea White "was simply them asking me what *my* goals were in music and whether Daemon could help those goals or not."[25] The fact that Daemon Records is a not-for-profit label may help explain why artists' needs and goals are central, something quite foreign to most labels. Everyone on the label gets a fair shake, and one artist is not promoted more than another out of some commercially driven objective. Ray explains that Daemon Records was born out of her "frustrations with the music industry. While reaping the benefits of a major label deal, I realized that all around me 'music' was getting lost among the checkbooks, executives, and mountains of paperwork that are all such a primary part of any major label."[26] The folks at Daemon adhere to a novel concept: profits go to the artist, not the record company.

Initially Decatur, Georgia-based Daemon recorded only Southern artists, and the aim for each signed artist was to establish a regional "root system" before launching out to a wider audience.[27] Amy Ray describes her
label in this way. "I sign stuff that's kinda regional, stuff from the southeast, usually bands that are going to tour a lot."[28] Rose Polenzani found that
out when Ray called her out of the blue and asked her if she had a major
label deal yet. When Rose said no, Amy offered to make a contact for her at
Mercury. Although Ray's contact at the label was "really, really interested,"
Mercury was busy morphing into Polygram. "And so I decided not to do
it." Sure enough, the Mercury A&R person disappeared in the label change,
and Ray decided to extend an offer to Polenzani to come to Daemon. "Well,
this is just ridiculous," she recalls Amy saying. "You know, maybe we should
try putting somebody out on Daemon that's not from the South." Polenzani
knows she has done well for Daemon; her records are reaching audiences
even the other Daemon artists do not find. And she still cherishes that first
phone call from Amy Ray, that unsolicited, unforeseen expression of interest in her music. "I just remember that somebody I really love did call me
up and said, 'You're really good. I really like your stuff.' So that definitely has
carried me through lots of different situations."[29]

When Amy Ray recorded her own 2001 release, *Stag,* for her Daemon
label, she adhered to the same financial guidelines she has used for artists
such as Rose Polenzani. Ray says, "I put limits on myself financially, because
it's just not fair to spend five times more on my record than we do for the
other artists."[30] Holding the budget for *Stag* to $10,000, Ray stepped outside
of her role as CEO to view the indie industry from an artist's perspective.
No doubt, the process had to go much faster than she was accustomed to,
and she was not able to enjoy the luxury of her usual perfectionism. However, she learned that "you don't have to spend thousands of dollars to make
a good record. You have to trust yourself and not overthink things."[31] Being
CEO had its advantages, as Ray was able to assemble her "dream team" for
Stag, collaborating with Joan Jett, Kate Schellenbach, and Josephine Wiggs
of the Breeders, possibly renewing a little riot grrl fervor.

Amy Ray as a solo artist and the Indigo Girls as a duo both benefit
from years of spade work in building an audience that cares about their
music and supports the directions they choose to take. Their work as big
artists has allowed them to rediscover the advantages of small-scale art-
making, whether it be putting out a ten-thousand-dollar CD or performing
at a local benefit that draws fifty people who are then inspired to go and do
likewise. Amy Ray wants budding artists to understand what they are up
against, no matter what label they sign with and what the size of their audi-

ence. "I'm a big supporter of the Future of Music Coalition, because they're trying to educate people about the way the machine works. You have to know that before you can accomplish your art within the framework of consumerism. It also helps you accomplish your activism better because if you're smart about the way this machine works, you're going to understand the way other corporate structures work and you'll understand how to approach them."[32]

Ani DiFranco's philosophy of the industry is similar to Ray's. Her Buffalo-based Righteous Babe label "has evolved from a one-woman shop into a successful multi-artist company by emphasizing music before business and product over profit." A shoestring operation was born in 1990 when twenty-year-old DiFranco put out her self-titled album on the label. Until then, she sold cassette tapes at her appearances. Initially recording one album a year, by the mid-1990s Righteous Babe had moved into its own office and taken on sales and marketing staff. At the turn of the century, Righteous Babe has fifteen people in the office and twelve on the road crew.[33] Scot Fisher runs the home operation, which allows Ani some measure of space for her own creative career.

"I guess if there is anything a little inspirational in my story," DiFranco told Billboard in 2000, "it is in showing that there are truly viable alternatives to playing the industry game." She added, "I just don't think that you can say something meaningful within the corporate music structure." When the label began to take on new artists in 1996, its priority was to "put out records," not make money—though it has. DiFranco has maintained creative and business independence in the face of interest from a number of larger labels: interest spawned by DiFranco's signal success at posting a profit.[34] With Grammy nominations and major network television appearances under her belt, her folk-punk songs have been featured in films, both independent and studio. By 2003 she had produced nineteen albums of her own and label record sales were pushing four million. She has been a cover girl on magazines worldwide and her politics and social activism from gun control to abortion, so evident in her music, have reached millions.

Ani DiFranco's passionate message as a songwriter permeates her business practice. Amy Ray compares her label to DiFranco's. "The expression of our agendas is different although the agendas are similar." Ray notes that their politics are the same, though they work in "a different way politically. . . . We do a lot of benefits and active things, she sort of runs her business socially consciously all the time." Contrasting their labels, Ray explains, "She started Righteous Babe to put her own stuff out while we started Daemon to put other people's out. Then I released my own record on Daemon and now she's releasing other people's records. We did it oppositely."[35]

Jann Arden shares a story of a fellow musician who owns her own record company and her own management company. This woman was "dangled the carrot" of a big label, but she responded, " 'You know what? If I sell even a third of what you think I can sell, I'm still gonna make more money than what you're gonna give me.' It wasn't about three million records to her. It was about, 'You know what? I can do one million records and be quite satisfied with that and control my world and my life.' "[36] Independence is key to her and many other artists, even if that means less distribution.

DIY: Do It Yourself

New technology has influenced the direction many musicians have taken with recording. It seems increasingly about bringing it all back home. "I think the record industry is falling apart," Ferron told us. "I think the CD industry is falling apart. And so it really comes back to what it once was, songs around a fire and making your mixes of your favorite things and sending it off to your friends. You know sometimes when I'm working, I turn the radio on here, and I'm astonished. There's probably only eight or ten people that they play all day long, over and over and over. And you know, we're more than that." How then do unrecognized artists get their music out? "Don't be afraid of the technology," Ferron suggests, "because the technology is the way. I mean I can make a whole CD at home, you know?"[37]

Madeline Puckette has grown up with the technology. Now a student at the California Institute of the Arts, she is learning the fancy versions of what she used to run in her Oregon bedroom. She got into the institute with a demo CD of her own work, one track done at a professional studio and two done on her home studio. She loves fronting a band; she is a charismatic performer, and was selected among other honors to be the rockin'-out spokesperson for the Lane (County, Oregon) Transit District, singing her own song on a television advertisement to increase ridership on the "LTD." But she has also worked with the keyboard in order to increase her skill at laying down her own tracks for home production. "I really like creating a whole piece of music, from start to finish."[38]

The digital revolution has allowed many artists to produce and promote their own music. The artists are certainly in many ways and at many levels necessarily complicit with the record companies. Needing to eat, wanting to spread their music as widely as possible, they are caught on the horns of a dilemma. "I can remember being on a show," Ferron told us, bemused, "and some young gal coming up to me and saying, 'I just uploaded your whole CD onto Napster.' And I was like, 'Oh! Great!' I mean she was telling me something else. She was saying 'I love you!' Right? And some part of me was responding from understanding that the business was falling apart." If the business falls apart, what is left? "The most important part was that she loved me," Ferron concludes, and with love, all things are possible. "And so that's what I'm saying about it's gonna start anew. The technology means that we can sing in our homes, make our CD, give it to our friends, they can do the same. [T]here's a whole new world out there, [and] it's not owned by a bunch of men in suits."

What financial and practical impact has the digital revolution had on artists who have not landed a deal, either with a major label or an independent one? Even though Ferron has been attached to the Warner Brothers label, she explains, " 'Indie' at some point is going to mean 'individual.' . . . For $3,000, or if you get it second-hand $1,500, you can sit at home with a Yamaha 4416, write your songs, get your friends over, burn it, and send it. That's 'indie' for 'individual.' . . . I mean, I'm going to make my next record that way."[39]

In 1997 Kim Gordon told *Rolling Stone,* "The whole do-it-yourself thing took a lot of ideas from feminism."[40] She is right, especially if power over and control of one's music are the key issues. Janis Ian believes the recording industry today has failed to explore "new frontiers," especially in terms of the digital revolution. The industry's emphasis on "protecting its assets" contributes to a reluctance to respond to changing times. Ian recalls that the industry's response to the advent of cassette tapes was " 'no one will ever get paid royalties again!' " and she believes executives today have a similar rejoinder "to the Internet, Liquid Audio, MP3, digital publishing, and everything else that gives the little guy a chance." She adds, "I'm completely disheartened that after all these years, songwriters still have no union, and artists have no power."[41]

Perhaps that kind of union could help artists such as bassist and singer Leah Hinchcliff. She shared with us her frustration with the way her bands Swamp Mama Johnson, Souljonz, and Sistershake have been treated. "I really have a problem with how artists aren't treated well in this culture, in America especially." When the band tells bookers their rates, the all-too-frequent response is " 'can't you just do it for a little less?' It's like, 'No, we can't actually. Can you charge less for your hamburger? Can't you just charge a little less for that? You know people really want it.' And it's like, 'No, would you ask the people that supply your food for the restaurant to take less?' No. So in that way we address it every single day, just trying to raise people's awareness that if you want art, and if you want good art, you have to be willing to pay the artists what they're worth." Leah describes a common problem, not only among club owners but also among music executives at the big labels. "It has been frustrating over and over that people just assume if you're a musician, that you'll play for nothing or that you're worth nothing."[42]

Leah wants a fair wage— a fair wage and respect as an artist. Ferron's advice to "do it yourself" will not necessarily make consumers value artists more, but her suggestion certainly eliminates the middleperson. DIY artists obviously reap the benefits Amy Ray desires for the talent on her label; the profits go to the artists, not the music executives, most of whom are men.

Hall of Fame Frustrations

Mary Wilson of The Supremes expresses frustration over continued male domination of the industry. Her beef moves from money to recognition. "I'll just go ahead and say it," she told us, "and they'll probably kill me about this. But I really don't care because it bothers me a lot, but it's the Rock and Roll Hall of Fame. And I really, I mean I really feel that they cater to the male artists. . . . And it really bugs the heck out of me. [43] The Rock and Roll Hall of Fame, which began inducting artists in 1986, requires that a musician, group, or band release a record at least twenty-five years prior to their induction. Mary was one of the lucky ones. Her group, The Supremes, did make it into the Hall in 1988. However, she does not enjoy much female company there. Of the inductees in the "performer" category, from 1986 to 2003, fewer than 15 percent have been women or groups/bands including women. Females honored by induction are Aretha Franklin in 1987, The Supremes in 1988, LaVern Baker and Tina Turner (along with Ike) in 1991, Ruth Brown, Etta James, and Rose Stone and Cynthia Robinson of Sly and the Family Stone in 1993, Janis Joplin and Martha and the Vandellas in 1995, and Gladys Knight (and the Pips) and The Shirelles in 1996. That year Maureen (Moe) Tucker was also included as part of the Velvet Underground. Joni Mitchell was an inductee in 1997, Christine McVie and Stevie Nicks of Fleetwood Mac along with Cass Elliot and Michelle Phillips of the Mamas and the Papas in 1998, Dusty Springfield and Cleotha, Mavis and Yvonne Staples of the Staple Singers in 1999, Bonnie Raitt in 2000, and Brenda Lee in 2002. No females made the cut in 2003. In the Hall's "early influences" category, the numbers are not much better for women, standing at 17 percent. These women include Bessie Smith in 1989, Ma Rainey in 1990, Dinah Washington in 1993, Mahalia Jackson in 1997, and Billie Holiday in 2000. No women, not even the legendary Carol Kaye, are included in the "sidemen" category. Carole King is the only woman included in the "non-performer" list, sharing her award in 1990 with former husband and cowriter Gerry Goffin.[44]

No wonder Mary Wilson is upset that more of her sisters do not share inductee status with The Supremes. She elaborates on why some women remain quiet about this gender differential, not only in the Rock and Roll Hall of Fame but also in the industry in general. "I think men are afraid. But then it leaves a lot of us after that sort of alone because when men become afraid, they leave you. So then you end up this woman out there who's fighting and you're alone. You know, you scare them off."[45]

This sentiment is not confined to women like Mary Wilson who began to declare their independence in the 1960s and 1970s. Younger artists, even the ones who project total control of their lives and careers, found themselves in the same boat at the turn of this century. In 2001 Madonna told Ingrid Sischy that her generation had been told to "grab life by the balls, be super-independent, get a great education, follow your dreams, kick ass, all that stuff." That was all fine for her until the equation included a relationship. Then, Madonna says, "I feel like I woke up one day holding the golden ring and realized that smart, sassy girls who accomplish a lot and have their own cash and are independent are frightening to men." If only Mary Wilson could have prepared Madonna, who asks, "Why didn't somebody tell me? Why didn't somebody warn me?" That frustration, "swallowing that bitter pill," is expressed in Madonna's song "What It Feels Like for a Girl" on her 2000 *Music* album.[46]

"They're strong as long as they can keep you quiet," continues Mary Wilson. "But then once they can't keep you quiet, they go to the ones that they can rule."[47] Have women been vocal enough in demanding fair and equal treatment? Is fear of losing her man to a more submissive woman part of the problem, at least for the heterosexuals? Does this produce a competition where some women join men in perpetuating gender differentials that keep women out of male-dominated lists and careers? In the early 1980s Janet Penfield suggested that one thing that keeps women quietly in their place is fear of one another based on competition for the support of men. Rather than raising a ruckus over being excluded, some women chose to maintain accustomed ways.[48] If Penfield had a good case in the 1980s, have things changed considerably since? Even Madonna made the first compromise with her son's father when she packed up her daughter Lourdes and moved to London to be near Guy Ritchie. Regarding the compromise, Madonna said, "It's that extra thing that women have. I don't think that we're better than men, but I believe there's an extra accommodating chromosome that we have."[49] If this is the independent Madonna speaking, women may have a long haul before they arrive at equity with men. With her first album's release in 1983, Madonna becomes eligible for induction into the Rock and Roll Hall of Fame in 2008. We wait to see how quickly she will be acknowledged in the Hall for being what Liz Phair called the speedboat pulling "the rest of us" who "are just the Go-Go's on waterskis."[50]

Women's Influence on Marketing

One dynamic that has certainly changed since the 1980s is women's access to cash and the Internet. Women often vote with their cash, and more and more, they are using the Internet as a vehicle for spending it. Perhaps the male-dominated music industry should take notice. In chapter 3 we looked at the conception of Lilith Fair, largely a reaction to producers' and promoters' "one woman" rule. Sarah McLachlan discovered in the 1990s, as she started to promote her album *Fumbling Toward Ecstasy,* that DJs were pitting her against Tori Amos's *Under the Pink* for radio play. When she tried to tour with Paula Cole, promoters said, " 'You can't put two women on a single bill.' " Why not? McLachlan asked rhetorically. "Are we going to have catfights backstage?"[51] Not only did she eventually tour with Paula Cole, she put together a three-year touring extravaganza of women that would make rock and roll history, and the Internet contributed to that success. During the first summer of Lilith Fair in 1997, the tour's Web site received as many as 300,000 hits a day.[52] If the majority of the hits were from females, that puts a dent in the notion, already problematic, that girls do not like computers. Even if labels did not directly target girls, "web sites like estrogenmusic.com and femalemusician.com" did at the turn of the century.[53] If women did not like what they saw on MTV and VH1, they could satisfy their desires with the click of a mouse. Ann Powers's comment on the Internet's influence on adolescents could apply equally to women. "With the internet," she writes, "it's ever more possible to find your own thing and completely avoid this monolithic corporate culture of television and music television."[54] Sites such as daisymusic.com continue to offer girls an alternative for buying their pink guitars online rather than being intimidated by walking into a music store. As Melissa Ferrick observed, entire shows are sometimes run by the Internet, giving fans unbelievable access to tour dates, news, photos, discography, lyrics, downloads, merchandise, and the artists.

Marketing to females and women's purchasing power became significantly more of an issue after 1997 (the first year of Lilith Fair) when "the

Recording Industry Association of America reported that for the first time in the history of the $12 billion U.S. music industry," women bought more music than men that year.[55] In 2002 women purchased 50.6 percent of music.[56] Women were gaining increasing influence, through buying concert tickets and CDs and by mastering their Macs and PCs.[57] What influence this ultimately will have on labels and music executives remains to be seen. However, as more and more women artists take the indie and "do it yourself" route, the more irrelevant the question may become.

How Do You Spell Success?

Fortunately not all the artists we talked with use their images or their bank accounts as a measure of success. Neither are they willing to be molded by a man—or a woman, for that matter—sitting in a plush office financed by the artists signed by the company. Jann Arden told us that she never went into the music business for the money. She says, "I just want to be able to support my life, look after my folks. You know, just enjoy myself. And I do."

Typical of women across a spectrum of businesses, the musicians we interviewed suggest that they do not measure success in terms of money and material goods.[58] While they want to make a decent living, becoming rich is not a goal for the majority of these women. For them, success is much more about being able to do what they love, make the music they want to make, and have an impact for good on the world.

In particular, success as defined by the artist often differs drastically from a record company's definition. Arden comments of her label, which incidentally employs many of her friends, "I mean, they get my records, and they always say to me, 'We don't hear any hits.' And I'm like, 'Well, I must be on the right track then. Go release it. Take your chances.'" Jann told us that Sheryl Crow hated her hit "All I Want to Do" and didn't want to have it on the record. "And there's just a great story of one of the A&R guys there just saying, 'You know, put it on there.' And I think it probably baffled her that it was as big as it was, but it made her career at the time. And she's tried to shake it ever since."[59] Hits can be blessings and curses, at least from the artist's perspective. Success can bring unwanted boxes and categories, not to mention executives' and the public's expectations.

In chapter 6 we looked at how many artists avoid that encumbrance by constantly evolving. Often an artist's label fears this. How will a haircut or more skin affect sales? What is "playing well" this year or this month? The executives are often as fickle as the buying public and sometimes have a limited idea of what sells. Often other politics come into play in promoting a certain image. When Mariah Carey was married to her boss, Tommy Mottola, president of Sony Records, he had a lot to say about her public image. Her 1996 *Daydream* had earned $250 million for Sony, and Mottola wanted to protect his asset and his wife's virtue, to the point that observers could call her a "puppet." "They dictated her look, everything" Gerri Hirshey quotes makeup artist Billy B. "—right down to her makeup."[60] After her divorce, life at Sony was dicey for Carey, but her presentation changed—she says by her choice— toward a sexier, more unbuttoned image.

Many artists cop an unconventional, anti-image posture or appearance. Jann Arden says adamantly, "I can't imagine anyone telling me how to dress. I think I'd burst out laughing."[61] This is usually easier, particularly for women, when they are not signed to a major label, with a major investment in their careers.

How does an executive create new talent? Often driven by the "right image," Berry Gordy certainly seemed to have a knack for producing commercially successful acts, giving the buying public what he felt it wanted. As discussed in chapter 2, he and Maxine Powell looked for a certain charm, even cultivated it in the girl groups of the 1960s. The teasing or demure charm and polish of those days were a far cry from the glitz and sex that became the standard by the 1980s. Gone were the days of selling girlish innocence. Poise, good grooming, and subtle dance steps gave way to navels, cleavage, and grinding. The perfectly coiffed " 'do" was replaced by the windblown look. Because Britney Spears fit the bill on the eve of the millennium, she pioneered the "naughty schoolgirl" look. When the press began to attack her, none other than Madonna came to her defense. "Even though she's terribly successful," said the veteran performer, "for some reason I think of her as an underdog."[62] Speculation about Britney's sporadic relationship with Justin Timberlake added to her declaration in her second album's title track, "Oops, I Did It Again," that she was "not that innocent."

Like many of the artists we interviewed, Britney Spears has been performing since childhood. She and her family chose a high-profile preparation for life in "show biz"; after singing at her kindergarten graduation and winning talent shows, she attended the Professional Performing Arts School in New York for three summers, and was a Mouseketeer for two seasons. She did *Star Search* with Ed McMahon in 1992. Because she could "deliver emotional content and commercial appeal," A&R man Jeff Fenster told *Rolling Stone*, and was remarkably "self-motivated," Jive Records signed her and began an advertising campaign complete with Web site and mall appearances. Kim Kaiman, Jive's marketing director, said, "One of the reasons that radio fell in love with her is that she's so very Southern, so sweet and gracious."[63] Her girlie-yet-athletic looks —cheerleader looks—have been perfect for a television market in which teens figure so heavily.

When Britney discovered the "Power Ranger-y" storyboards for " . . . Baby One More Time," she objected. She had a cannier sense of her peer group's taste than the video's producers. It was her idea to go with the "schoolgirl" theme; the tied-up shirts were meant to "give it a little attitude."[64] As we write, her popularity may have run its course; it remains to be seen if she can reinvent herself. By 2001 if not before, a Britney backlash had begun. As Rebecca Boone points out, although Britney and Madonna may have caused equal angst for the mothers of teenage girls, their songs carried strikingly different messages. Madonna's lyrics encouraged female autonomy and directed them to take control of their lives while Britney often sang more docile words that some believed set feminism back. Madonna, too, drew her share of feminist critique, but she left no question that she masterminded her own career. Boone suggests that Britney's "come hither but don't touch" lyrics and posture send mixed messages, to both the girls and the boys. Boone asked in 2002, "Is the cynical marketing and one-dimensional 'girl power' of Spears, the Spice Girls and Destiny's Child part of a backlash against the genuinely independent women of '80's pop?"[65] Were consumers growing weary of the independence of Joan Jett in the 1980s or the anger of Alanis Morissette in the 1990s?

Britney's popularity begin to slip even before Norah Jones, only two years older, became number one at amazon.com and won five Grammy Awards in early 2003. Britney had lost her spokesperson job at Pepsi, and her second album's sales paled in comparison to her debut hit. Madonna casts Britney as a victim of what Ingrid Sischy in *Interview* calls a "type of snobbery." When asked whether she defended Britney when people began making fun of her, Madonna responded, "Totally. It's like when you go to a party and there's a girl, and everyone's avoiding her because she's really pretty, or whatever. I always want to go over and talk to that person. It's kind of like that." Feeling the effects of a similar snobbery herself, Madonna said that often people dismissed her talent: "And now I just see everybody doing it to her, so I feel defensive of her and protective of her."[66]

"Sugar-coated pop is over," *Newsweek* predicted in early 2003.[67] How much did image contribute to the turning tide? Norah Jones, influenced by the incredible Billie Holiday, looked more like the girl next door rather than the one who had been around the block a few times. Part of Norah's success, however, was due to her popularity among over-thirty adults. "Sugar-pop acts" began to languish as younger listeners opted for new acts such as Michelle Branch, Vanessa Carlton, and Avril Lavigne. The popularity of Avril and her lyrics reflects a closer identification with her audience, says Arista CEO Antonio (LA) Reid, who signed Lavigne. "Kids feel they can identify with Avril. They wear the same T shirt, the same jeans, have the same kind of nonchalant attitude."[68] Lavigne sold more than four million copies of her 2002 *Let Go.* Were even young buyers becoming more discriminating, looking for meaning rather than image?[69]

Regarding the market, Ann Powers says, "It's not moral. It doesn't have politics. It is an empty machine that we feed." The buying public was getting more savvy. "What I think you can see that's different now, . . . is that the consumer, the fan, is so much more aware of the machine."[70] That machine was put on a diet and began to slow considerably, according to Nielson SoundScan, when CD sales dropped "from 763 million in 2001 to 681 million" in 2002. From 2000 to 2002, albums selling more than four million copies dropped from eight to three, one being Lavigne's. Part of the decline certainly could be attributed to a bear economy, illegal downloading, and the mammoth increase in the sale of blank CDs, which surpassed recorded ones in 2001.[71] But perhaps many buyers were simply becoming fed up with music executives' focus on the next big act.

Advice to the Novice

Like the buying public, female artists have gotten more business savvy. They know the industry better now and have learned from their older sisters. However, getting money and holding on to it seemed to be issues for many of the artists we interviewed. Commercially successful artists often found themselves not reaping the benefits of hits. Shirley Alston Reeves and the Shirelles received some advice from wise mentors in the business during the late 1950s. Because the girls were so young when they began to tour, their mothers insisted that chaperones accompany them on their trips. Older Ruth Brown and Etta James, also on the tour, drew that assignment and offered the girls invaluable counsel. Shirley told us, "Well, Etta James was very nice to us because we didn't know how to manage our moneys and how to live on the road. . . . So, you know, naturally when we'd get paid, we'd go out and we'd want to buy ourselves big dinners and all the stuff. So she was like observing us, you know. . . . She said, 'You can't do that out there.' She said, 'You have to save your money, and you have to budget your money,' because we weren't making a lot of money. We, of course, had the hit records and no money. . . . She said, 'I'll show you how to, to live out here. . . . Otherwise, you won't make it.' "

Wanting to pass Etta James's advice on to others, Shirley says to new artists, "Learn the business. If you're going to be in this business you've got to learn something about it." She and the Shirelles were unable to do that because promoters kept them on the road most of the time. "And being young, bright-eyed, happy to be out there singing with all those stars and people, we'd say, 'Oh boy, we're with Chuck Berry on this tour!' " Tickled that they were a part of such a popular crowd, they enjoyed the ride without understanding where the money was going. Regarding artists today she adds, "But I don't have to tell them now because all of the artists have learned from our experience that . . . you're not gonna make it if you don't know what you're doing. . . . You may make it and be a success record-wise, but your bank account is not going to go along with your success. You must learn the business, the ins and the outs and the little things, so that way you can handle your own destiny."[72]

Ann Powers agrees with Alston Reeves that girls do know much more than their forerunners did. "Even the youngest people, 12-year-olds, 14-year-olds, they know what a manager is. They know what a VP executive is."[73] Shirley says that she and others who fell prey to executives do not try to hide the fact that they were wronged. "I let them know that, we all have. I even got chastised by the woman [Florence Greenberg] who owned the company who started us out. I said, 'Look, I love you for what you did for us because . . . we probably never would have been recording artists had your daughter [Mary Jane] not been there. But,' I said, 'at the same time there still was something wrong.' "[74]

Canadian star Jann Arden echoes Shirley's advice to learn the business and maintain control. "I answer to no one. I do exactly what I want to do. I own my own management company. I do my own artwork. I shoot my own videos. We control our Web site. I don't, I mean I'm part of a big company that has no intention of ever releasing me. But I'm my own person, savvy to what's going on around me." Jann learned this the hard way. "Well, and I was so foolish when I was twenty-nine and signing this contract. I don't think my management at the time really understood what we were doing, but I signed for ten records," something she later regretted. Though she likes the people she works with—or for—she says, "I want to wring their necks half the time. But I'm sure they want to wring mine. And I tried to get out of the record deal." Her company refused to let her go as long as they were still making money from her records. "And I know that they're terribly proud of me. And I know that me being on their label gives them credibility." She gets to control production at every level because the label head has abdicated. " 'You do it,' he said, 'We know we can't A&R you any more.' " And she does, adding that having her records sent all over the world is a thrill.[75]

She advises other women, "Hang on to your money and be smart, because this is such a fleeting thing. Very few people can get past the sophomore record and continue on. They really don't. I mean, I know fifteen other acts that started out with me on A&M ten years ago, and . . . they're gone." When she and Sheryl Crow had records come out at the same time, Jann says, "I remember seeing her and, I mean she's a far different story in the States than I am, but I always think, 'Good for you, Sheryl, for adapting and doing your own thing and being so tenacious.' "[76]

Martha Reeves of Martha and the Vandellas understands the business and shares these humorous words of advice: "You got to sacrifice, and it's not a lonely place either because any time I feel like I need companionship, I just pop in one of my records." Her music empowers her, she adds: "That's all I got. That's all I really know how to do. And now that I've produced this album, I think I've got another hat." Wanting to pass on a legacy, she says, "I'm anxious to get somebody across the board, have them bound to that microphone, and help them do what producers have helped me do all of my life."[77] Mentoring younger artists is important to this veteran.

Here Martha Reeves illustrates what Erik Erikson would call "generativity." Erikson believed that each of his theorized eight stages of psychosocial development has an emergent strength. In middle adulthood, one may either achieve generativity, characterized by a need and a willingness to produce or create, and to establish and guide the younger generation, or one will become stagnant, not producing anything and not caring about the next generation. With generativity, the emergent strength is "care."[78] We found that for many of our informants, not just the middle-aged ones, this type of care and mentoring was a crucial issue, a subject that will be explored more fully in the following chapter.

CHAPTER 8

SURVIVAL
("PRETTY GOOD FOR A GIRL")

You should be very careful that you don't build everything
you have around how cute you are or how sexy you are,
because, unfortunately, no matter how cute you are or how
sexy you are, in fifteen years, that won't be the most important part of your music.

—*Stevie Nicks,* Rolling Stone *(2001)*

The most important thing we have learned from talking with our informants, from the seventeen-year-old music student to the sixty-year-old veteran, is that making popular music is hard work. It is work of the body, the
mind, and the emotions—most of all, the emotions. Making music central
to her life is something the musician does and something that is done to
her. Both events are painful. "Most of the musicians that I know, or
songwriters that I know, have always wanted to do this. And the idea of
doing something else just doesn't even enter into the brain," Janis Ian tells
us.[1] "I think I was born to be a musician because I'm really not interested in
anything else at all," Rana Ross said.[2] To carry around that feeling of inevi-
tability is a blessing and a curse, a relief and a burden. It becomes the life's
work to sustain that drive, that certainty, in the midst of all the mantras of
defeat.[3] *You cannot make it. You are not good enough. Plenty of people are
already out there doing what you do, only better. You'll never succeed without
an agent. You'll never get an agent. You need to build an audience. People won't
like the things you do. Your songs won't sell. You won't get a recording contract.
You don't sound like anybody else.*

She does not sound like anybody else. The logic of creativity suggests that such a condition might be a key ingredient of success. But popular music, as we have seen, is about many things, only one of which is creative originality. One of rock history's ironies is that the artists with true longevity are the ones that, despite the industry's plea for more of the same, evolve in their own direction to the beat of their own drummer. The Beatles, the Rolling Stones, Bruce Springsteen, Metallica, B. B. King, Ray Charles, Tina Turner, Joni Mitchell, Bonnie Raitt, Michael Jackson, James Taylor, Kathleen Hanna, Madonna: here is a wildly incomplete list of famous rock musicians who have struggled to sing in their own voices. And the audiences *have* listened. But it has never been easy.

To shape one's identity as a rock musician against the expectations and constraints of a male-identified genre requires vision, hard work, persistence, and a dogged commitment to one's art. For the women we spoke with, music is a calling and a vocation; it is what they must do. The identity they have forged as rock musicians has been about their music—not about the expectations of others nor the demands of the music industry, though these have certainly played a role in the ways these women have constructed their identities. At the center of who they are, ultimately, is their music.

Rana Ross was only in her early thirties when we spoke with her. She talked and obviously felt like a veteran, though she was arguably early on in a musical career that a year later would be ended by the ravages of a chronic disease. She began with a punk band at sixteen, with a couple of other girls, playing in Manhattan. In her early twenties she met members of Vixen and helped them make demos to get re-signed after EMI dropped them. When their regular bassist didn't want to tour, she joined up and saw the country. She also began to find her audience. After that, she started her own group, Sinboy, and gave it her best shot for three years. "What happened to me is the same story that happened to a million other bands, you know. There was interfighting. There was this. There was that. Personal issues in people's lives, whatever. And the band broke up." She spoke regretfully about missing opportunities to tour with other bands. "I turned down so much stuff to do my own band. . . . And if you're not out there, you know, people forget about you." This in-danger-of-being-"forgotten" bassist made the cover of *Bassics* magazine in March/April 2000, and won several Los Angeles–area polls for best female bassist, and then, in 2000, best bassist. "It was not gender specific," she told us proudly. "It was best bassist, the guys, the girls, over everybody."[4]

For Rana, as we have seen, music began in the school years. She grew up poor, in a cold-water flat in Brooklyn. Her "hippie-like mom" introduced her to Led Zeppelin, Sly and the Family Stone, and Earth, Wind, and Fire. She joined gangs and fought in the streets. She also played the viola at school, then the cello, and then gave herself to music at fifteen when she discovered the bass.

> On one fateful night an angel came from the stars
> He told me in my dreams to play the Bass Guitar
> Play it down, Sister, till your fingers bleed
> Because you've got the drive and you've got the need[5]

Suddenly the "grooves," as she called the sound and feel of the bass, were everywhere. "Even sitting here, you know, there's grooves happening. There's the sound of the cars and there's the sound of turning the paper, and you know, there's grooves. And that's why people love when there's just bass and drums in the music because it has something to do with us inside."

Ross didn't feel like a prodigy, "even though I did start at four." She attributed her success to work. "I worked really hard. I was not given a God-given talent. I worked my ass off." She worked straight through that demon chorus. "I really used to care what people thought . . . of me." In a sense, the voices kept her home—not to hibernate, but to work. She became a poster child for the old joke about how to get to Carnegie Hall. "I stayed home a lot and practiced." She also built up her defenses for the career she planned. When she became comfortable inside her musician's skin, she heard the voices differently. "All I want is for somebody to walk out of a show and be like, 'Wow, that music was amazing. That music touched me. That bass player was amazing. Wow! Who is that chick?'"

Rana Ross sounded a bit like Carol Kaye in welcoming comparison with men, and in believing in a male-set standard of technical and creative excellence in her instrument. Also like Kaye, she found proof every day that women have a tougher time emerging from the obscurity of practice in the basement at home into the light of a public career. This idea found poignant demonstration for Ross in that she did not know who Carol Kaye was until long after she started absorbing Kaye's influence. "Here's a woman that did all the Motown stuff, all the stuff I probably was listening to and took, you know, stole all of her ideas because that's all a musician does." She rectified the oversight at a NAMM (National Association of Music Merchants) show in 2000, where she spotted Kaye. She hurried over. "'I have to touch you,' I said. 'Ms. Kaye . . . thank you so much for opening the doors.' And to me," Ross continued, "she is like the great-, great-, great-grandmother because I feel that my generation of musicians, of bassists and guitarists and drummers, . . . are the grandmas." In this vision of musical generations, it becomes clear why Rana Ross felt old at thirty-two, with her task of "opening the doors for the younger girls to come in." The inequalities between men's and women's opportunities, she believed, are destined to continue "for many generations to come." Sick of being asked to "show the calluses" on her tiny hands in order to prove she really plays the bass, she was delighted when Phil Chin (of Irie) wanted to compare small hands.[6]

Becoming Mentors

Like Carol Kaye, Rana Ross believed in her mission to mentor younger women players.[7] Kaye has mentored musicians not only through years of offering lessons, but also through a series of instructional books and videos.[8] Ross happily did events like the Rockrgrrl Conference in Seattle in 2000, where she appeared on a panel about endorsements. (She had endorsements from Hohner, LaBella, and SWR, among others.) But she found that music itself was her best vehicle for making a difference, further illustrating Erikson's idea of generativity, mentioned in the previous chapter. "You're a caregiver in a different kind of way," she said, thinking of situations in which a song makes a difference in a girl's life. "I can give back by having people listen to what I do and bring up something inside of them or bring up something socially, bring up something emotionally."[9]

Melissa Auf der Maur expresses the same kind of longing to make a difference through the music itself. Auf der Maur has recently decided to reach out in more ways to women. One of the reasons she is talking with us, she says, is that she hopes her story will make it to a young girl who will take inspiration from it. "I will take time out any time a young woman wants to talk to me about life."

Auf der Maur voices the same frustration we heard from Rana Ross that they do not encounter more peers as women musicians active with headlining rock bands. "I can't believe that after ten years of doing this." The peers they find can become precious sources of support and inspiration. Melissa Auf der Maur and Paz Lenchantin met each other on the road, as the only women on the Smashing Pumpkins/A Perfect Circle tour. They were soul mates, and now support each other's musical and artistic efforts (Auf der Maur is a photographer as well as a bassist). "It's a revelation that we found each other. . . . And we, I'd say, are guiding each other in many ways as women, as like-minded spirits."[10]

Often the first contact between women musicians is from mouth to ear, through some recorded medium. On the DVD compilation of *Lilith*

Fair performances, Meredith Brooks tells the story of how she went through a phase of disillusionment and exhaustion with music, which manifested in her refusing to listen to other artists at all—until one day her manager begged her to put a new CD into her machine. Brooks tears up and her voice catches as she tells about hearing Sarah McLachlan's "Ice Cream" for the first time. Every song on that album, *Fumbling Toward Ecstasy,* came to her as a revelation. She wore out the CD. Somehow the songs transcended the threat that others' harvested crops can pose to each of us laboring in our own fields; instead they took her home to her own musical self.[11]

Sarah Dash spoke of listening to The Shirelles and Brenda Lee on the radio. Jean Millington remembered learning to play bass by learning songs by the Supremes and Ronettes. Madeline Puckette loves Kate Schellenbach's drumming; Melissa Auf der Maur listened to Blondie; Stacey Board to Chrissie Hynde and Pat Benatar. Leah Hinchcliff mentions Joni Mitchell and Carol Kaye; the Indigo Girls mention Carole King; Emily White mentions the Indigo Girls. Kate Campbell played Janis Joplin's "Me and Bobby McGee" over and over; "and to this day," she adds, "I can sing every part." Laya Fisher, a New Jersey musician transplanted to Australia, says she became a musician because "I listened to Tori Amos for an entire summer in '94 and knew I wanted to make people feel the way she was making me feel."[12] Erin O'Hara was working nights as a janitor at a law firm when she moved the radio dial from the classical station to a Syracuse University station that played a Kate Bush song. "I was just stopped in my tracks," Erin explains, "like I was just blown away. I just went and turned it up and stopped what I was doing, and then I went out and bought the record, and I used to play it at, like, tremendous volume in my house over and over because I just had never heard anything like that. I had never heard a woman use her voice like that. I had never heard songwriting like that, and all the drums and . . . it was just very powerful."[13]

For other interviewees, their first connection with other women musicians came at a concert. When we asked Lynn Frances Anderson who were her rock role models, she began with Helen Reddy. "Why Helen Reddy?" we asked. " 'I Am Woman!' " Lynn laughed. "When I was in the fourth grade, my grandpa took me to see Helen Reddy at the Lane County Fair, and I cried. I was so excited to see her. . . . And then when I was in college, a friend of mine and I went and saw Judy Collins at the Lane County Fair. And I cried again."[14] Jonatha Brooke recalls seeing Bonnie Raitt a couple of times when she was in college and "being just completely smitten, you know, just totally into what she was doing and how cool she was and how powerful and strong. . . . And when I finally met her, I was really psyched that she was normal. You know, she was really cool and very gracious. And I was really pleased to have seen that journey for her and then talk to her and find out that I really like her too."[15]

Our informants often mentioned Bonnie Raitt. The Indigo Girls told us she was an inspiration to them politically. Lynn Frances Anderson said she went to all three Portland concerts Bonnie did for her *Road Tested* album. She continued, "But the other thing that going to concerts and seeing entertainers like Bonnie Raitt does for me is it inspires me and it teaches me something. Because every time I see something happen at a concert, like during the middle of Bonnie Raitt singing 'Angel from Montgomery,' the power went out. And you could hear this big pop, and she didn't move; she didn't blink. She just kept singing. And the power came back on and she finished the song. And it just, it's like a lesson in how to respond when the power goes off. You know, just keep singing. And that's true about life, right? When things don't go right, for me, music is so much about just keep singing because life can go to shit, you know, to hell in a hand basket really fast. But if you have some creative outlet, I think it can save you. . . . And if we don't have it then we are always looking for it. . . . Bonnie Raitt, I love her."[16]

Artist to Artist: Shared Vision

Musicians often touch each other directly. Though it is often a lover or a parent or a friend or a manager who comes to the rescue of a musician in crisis, sometimes it takes another artist to understand. Ferron went through a bad time in the mid-1990s when her life partnership broke up at the same time that her brief relationship with Warner Brothers went on the skids ("and *they* wooed *me*," she says ruefully). She fell apart. "I had a spiritual breakdown," she says. "You know, I was so broken and lost confidence in myself since I had done something that I considered to be so bad for me." June Millington and Ann Hackler urged Ferron to come to Bodega, California, and teach writing at the Institute for the Musical Arts. "I lived with them for three years. I was their in-house writer." Working at IMA, Ferron came to a new place. "What I needed out of it was to come down to earth or to come up to earth." She also reached a new understanding of her role in the lives of other women, and that it might begin just with listening: hearing people's stories, which allowed them to hear themselves. "I started to see that women still didn't really have a voice. And I know that because when I sat with women and they finally read their story, the first thing they do is weep." She remembered her own experience. "The first time I ever sang a song in front of somebody, I burst into tears. It was like I heard myself. . . . I wasn't silent inside of a brass ball. And so sometimes I cry too when other people read their stories."[17]

Hackler and Millington's IMA has addressed the needs of many women musicians, with the ultimate vision of changing the popular music paradigm in our culture. "*What if . . . ,*" the IMA Web site challenges its visitors, "artists like Tracy Chapman were the norm, rather than the exception in mainstream music? What if an artist the stature of Ani DiFranco could actually get mainstream radio air-play? What if all-female bands were as common as all-male bands or if fifty percent of all professional symphony orchestras were composed of women? What if we could all name three Native-, Latin-, & Asian-American musicians without thinking twice? What if it was ordinary to see women running the sound at a concert, or if female producers & engineers weren't anomalies? What if there were more women at the top of record companies? Each day the Institute for the Musical Arts brings these dreams a bit closer to reality."[18] Founded in 1987 in Bodega, the IMA began sponsoring workshops and performances to teach women how to do the things that somehow men learn to do without special institutions—or in the mainstream institutions and organizations, from guitar stores to sound companies to junior high shop classes—that have been hostile to women. Songwriting and composition; guitar, drum, and voice performance; booking and promotion; album development; sound; production—these have been some of the workshops sponsored over the years and taught by Ferron, the Millingtons, Holly Near, Cris Williamson, Tret Fure, Erika Luckett, Bitch and Animal, and many others. In 1999 the IMA, shaken by the threatened end of its long-term lease in Bodega, began an attempt to become bicoastal by moving many of its activities to temporary quarters in Northampton, Massachusetts, the site of strong music and women's communities. A number of the artists we spoke with have encountered the IMA, as teachers, performers, students, and artists passing through.

The IMA tries to institutionalize the kind of network that the women's music festivals began facilitating in the mid-1970s. The IMA has been sponsoring its own festival, called DivaFest, every summer in Guerneville, California, to raise money for IMA workshops and functions and also to bring together veteran women musicians with newbies. DivaFest, like most other established music festivals, takes its cue from Tanglewood on the classical side and Newport on the popular side, returning to the same performance space every year, which creates a tradition rooted in place. Advantages include returning audience members and performers, and usually ever more experienced producers and public relations personnel.

In August 2000 a new phenomenon emanated from Olympia, Washington, home of the DIY spirit in punk music, home of the riot grrls movement, home of unconventional Evergreen College, and home to a group of bold women who pushed past the intimidating aura of doing something completely new, and doing it just once. They organized LadyFest, a music-art-film-writing and gender-politics festival run by women, for women, and meant to serve as a template for other grassroots festivals. At this writing, LadyFests have occurred or are being planned literally all over the Western world, from every corner of the United States to Canada, the United Kingdom, Belgium, Germany, the Netherlands, France, and Australia. There are no super-organizers; rather, each group learns from the model and mistakes of previous groups. While we were working on this book, we attended two LadyFests.

The LadyFest phenomenon is more complicated than the passing of a torch, or a checklist, from one generation to another. It is a bubbling-over of shared experiences from older to younger, and from younger to older. Mina experienced this too-little-acknowledged kind of exchange in mid-August 2001, when she flew to Chicago for LadyFest Midwest. As budget-conscious and wannabe bohemian as most academic researchers, she made reservations at the Three Arts Club, a Chicago institution founded in 1912 by Progressive Era women reformers like Jane Addams for the care and protection of young women art students, footloose and poor in the big city.

As it happened, the Three Arts Club was a perfect staging ground for attending a festival celebrating women in the arts. The building is impressive, planted on a corner in the Gold Coast surrounded by turn-of-the-century apartment buildings, and a short walk to the nearest Chicago Transit Authority stop. The ground floor is arrayed around a courtyard with benches and statuary, reminiscent of the settlement houses and women's colleges of that era. In fact the Three Arts Club is very much like a settlement house for middle-class kids wanting to live the artist's life in a somewhat more predictable and sheltered, but still inexpensive, way. In the summer it becomes a coed hostel catering to short-term visitors and summer school students, but if there were men in residence this August weekend, they stayed out of sight. The rooms off the courtyard are grand: two large living rooms or *salons,* a small auditorium, and the dining room and kitchen at the back.

There are many pianos here: a grand piano in one living room, several uprights stored on the auditorium stage, and more pianos crammed, comically, into the communal bathrooms on the floors above. It is hard not to plunk the keys as one enters and exits on other business. Apparently the pianos are, or have been, available for rent to individual residents. What a luxury it seems to have a piano in one's room! And that is certainly where the luxuries end in the upstairs rooms. The grand ground floor does not prepare the new arrival for these residential floors, as dark and simple as any older college dormitory: the lives of the residents intermittently noisy yet hidden behind closed doors.

Bulletin boards on every landing of the iron stairway hint at the hope-filled lives of the current women residents. Their comings and goings are subtle, shall we say, unobtrusive, and yet the residents are clearly around. Some eat the breakfast or dinner included in their monthly rent. Others chat in the crowded storage room used as an office and reception area. The women may live in the club as long-term residents or short-term guests. All residents must apply and be accepted. They may pursue their arts in classes or studios, in the hours between stints as *baristas* or temps, or in their rooms. Quiet hours are enforced. You may not practice the flute or the electric bass in your room in the wee hours of the morning. Rooms come in different sizes and are differently furnished—but to begin with, each room has, more or less, a sink, a single bed, a dresser with a mirror, a small bookcase, and an old-fashioned steam radiator. There is a plug-in fan, but no air conditioner. Mina knows a lot about Jane Addams, having spent a summer in Chicago twenty years earlier researching another book about young women making their own lives. She imagines the fresh-faced women running up and down the Three Arts stairs with their bobbed hair and long-waisted dresses in the new world of the Roaring Twenties.

A number of the Three Arts denizens will undoubtedly attend LadyFest. Mina tries to catch up with a woman at the Three Arts Club, a musician with the group Apartment who she learns from the receptionist has been working on LadyFest. (They exchange notes but never do connect face-to-face.) She plunges underground to find the headquarters that first after-noon: the Congress Theater on North Milwaukee. Musicians play in the transit station, welcomed by and confined to boxes painted onto the train platform. A two-block walk from the California stop, the Congress is a grand old theater that now hosts rock concerts and other events willing to brave the old facilities. Girls, girls, girls, and a few boys are lined up outside the door in the gray summer afternoon. Mina feels a bit old and out of place—not that the younger women are rude or even take notice of her at all. (Un-like Tisa, she is not politely challenged to say that this is her intended destination—but surely not because she blends in any better.) The girls chat in groups of two or three as they wait. They have multicolored hair, body piercings, messenger bags with special cell phone pockets, and the kind of clothing that would have saved older women a lot of angst and money dur-ing their own leaving-their-parents'-houses years. While the researcher's generation wore denim, these young people wear—denim. The rule is to layer whatever you find at Goodwill, which had just begun to find its natural middle-class clientele in the 1960s. The wardrobe staple is generally a T-shirt with a funny slogan or personally significant name of a coffee shop, band, or more rarely, a university or clothing brand. Girls wear small shirts, bellbottoms (knockoffs of the 1960s version), and pieces of old accountants' suits that probably did not fit their first owners well, and were certainly never before worn with such élan. Accessories flirt with biker/S&M motifs: chains, leather belts, steel hoops and studs in ears, noses, tongues, and belly buttons. Some girls wear dresses, often the kind with waistbands and patterned material, over Doc Martens or canvas basketball sneakers. Not these girls with dresses, but others, look like boys, and many of the boys look like girls. This is what sixties parents said about sixties kids—only now it is really, really true.

When the line moves, it is clear that the organizers have made it simple for attendees to report their names and get their wristbands. (Things seem to go well not only here and now, but pretty much everywhere throughout the weekend.) The music has begun. Inside the theater's great foyer, display tables carry artists' CDs, T-shirts, sample copies of music zines and newspapers, pamphlets from organizations for musicians, organizations for survivors, for political women, for the arts. There is a message board and a board with a map where you can stick a pin to show where you are from. There are a couple of snack bars with popcorn, nachos, candy, soda, and innocuous midwestern beer. The music is loud: very, very loud inside the theater. Down in the mosh pit near the stage, nobody is moshing yet. The afternoon is split between Chicago favorites and out-of-town headliners. Summer Chance, the Hissyfits, Tami Hart. Amy Ray is backed by the Butchies, who have also backed her on *Stag*.

Everybody seems happy. More girls in retro glasses and rude T-shirts arrive. They themselves are not rude. The girls still far outnumber the men, who it must be said seem quite brave but also fortunate to be joining the scene. Even though this is probably a punker scene than Lilith Fair, men might find here the same advantages of going to a concert with mainly girls—although guys never seem to have a problem getting in and out of bathrooms between sets. The crowd grows, but not enough to keep the gals very far away from their idols. Amy Ray and the Butchies are favorites; they are a big deal, very big celebrities, and it is nice how close members of the audience can get, unconfined to seats.

Smoke fogs the theater, even though smoking is confined to the lobby. The performers know each other and share sets. Amy Ray calls out Danielle

Howle, a Daemon artist, and Tami Hart, who records with Mr. Lady, from backstage to join in on certain numbers. During her own earlier set, Tami had invited people to come up onstage and dance. She was overwhelmed by the enthusiastic response—a sea of colored bodies. "Hm, OK, no more dancing," she orders amiably. "You guys just dance out here" [pointing to the mosh pit]. Later the brash, talented eighteen-year-old calls into the mike, "How many of you are queer tonight?" Between sets there are short movies, including *My Name is Gal,* a sweetly comic lip-sync performance by KJ Mohr and Kelly Hayes, set in Rio de Janeiro against the Christ statue and other public monuments.

In this sprawling city, attendees rely on the printed program and whatever local maps they can pick up to find the festival's far-flung venues. The Congress Theater is the central gathering spot, but still LadyFest does not feel entirely "centered" here, partly because this is a performance place, not a hotel, and neighborhood restaurants are actually sparse. The next day Mina explores another venue twenty minutes' walk down Milwaukee from the Congress (or one El stop closer in). The Local Grind is a warm, high-ceilinged space with oddly angled walls and deep couches.[19] The performers are tucked up next to the plate-glass window, so passers-by can see there is something going on. These are the folkie sets. The appreciative audience—many obviously friends and family—sprawls on the couches and applauds the performers, several of them young novices, while others are experienced hands around Chicago. The organizers move things along from their base on a central couch. They watch for arriving performers, warmly greet them, and make sure they have the necessary sound equipment. The bill is actually running short, not long, so Ellen Rosner, one of the organizers and a seasoned performer around Chicago, does a short set while the next performer is catching her breath.

Rosner has a big, bluesy voice. She is comfortable performing. She and Rose Polenzani will trade sets the next evening at Schuba's, a favorite Chicago bar-restaurant with a dedicated performance space. At the Local Grind this afternoon she accompanies herself on guitar, though she usually sings in front of a band. The next afternoon Mina sits down with Rosner during her work shift back at the Congress Theater. In a noisy, cramped backstage room, they talk, among other things, about mentorship. Ellen has become passionate about the need for artists to teach each other what a career in popular music is all about—perhaps most of all, that such a career is possible. Her own day jobs have been with arts organizations, where she has learned, ironically, how little musicians' lives are understood by individuals making careers in arts administration. One of her supervisors refers to Ellen's touring as going on "vacation." In another job, Ellen had a phone conversation with an arts funder who suggested that popular music was not a viable art form (and thus not fundable), because it was inherently "commercial"—one could make money from it. "Well, so, artists," she asked the woman, "when they get to a certain level, like when they're garnering a hundred thousand dollars per painting, no longer are artists because they're commercial?" Ellen admits that she put the woman on the spot because her narrowness "really, really made me irate. But it also made me want to change it as much as I could."

For Rosner, LadyFest Midwest posed a perfect opportunity to put her passion to the test. In LadyFest, "we're all learning together how to do this. There's nobody coming in" to tell them how to organize a conference, solicit workshops, produce a concert. Some came to the table with a great deal of experience, and many with none at all. "It's somebody even like just one half-step ahead of you, sharing that information."[20]

Erin O'Hara echoed that urge for demystification when we spoke with her a month later during LadyFest East in New York (in retrospect, of course, one of the last innocent celebrations before the sky turned black in lower Manhattan). A New York City musician, she joined the vocal faculty at the Rock and Roll Camp for Girls in Portland that August in order to pass her knowledge to the next musical generation. Rock and roll is not difficult, she asserts. It is all about access. She comments gently, "In my experience, I think a lot of information wasn't really forthcoming from a lot of the men that I worked with." Her analysis becomes more pointed: "That was to kind of protect their own sense of their thing, their power, their—and then when I started gaining more information, like whether it was from other women or from really open-minded men, I realized like, God, this is easy. It made me kind of angry that I didn't have access to it earlier, and so, like seeing those girls at the rock camp . . . it took me ten years to learn all the things that these girls [in the sound workshop] are learning in a week. . . . Just to have somebody be saying," she says, her memory interweaving the practical and spiritual directives, " 'here. This is how you do this. . . . It's this simple. Put your fingers here. Do this. Sing from here. Say whatever you want to say. Say what you feel. [T]ell the truth about a situation. Um, plug this cable into here. Here, this is a trick so you don't pop your Ps and your Bs into the microphone.' . . . To watch so many women doing that . . . it was like heaven."[21]

This was not Erin's first mentoring experience. Drawing from her own youthful struggles with social isolation, her Catholic school education (with all its messages about the female body), and, in mitigation, her close relationships with her sisters in their rural New York setting, she has developed a philosophy about what girls need in order to flourish. "Just listening to them I think is one of the most important things and . . . exposing them to things, like I said before, like access." As a girl, Erin tells us, she went to a lot of movies alone, because she could learn about "alternative" ways of being: "alternative universes, alternative kinds of worlds, alternative families, alternative ways of communicating, and so they sort of served as nurturers to me in a weird way." Girls are still kept back by social structure and design; but then again, "girls are smarter . . . they'll figure it out and find their way if, if they're given access to information and if they're . . . heard." She plays with a pun. What girls need is to be "allowed in every way—allowed in the a-l-l-o-w-e-d but aloud, you know, like, to be *loud*. [In] the traditional sense of raising girls, you know, you're encouraged to be kind of polite and quiet and ladylike, and to be a*loud*, to be truer than that is . . . it's gonna change."[22]

For Erin, too, LadyFest East was a chance to see if there could be more community among musicians. Having scored films, she had already become part of New York Women in Film and Television, and she was seeking a similar women musicians' network. New York is difficult, she acceded, more "fractured" than other cities, perhaps because it takes a lot of energy just to "make your rent." When we talked with her, she had just brought out *Indestructible Joy*, her CD that celebrates the process of becoming strong against the barriers she discussed with us. On the CD cover, Erin flexes a strong arm proudly against the blue Manhattan sky:

> I am here to take back what you stole
> My birthright, my very soul
> I am here to take back my velvet night
> My hopeful morning, my strong sight
> Let star bright stab through a dark dream
> Learn to sew the deepest holes clean
> My indestructible joy is too big to be beaten down[23]

Janis Ian has devoted much of her long career to helping other musicians along. She claims she would not have the patience to coach individual students. "I'm not nearly nice enough," she insists. But she runs master classes, and reaches even more musicians through her writing, including for several years a monthly column in *Performing Songwriter*, "Risky Business," devoted to central issues in "the business": everything from whether to have a manager, to recording with indie versus major labels versus DIY, to touring woes, to cowriting, to more crucial intangibles like what "truthfulness" means in personal presentation, and what happened to her music and her insides after her mother's death. Recording "Society's Child" at fourteen, she has forged a career over almost four decades (when you start that young, the numbers roll up in an awesome way). Growing up in a jazz-oriented family, she broke through—at thirteen— with a folk performance at the Village Gate, to an audience including Tom Paxton, Eric Anderson, Phil Ochs, and Judy Collins. It is not surprising that as for so many of our respondents, it was love at first mic. "I thought it was the coolest thing that had ever happened in the entire history of the universe. . . . I was sure that every record company in the world was gonna want to sign me immediately, and that within a matter of moments." Those illusions dashed, as we recounted in chapter 7, Ian made the career that she could hardly avoid, driven by songs that told the truth as she saw it. Her career differs from some others—but puts her on the list of greats near the beginning of this chapter— because she spoke the truth in love and also made noted albums, as well as writing songs others would take up the charts. There was one ten-year hiatus in her career, from 1983 to 1993, when she pursued the other arts, primarily acting, that she had been exploring off and on all her life. Then she roared back into popular music with *Breaking Silence,* which earned a Grammy nomination.[24] When we asked her about her artistic vision she told us that she doesn't think she has one; that what she thinks about is "Does this song need a third verse?" But she also directed us to this lyric, "Take No Prisoners," which captures, she said, "pretty much everything I have to say about being an artist":

The writer wrote. The singer sung.
The record broke. The audience was stunned.
Some they begged for mercy, others even cried
Some fled, left for dead, some said it changed their lives.
And the writer said "I wish you'd known me
When I still believed in the truth
Now it's all I have left along with my debts
And lack of youth." He said—

Take no prisoners. Tell no lies.
No pretty songs of compromise.
Take no prisoners. Tell no lies.
It's a good day to die.[25]

Born a decade later, Jill Sobule did not find her public voice as early as Janis Ian. Inducted into rock by an amiable older brother who showed her some chords and let her listen in on his band rehearsals in the family's Denver basement, she began to play drums, then settled into guitar study with a blues artist she loved, who died after she had taken five lessons from him. "I tell people today, I don't know anything more than I did in eighth grade." She loved electric guitar, and didn't give in until several years later to a general pressure to take up the acoustic guitar as a more gender-appropriate instrument. Though she felt pretty great up there onstage with her Gibson SG and her brother's Marshall stack amp, "I didn't get like 'She's cool.' I got more like, 'She's a freak. She's not feminine.' You know, you don't get dates." She played on in various bands, diffidently. She didn't use her voice. "I thought I had a horrible voice." She started writing songs, but she thought of them as a kind of private journal, and never played them for anybody. In college she studied international affairs ("it sounded so frigging cool") and took a junior year abroad in Spain. There she turned a musical corner. Another visiting student, a flute player, suggested they busk on the streets "for a goof." It was the first time she had ever played and sung her own songs. A man walked by and asked the duo if they would like to play in his nightclub. "At first we were like, 'Yeah, right. What club?'" But it was a real club, and a real gig, and Jill ended up dropping out of school and playing that club for three months. The language "barrier" became her liberation. "You can totally re-create yourself and write these words and sing these words that probably three-fourths of the people don't even understand." She returned to hometown Denver. The bug had bitten her and she began to play open mics. Her father came with her. She got club dates and grew into a pretty big fish in the relatively small pond of Denver music. One foot out the door to New York, she was stopped by an A&R guy from MCA who wanted to get her a major label deal. She moved to New York, then commuted occasionally to Nashville as a working musician will do, and actually got signed at a big showcase, the Nashville Extravaganza. It was a dream come true, with all the accoutrements, including a first album produced by Todd Rundgren—which would have been terrific except that Rundgren "just doesn't have good bedside manners, and it kind of freaked me out." Jill finally turned to Todd's girlfriend for interpretation. "Well, for Todd," she explained to the quaking first-time recording artist, " 'adequate' means 'really good.'" The first MCA album, *Things Here Are Different,* came out. The second album ended up in the vault. "Way deep in the vault," Jill clarifies. MCA dropped her, so she moved to Los Angeles and stayed for a couple of years to cowrite and see what happened. Those years were "fairly difficult," she deadpans. She worked as a wedding photographer's assistant and kept making demos. "I didn't know; I was all fucked up. I didn't know what to do."[26]

Another chance encounter with a producer—as "chancy" as these encounters are for gigging musicians keeping a career afloat—got her another backhanded compliment (" 'I wasn't sure if I liked you or that band before you was so bad' "), and a deal with Atlantic. Jill did two albums with Atlantic, and had her one chart hit, "I Kissed a Girl," before she was dropped. She comments that she will not go with a major label again unless she gets a "Mariah Carey" level of advance. (We assumed that did not mean she wants the wedding thrown in, too.) "I really don't care about going on a major because I never saw a penny [from] the 'Kissed a Girl' record. . . . The only time I've ever made any money," she echoes so many of our other informants, "was just selling out of my van, my CDs at live shows."[27]

Sobule has become a celebrity in a way that must be both frustrating and gratifying. VH1 features her—respectfully—on its *Pop-Up Video* show for her "one-hit wonder" of 1995, "I Kissed A Girl." She has friends throughout the industry, has opened for Don Henley, and toured as a sideman with Lloyd Cole. Jill Sobule is liked *and* respected by fellow musicians. Her songs are often hilarious and poignant within the same verse. Her lyrics have an effortless quality that eventually brings them around to smack the listener upside the head. She has fought for everything she has, and for a cheerful woman, sometimes she sounds pretty world-weary. She has worked through at least two big writing blocks—one of them after being dropped from Atlantic in 1997, when she just about gave up music until she rediscovered the drums, her first love as a kid. She also took a job as a topical songwriter for the New York NPR affiliate, WFUV-FM. "I had to get up in the morning and come up with something to sing that day."[28] These days, she calls herself a "touring machine," and explains that the intensity of touring forced her to develop her effervescent, free-associative stage persona. "You know at first I was so uptight and a very serious singer/songwriter. You know . . . like, when you see Tracy Chapman." But touring wore her down to her essence. "When you get really tired, your real personality comes out. And I was like, 'Oh, this is way more fun and it's kinda working better.' "

It seems emblematic of her journey that her favorite guitar teacher, the one she learned the most from, died shortly after taking Jill as a student—of still mysterious causes. ("Someone told me later he'd died of a heroin overdose. I don't know.") Her other guitar teacher wanted her to use Mel Bay and play "When the Saints Go Marching In" one note at a time. "I just couldn't get into it. It was not there." Women mentors? Her brother had a Fanny album. "I thought that was really cool 'cause there [were] girls playing guitars." As for women rockers, she did not encounter any in the flesh, in Denver. "There were some real folkie people. There [were] jazz singers I knew."[29] She too has reached out to lesser-known musicians, producing her friend Mary Kate O'Neil's first CD and touring with her. She does not present her role as that of mentor; a number of our informants are diffident about admitting to their importance in other musicians' lives, though they are grateful to be mentioned by others.

Shirley Alston Reeves credits Ruth Brown and Etta James with mentoring the Shirelles. When we ask her what young artists she thinks have been influenced by The Shirelles, she says, "Well, we've been told that, you know, by different groups, like En Vogue, . . . they tell us that, you know, we're their mentors." "Destiny's Child?" we ask. "Well," Shirley responds, "I would think that they pattern themselves a little more probably after maybe The Supremes. . . . But I think the En Vogue girls . . . were a little more patterned from The Shirelles. And they actually did a tribute to us on the TV show that we did with Dionne Warwick. They were actually nervous to sing, and we laughed our heads off about that because we knew that our harmony is definitely not as good as theirs, not as tight."[30]

We ask the Indigo Girls if they are mentoring anybody, and Amy bursts out, "Nobody. I hope nobody!" she laughs. Amy Ray!—whose Daemon Records has nurtured so many talents by asking what they need and trying to get it for them. We ask Ferron whether she is mentoring other musicians, and she says, wryly, "Well, no one follows me around." We prod her by telling her that Amy and Emily have mentioned her influence. "Oh yeah," she says, "but they were wonderful to me." For Ferron, the favor ran the other way. "At the point just before Maya was born, they took me out on the road with them and paid me to be their warm-up act." It sounds like one of those golden moments in musical history when suddenly there's no "newer" and "older," "mentor" and "protégée," but just peers. "They just wanted to hang around. And we had a great time, but I'd felt a little retired compared to, you know, they were still burning, going out."[31]

The Long Haul

As mentioned previously, Bonnie Raitt's name surfaced repeatedly when we asked our informants to comment on their musical influences. Her determination, musical longevity, and vigorous talent have inspired countless artists, some successful and others struggling. Since her early twenties, Raitt has played and recorded with blues legends including Sippie Wallace, her "sassy grandmother," who certainly rubbed off on the self-described tomboy.[32] "I never saw music in terms of men and women or black and white," she told *Rolling Stone*. "There was just cool and uncool."[33] While her albums enjoyed critical acclaim in the seventies, she was off-loaded by Warner Brothers in 1983. She signed with Capitol in 1989, and in 1990 she reached a new level of public notice with four Grammys for the aptly named *Nick of Time*. She earned three more Grammys for *Luck of the Draw* in 1991, and another for *Longing in Their Hearts* in 1993. Blending the blues with pop and rock, all three albums went multi-platinum, quite an accomplishment for an artist who had been dropped from her first label.[34] Warner Brothers' loss was Capitol Records' gain, propelling her from cult icon to major star status as Raitt broke down barriers of gender and genre. Bonnie Raitt as much as any other artist has *created* a space, as a sexy, vibrant, brilliant artist, for post-forty women rockers.

Bonnie received her first guitar for Christmas when she was eight. During summers at a Quaker camp in the Adirondacks, she listened to Odetta records and taught herself to play guitar. Uninterested in her native California beach scene, she fell in love with the East Coast antiwar and civil rights scenes, which included the urban folk music movement. Attracted to Joan Baez's New England roots in Cambridge, Massachusetts, Bonnie chose to attend college at Radcliffe. In local clubs she met and performed with some of her blues idols. Along with Buddy Guy and Junior Wells, Bonnie opened for the Rolling Stones when she was only twenty years old.[35] During her junior year, she dropped out of Radcliffe, opting for touring and gaining attention playing her trademark slide guitar. At age twenty-one she signed that coveted deal with Warner Brothers.[36]

During this time, unlike many fellow female artists, Bonnie enjoyed the respect of her male peers. She wanted to be the best, but fitting in with the boys took its toll. In a 1990 *Rolling Stone* interview, she confessed, "There was a romance about drinking and doing blues."[37] In 1987, Patricia Romanowski writes, Raitt faced and beat her drinking problem. Two years later she was in the studio with *Nick of Time*.

Sensitive to hard times at both the cultural and personal levels, for decades Raitt has been an activist, working for the environment, for racial justice, for women's issues. She also focuses on the past and future of the music industry; she assists legendary artists needing a secure retirement (many have nothing material to show for decades of musical contributions), and with her royalties from sales of her signature Fender Stratocaster electric guitar, she has funded free guitar lessons for girls.[38] She was inducted into the Rock and Roll Hall of Fame in 2000, and her sixteenth album was released in May 2003. Raitt has survived and her music has thrived.

Bonnie Raitt often deflects applause to those playing onstage with her, artists such as Shawn Colvin.[39] Like Raitt, Colvin started playing guitar as a youngster, in 1968. From performing in a local hard rock band as a teenager and playing in Austin clubs to winning Grammy Awards, this smart singer-songwriter with her own sound and style has staying power. "Shawn Colvin is one of those overnight success stories that's taken many, many years," Don Henley commented in *Billboard*.[40]

When college and playing hard rock in Illinois proved unfulfilling, she joined the Dixie Diesels in Texas and then the Buddy Miller Band in New York by way of San Francisco.[41] Columbia Records signed her after her European tour with Suzanne Vega's band in 1987. Colvin won a folk Grammy in 1990 for *Steady On*. The work continued. *A Few Small Repairs* hit big in 1997, and Colvin won two more Grammys, for the album and for the single "Sunny Came Home," which topped out three industry charts.[42] Three decades of work developing a career brought well-deserved rewards.

Crediting Joni Mitchell as her first musical influence, Colvin is a powerful guitarist and songwriter, drawing on the personal while creating "short-story" songs. She often collaborates with John Leventhal, particularly on lyrics; she has called the collaboration a "moving experience," playing with the twinned concepts of emotion and creative process.[43] Her characters live bleak lives that they often describe in disconcertingly upbeat melodies, as in the unshakeable "Sunny Came Home." *Whole New You,* her 2001 album, was released more than two decades after her first professional performances in college, and significantly, after her daughter was born. She told *Performing Songwriter* in 2001 that she wrote the material for that album with trepidation. "It was like the poetry was gone," she says, speaking of the frightening ironies of early motherhood. "I had no poetry. And there was poetry in *every breath I was taking,* so to speak, you know?"[44] In "One Small Year," an aching, simple report from the inside, she captures the great transformations that seize our lives in daily increments. She says finishing that song, for which the first verse came in all of two seconds, was "complete and utter hideous hell."[45] The stamina to work through that hell, with all the courage it takes to face down the inner voices of disparagement (and in this case, the outer voice of a dubious collaborator), marks the musical survivor. Shawn Colvin's longevity in the business is due, at least in part, to her cleaving to her own vision and her own timing.

This is one of the hardest jobs in the world; there are bad days, and bad months, but unlike other careers or professions, there are few bad years, and almost no bad decades—because you cannot last that long as a professional without doing good work, meaning work that somebody likes enough to pay for. If you stop making music someone will buy, you need to find another way to make a living. And only a small fraction of pop musicians make a living entirely from music. When we asked Jonatha Brooke what advice she would give to new musicians just starting out, she said, "Make sure this is what you have to do. Make sure it's what you really have to do to breathe because it's really tough. It's really, really hard to make ends meet and to make an impression, I think."[46]

A Sense of Purpose

Brooke's advice illustrates what psychologist Abraham Maslow would call "self-actualization" in his hierarchy of needs. At times forsaking lower-level "deficiency needs" such as food and safety, many artists are driven to do what they feel they must do: make music. Self-actualization, one of the "being needs," tops Maslow's hierarchy. Unlike the deficiency needs such as water and oxygen, which are satisfied when met, being needs become stronger when discovered.[47] The hunger to make music or, as Maslow would say, to continue to self-actualize grows. Music for many of our informants is who they are, and without it many of them would have no self-recognizable identity.

While making music is fulfilling within itself, without a fan base one cannot survive in the business. When we asked our informants what they hoped their music did for their fans, the responses varied considerably. But nearly all responses connoted a sense of purpose, a connection, and a move toward self-actualization. For Shirley Alston Reeves the sincerity of the performance was key, but another response from her evoked tears during the interview, both from Tisa and Shirley. Commenting on what "a doll" Dick Clark had been as he tried to run interference and smooth tensions in the Jim Crow South as The Shirelles and other black performers toured, she said that even when Dick Clark told hotel clerks who he was, the door was shut in his face because of the "mixed bus" outside. "Thank God things have changed!" Shirley exclaimed. "But you know what? That's what I was going to tell you. Music is what changed it. Music has so much to do with change."[48]

"Just some moment of happiness" is what Carol Kaye hopes her music offers.[49] Likewise, Holly Near wants to "invite people to feel better about themselves when they walk out than they did when they walked in and encourage them to do one thing that will alter the outcome."[50] Kitzie Pippin Stern has a similar goal. She wants her fans to feel uplifted and joyful, "to really have it touch something deep inside that makes people feel good." She adds, " . . . if you want to put it into spiritual terms, which is where it's been living for the last couple of years, I really wanted to express God or

Spirit or that universal truth that is in all."[51] Bitch and Animal told us they hope they are inspiring creativity and spreading love with their music. Animal explains, "I just want them to feel inspired to be themselves, because to me the world would be so much fun and interesting if people were creative and did their own thing."[52] Likewise, Paz Lenchantin sees creativity as a goal. Fans send her their music and comment on being inspired and pushed by her music "to keep being creative."[53]

Connection to the past is important to many artists. To touch people emotionally is Brenda Lee's purpose. She says, "You know, they'll always remember what they were doing at the point that that song made a difference in their life."[54] Similarly, Wanda Jackson hopes her music helps her fans remember an earlier time as "the best era to have lived." She explains that she wants to "take them back to a time that most of them didn't live in but they know a lot about through movies and pictures and songs . . . and documentaries, that takes them back to a more innocent time in America."[55]

Giving their fans strength and courage, Janis Ian and Carey Colvin often articulate what their fans cannot say. Janis laughs as she says her music "maybe reminds them of things that they may have tried to forget" and "allows them to feel like there's someone who gives voice to what they can't say."[56] Carey wants listeners to say, "Hey, I've felt that! I get what she's saying here because I've lived this."[57] Healing is a large part of Lynn Frances Anderson's purpose: "I hope that there's someone out there who says 'Thank you for writing that song. It has helped me.'"[58] Likewise, Emily White's goal is to make her fans think. She hopes her music "offers them some sort of solace, truth, and understanding."[59] Rose Polenzani wants to convey a sense of hope, especially to "people who feel tormented."[60]

A number of informants commented that the performance itself was central to their music. As Rana Ross mentioned, the desire to make a lasting impression on an audience, to elicit the "Wow! Who is that chick?" response, can be a strong motivator. [61] Kate Schellenbach's music is pure entertainment: singing along, dancing, and having fun, "pretty simple" and "nothing too deep."[62] Mary Wilson hopes The Supremes were about more than music. "I hope that our legacy is one of grace and talent and shows that women are not only beautiful but talented and inspirational."[63]

Being a role model is crucial to some of the women we interviewed. For Melissa Auf der Maur, "if I can be a role model to young women who are trying to be honest, strong, brave, and independent, that would be, it's like as simple as it gets, I think."[64] While most of her music appeals more to young and middle adults, Robin Renée says she has been thinking about "wanting to reach a younger audience, and I would like to be what Jackson Brown was for me when I was growing up, . . . you know like when you hear something for the first time and it really affects you? I want to be that, and I would like to be that for all people." She adds, "I also would like to be a little fun."[65]

The importance of connecting with fans was also a common theme for many of our informants. While Emily Saliers told us that she is "not a very goal-oriented person," making music for her is about sharing. She says in playing for fans, "You get that swirling, reciprocal experience that's impossible to articulate, and that's making music." Amy Ray shares that sense of communing; "the idea of something that is really communicating and that's not selfish" is crucial for her.[66] Similarly, Leah Hinchcliff says, "Performing live, first of all you have all the people there who are responding to you, and you get this energy cycle going back and forth."[67]

Speaking of energy cycles, we end, for now, our journey through the capacious and astonishing hearts and minds of women in rock with one more woman-to-woman innovation: the Indiegrrl network (indiegrrl.com), founded in 1998 by Holly Figueroa, a singer-songwriter, mom, and cyber-mentor to more than a thousand members and lurkers who draw inspiration and assistance from each other through the indiegrrl mailing list. (Several of our artists are on the list, and we thank them here for their generosity in responding to us and telling their stories.)

Indiegrrls log on with celebrations, concerns, touring tips, and recording questions. One of the biggest favors they do each other is "vetting" promoters—people who promise the world and all its wonders to aspiring professionals. Is he on the up-and-up? Will he exploit us? Does he pledge more than anybody can deliver? The "grrls" also share contacts for gigs and stories about venues, good ones, bad ones. They recommend indestructible travel cases for guitars, and trade stories about the airlines: which allow guitars onboard, which hassle the touring artist. Musicians being who they are, Figueroa has had to limit gig postings to Fridays or the list would be inundated with the members' professional need to self-promote and network in far-flung places. (Yes, this is about ego, but we hope we have told this story well enough so that the reader understands that without healthy egos, women musicians would have continued to be those rare gender-constrained creatures of yore.) Indiegrrls meet in the flesh, too, sharing stages and living-room couches. Performing members are admitted to that coveted status by submitting a demo tape or CD to a panel that meets once a month and judges submissions—not evaluating press kit goodies, but the music itself. As a performing member, the Indiegrrl can, and indeed is expected to, make music happen for others as well as herself, join tours, promote events, and mentor other performers. "The cause, of course, is to ensure that musicians of both genders play on a level field," the Web site enjoins.[68]

The no-nonsense spirit of Indiegrrl.com captures the heart of women's rock today. To level the playing field—that is what women in rock want most. They do not want to be better than men, except in the sense that Bonnie Raitt wanted to be the best blues player around. They do not want to get rid of men, except the ones who are truly obnoxious. They are tired of being girls first and musicians second. They are tired of being "women in rock." They just want to make music. And they believe, with good reason, that they have already proven everything they need to prove.

Girls rock.

NOTES

Preface

1. *Cleveland Scene,* August 21, 2002; reproduced at *Scene,* http://www .clevescene.com/issues/2002-08-21/music.html/1/index.html.

2. Lucy O'Brien, *She Bop II: The Definitive History of Women in Rock, Pop and Soul* (London: Continuum, 2002), 1.

3. Gerri Hirshey, *We Gotta Get Out of This Place: The True, Tough Story of Women in Rock* (New York: Atlantic Monthly Press, 2001), 15.

Chapter 1

The White epigraph to this chapter is drawn from an email interview, May 7, 2002. The Carpenter epigraph is drawn from "Girls with Guitars," words and music by Mary Chapin Carpenter. Used by permission.

1. Wanda Jackson, telephone interview, September 18, 2001.

2. For an excellent documentary film on women in rockabilly, see *Welcome to the Club—The Women of Rockabilly,* producer Beth Harrington, 2002. For more information on the film and the women of rockabilly, see www.pbs.org/itvs/ welcometotheclub/. For more on rockabilly, see Craig Morrison, *Go Cat Go! Rockabilly Music and its Makers,* reissue ed. (Urbana: University of Illinois Press, 1999); Randy McNutt, *We Wanna Boogie: An Illustrated History of the American Rockabilly Movement* (np: Hamilton Hobby Press Books, 1988).

3. For more on women in the 1950s, see Georgeanne Scheiner, "Look at Me, I'm Sandra Dee," *Frontiers: A Journal of Women's Studies* 22 (2001): 87–106; Brett Harvey, *The Fifties: A Women's Oral History* (New York: HarperCollins, 1993); Benita Eisler, *Private Lives: Men and Women of the Fifties* (London: Franklin Watts, Inc., 1986); Eugenia Kaledin, *Mothers and More: American Women in the 1950s* (Boston: Twayne, 1984).

4. www.rockabillyhall.com/WandaJackson.html (cited March 27, 2003).

5. Mike Walsh, "Nitroglycerine!!!!! The Rock & Roll Eruption of Wanda Jackson," http://www.missioncreep.com/mw/jackson.html (cited March 27, 2003).

6. Mary Ann Clawson, "Masculinity and Skill Acquisition in the Adolescent

Rock Band," *Popular Music* 18 (January 1999): 99–115; Elizabeth L. Wollman, "Men, Music, and Marketing at Q 104.3 (WAXQ-FM New York)," *Popular Music & Society* 22 (Winter 1998): 1–23.

7. For more, see Bebe Buell with Victor Bockris, *Rebel Heart: An American Rock 'n' Roll Journey* (New York: St. Martin's, 2001); Lisa A. Lewis, *The Adoring Audience* (London: Routledge, 1992); Pamela Des Barres, *I'm With the Band: Confessions of a Groupie* (Beech Tree Books, 1987); Victoria Balfour, *Rock Wives: The Hard Lives and Good Times of the Wives, Girlfriends, and Groupies of Rock and Roll,* reprint ed. (New York: William Morrow & Company, 1987).

8. Quoted in Katherine Dunn and Peggy Sirota, "Courtney Love," *Rolling Stone* 773 (November 13, 1997): 164–166.

9. Mavis Bayton, "Women and the Electric Guitar," in *Sexing the Groove: Popular Music and Gender,* ed. Sheila Whiteley (London: Routledge, 1997). For an in-depth exploration of cultural norms of femininity, see Susan Brownmiller, *Femininity* (New York: Fawcett Columbine, 1984).

10. Rana Ross, interview, Los Angeles, August 29, 2001.

11. Philip Blumstein, "The Production of Selves in Personal Relationships," in *The Self-Society Dynamic: Cognition, Emotion, and Action,* ed. J. A. Howard and P. L. Callero (New York: Cambridge University Press, 1991), 305–322.

12. Judith A. Howard and Ramira M. Alamilla, "Gender and Identity," in *Gender Mosaics: Social Perspectives,* ed. Dana Vannoy (Los Angeles: Roxbury, 2001), 61.

13. Candace West and Don Zimmerman, "Doing Gender," *Gender and Society* 1 (1987): 125–151.

14. Susan A. O'Neill, Antonia Ivaldi, and Claire Fox, "Gendered Discourses in Musically 'Talented' Adolescent Females' Construction of Self," *Feminism & Psychology* 12 (May 2002): 153–159.

15. Lalo, email interview, December 8, 2002.

16. Leah Hinchcliff, interview, Portland, Oregon, August 23, 2001.

17. Quoted in Evelyn McDonnell and Cathrine Wessel, "Joan Jett," *Rolling Stone* 773 (November 13, 1997): 147.

18. Quoted in Jim Bessman, "Jett Enlists Riot Grrrls for Blackhearts' Warner Debut," *Billboard* 106 (May 7, 1994): 14–15.

19. Paz Lenchantin, interview, New York City, September 7, 2001.

20. Bitch and Animal, interview, New York City, September 6, 2001.

21. Scarlet Rivera, telephone interview, July 31, 2001.

22. Carey Colvin, email interview, September 27, 2001.

23. Lynn Frances Anderson, interview, Corvallis, Oregon, May 2001.

24. Lynn Ann Witting, email interview, August 17, 2001.

25. Madeline Puckett, interview, Corvallis, Oregon, July 24, 2001.

26. Kate Campbell, interview, Minneapolis, October 4, 2002.

27. Carol Kaye, interview, Los Angeles, August 27, 2001.

28. Quoted in Gillian Gaar, *She's a Rebel: The History of Women in Rock & Roll* (Seattle: Seal Press, 1992), 222.

29. Michelle Malone, telephone interview, August 19, 2002.

30. Gaar, *She's a Rebel,* 190–191.

31. Richard Stengel, "Singing for Herself," *Time* (March 12, 1990).

32. Indigo Girls, interview, Vienna, Virginia, August 7, 2001.

33. Leah Hinchcliff, interview, Portland, Oregon, August 23, 2001.

34. Amy Emerman, email interview, December 4, 2002.

35. Wendy Profit, email interview, December 5, 2002.

36. Jann Arden, telephone interview, September 18, 2002.

37. Michelle Malone, telephone interview, August 19, 2002.

38. Quoted in Rich Cohen, "Melissa Etheridge," *Rolling Stone* 698–699 (December 29, 1994): 110–115.

39. Quoted in Jancee Dunn and Peggy Sirota, "Melissa Etheridge Takes the Long Hard Road from the Heartland to Hollywood," *Rolling Stone* 709 (June 1, 1995): 38–43.

40. Quoted in Timothy White, "A Portrait of the Artist," *Billboard* 111, 49 (December 4, 1999): 14–17.

41. Ellen Rosner, interview, Chicago, August 18, 2001.

42. Quoted in Susan Hopkins, "Hole Lotta Attitude: Courtney Love and Guitar Feminism," *Social Alternatives* 18, 2 (April 1999): 11–14.

43. Janis Ian, "Of Guitars and Righteous Men," available at www.janisian.com (articles) (cited March 5, 2003).

44. Tom and Mary Anne Evans, *Guitars: Music, History, Construction, and Players from the Renaissance to Rock* (New York: Facts on File, 1977).

45. Ibid., 286–289.

46. Marcus Charles Tribbett, " 'Everybody wants to buy my kitty': Resistance and the articulation of the subject in the blues of Memphis Minnie," *Arkansas Review* 29, 1 (April 1998): 42ff.

47. Evans and Evans, *Guitars,* 314–315; Mark Zwonitzer, *Will You Miss Me When I'm Gone? The Carter Family and Their Legacy in American Music* (New York: Simon & Schuster, 2002).

48. For more on the history of the guitar, see Walter Carter, *Gibson Guitars: 100 Years of an American Icon* (Miami: Warner Brothers, 2003); James Tyler, *The Guitar and Its Music: From the Renaissance to the Classical Era* (Oxford: Oxford University Press, 2002); John Morrish, ed., *The Classical Guitar: A Complete History* (San Francisco: Backbeat Books, 2002); Tony Bacon, *History of the American Guitar* (New York: Friedman/Fairfax, 2001); Steve Waksman, *Instruments of Desire: The Electric Guitar and the Shaping of Musical Experience* (Cambridge: Harvard University Press, 1999).

49. Quoted in Thom Geier, "Girls with Guitars that Fit Just Right," *U.S. News & World Report* 122, 9 (March 10, 1997): 65.

50. "Kristin Hersh," in *Grrrls: Viva Rock Divas,* ed. Amy Raphael (New York: St. Martin's Griffin, 1995), 206.

51. Janis Ian, "Of Guitars and Righteous Men," available at www.janisian.com (articles) (cited March 5, 2003).

52. Erin O'Hara, interview, New York City, September 8, 2001.

53. Leah Hinchcliff, interview, Portland, Oregon, August 23, 2001.

54. Rana Ross, interview, Los Angeles, August 29, 2001.

55. Rose Polenzani, interview, Chicago, August 17, 2001.

56. Kate Schellenbach, interview, Los Angeles, August 29, 2001.

57. Lynn Witting, email interview, August 17, 2001.

58. Jill Gewirtz, email interview, July 29, 2001.

59. Melissa Auf der Maur, telephone interview, August 13, 2001.

60. For more on girls and family, see Mary Collins, *The Essential Daughter: Changing Expectations for Girls at Home, 1797 to Present* (Westport, CT: Praeger, 2002); Miriam Forman-Brunell, ed., *Girlhood in America: An Encyclopedia* (Santa Barbara, CA: ABC-CLIO, 2001).

61. Wanda Jackson, telephone interview, September 18, 2001.

62. Brenda Lee, telephone interview, July 19, 2002.

63. Carol Kaye, interview, Los Angeles, August 27, 2001.

64. Kitzie Pippin Stern, interview, Corvallis, Oregon, July 24, 2001.

65. Indigo Girls, interview, Vienna, Virginia, August 7, 2001.

66. Michelle Malone, telephone interview, August 19, 2002.

67. Kate Schellenbach, interview, Los Angeles, August 29, 2001.

68. Mary Wilson, telephone interview, October 16, 2001.

69. Rana Ross, interview, Los Angeles, August 29, 2001.

70. Melissa Auf der Maur, telephone interview, August 13, 2001.

71. Kitzie Pippin Stern, interview, Corvallis, Oregon, July 24, 2001.

72. Quoted in Gaar, *She's a Rebel,* 222.

73. Quoted in ibid., 222–223.

74. Jean Millington, telephone interview, October 16, 2001.

75. Ibid.

76. Jeff Hopkins, "Signs of Masculinism in an 'Uneasy' Place: Advertising for 'Big Brother,' " *Gender, Place and Culture* 7 (2000): 31–55; Anna Mehta and Liz Bondi, "Embodied Discourse: On Gender and Fear of Violence," *Gender, Place and Culture* 6 (1999): 67–84. Joel Sanders, "Introduction," in *Architectures of Masculinity,* ed. Joel Sanders (Princeton, NJ: Princeton University Press, 1996), 11–25; Peter Jackson, "The Cultural Politics of Masculinity: Towards a Social Geography," *Transactions of the Institute of British Geographers* 16 (1991): 199–213.

77. Michael S. Kimmel, *Manhood in America: A Cultural History* (New York: Free Press, 1996); Brownmiller, *Femininity.*

78. Erin O'Hara, interview, New York City, September 8, 2001.

79. Bitch and Animal, interview, New York City, September 6, 2001.

80. Carla DeSantis, Keynote Address, Rock and Roll Camp for Girls, Portland, Oregon, August 20, 2001.

81. Kristen Day, "Constructing Masculinity and Women's Fear in Public Space in Irvine, California," *Gender, Place and Culture* 8 (2001): 109–137; Leslie K. Weisman, *Discrimination by Design: A Feminist Critique of the Man-Made Environ-*

ment (Chicago: University of Illinois Press, 1992); Karen A. Franck and Lynn Paxson, "Women and Urban Public Spaces," in *Public Places and Spaces,* ed. Irwin Altman and Ervin Zube (New York: Plenum, 1989), 121–146.

82. Jill Sobule, telephone interview, July 17, 2002.

83. Emily White, email interview, May 7, 2002.

84. Quoted in Jill Hamilton and Mary Ellen Mark, "Ani DiFranco," *Rolling Stone* 773 (November 13, 1997): 150–151.

85. Kate Schellenbach, quoted in Mim Udovitch, "Mothers of Invention: Women In Rock Talk about Scents, Sensibility, and Sexism," *Rolling Stone* 692 (October 6, 1994): 49–54.

86. Beth Rippey, telephone interview, March 28, 2003.

87. Bitch and Animal, interview, New York City, September 6, 2001.

Chapter 2

The Mary Wilson epigraph to this chapter is drawn from a telephone interview, October 16, 2001.

1. Mary Wilson, telephone interview, October 16, 2001.

2. Shirley Alston Reeves, interview, Brevard, North Carolina, August 10, 2001; John Clemente, *Girl Groups: Fabulous Females That Rocked the World* (Iola, WI: Krause Publications, 2000), 200–205. Also see Gaar, *She's a Rebel,* 35–37.

3. Shirley Alston Reeves, interview, Brevard, North Carolina, August 10, 2001.

4. Ibid.

5. Martha Reeves, telephone interview, October 5, 2001.

6. Sarah Dash, telephone interview, October 14, 2002.

7. Quoted in Gerri Hirshey, *Nowhere to Run: The Story of Soul Music* (New York: Times Books, 1984), 144.

8. James Miller, *Flowers in the Dustbin: The Rise of Rock and Roll, 1947–1977* (New York: Simon & Schuster, 1999), 34–39, 57–67.

9. On the partnership of Goffin and King, see among others Roberta Burkely, "Carole King," in *Trouble Girls: The Rolling Stone Book of Women in Rock,* ed. Barbara O'Dair (New York: Rolling Stone Press, 1997), 83–86.

10. For a concise history of the male doo-wop phenomenon, see Paul Friedlander, *Rock and Roll: A Social History* (Boulder, CO: Westview Press, 1996), 63–68.

11. Mary Wilson, *Dreamgirl: My Life as a Supreme* (New York: St. Martin's Press, 1986), 27.

12. Ibid., 40.

13. "Jambalaya" had been recorded by Brenda Lee at the age of eleven in 1956.

14. Ronnie Spector, *Be My Baby: How I Survived Mascara, Miniskirts, and Madness, or My Life as a Fabulous Ronette* (New York: Harmony Books, 1990), 4–5.

15. Gospel emerged in the 1920s and 1930s as an emotionalist child of the spirituals of the nineteenth century. "In storefront Baptist churches, to the rhythm of handclapping, foot-stamping, rattling tambourines, and a thumping, tinny up-

right piano, black people sought to escape the deprivations of the lean years and find solace in the embrace of Jesus and the Lord, and to hope for a brighter future," writes Arnold Shaw, *Black Popular Music in America: From the Spirituals, Minstrels, and Ragtime to Soul, Disco, and Hip-Hop* (New York: Schirmer Books, 1986), 210.

Has there been a difference between white and black communities in terms of the salience of church music in youth musical training? Across the North American Protestant experience, the heritage of the Reformation cast a damping shadow, though there are now few churches that actually prohibit the use of music in services. The rising "Christian music" phenomenon, pop- and rock-inflected inspirational music prominent in fundamentalist and evangelical sects and denominations, has probably increased young white churchgoers' involvement in amateur music just as the schools have dropped the ball in recent decades.

16. Martha Reeves, telephone interview, October 5, 2001.

17. Sarah Dash, telephone interview, October 14, 2002.

18. Portia K. Maultsby, "The Impact of Gospel Music on the Secular Music Industry," in *Signifyin(g), Sanctifyin', and Slam Dunking: A Reader in African American Expressive Culture*, ed. Gena Dagel Caponi (Amherst: University of Massachusetts Press, 1999), 176–177.

19. Lucy O'Brien, *She Bop: The Definitive History of Women in Rock, Pop, and Soul* (New York: Penguin, 1995), 84.

20. Alan Young, *Woke Me Up This Morning: Black Gospel Singers and the Gospel Life* (Jackson: University Press of Mississippi, 1997), 107–109.

21. Horace Clarence Boyer, "Foreword," in Willa Ward-Royster and Toni Rose, *How I Got Over: Clara Ward and the World-Famous Ward Singers* (Philadelphia: Temple University Press, 1997), viii–ix.

22. Clara Ward, "How a Visit to the Holy Land Changed My Life," *Color* (May 1956): 16.

23. For more information on Mahalia Jackson, see Jules Schwerin, *Got To Tell It: Mahalia Jackson, Queen of Gospel* (New York: Oxford University Press, 1992).

24. Quoted in Hettie Jones, *Big Star Fallin' Mama: Five Women in Black Music* (New York: Viking, 1974), 80.

25. Quoted in O'Brien, *She Bop,* 84.

26. Jones, *Big Star Fallin' Mama,* 122–123.

27. Quoted in Gaar, *She's a Rebel,* 87.

28. Mary Wilson, telephone interview, October 16, 2001.

29. Martha Reeves, telephone interview, October 5, 2001.

30. Shirley Alston Reeves, interview, Brevard, North Carolina, August 10, 2001.

31. Mary Wilson, telephone interview, October 16, 2001.

32. Spector, *Be My Baby,* 16.

33. Hirshey, *Nowhere to Run,* 140.

34. Ibid., 142.

35. Gerald Posner offers a well-researched look behind the Motown curtains in *Motown: Music, Money, Sex, and Power* (New York: Random House, 2002). Espe-

cially interesting in this context is Posner's discussion of Gordy's management decisions in the chapter "Color-Blind," 167–171.

36. Among other sources, O'Brien, *She Bop,* 78; Wilson, *Dreamgirl,* 63–67.

37. Wilson, *Dreamgirl,* 69.

38. Mary Wilson, *Supreme Faith: Someday We'll Be Together* (New York: Harper Collins, 1990).

39. Quoted in Hirshey, *We Gotta Get Out of This Place,* 51.

40. Wilson, *Dreamgirl,* 181.

41. Quoted in O'Brien, *She Bop,* 77.

42. Quoted in Hirshey, *Nowhere to Run,* 151.

43. Quoted in O'Brien, *She Bop,* 77.

44. O'Brien, *She Bop,* 79.

45. On the tensions within the Supremes and between Gordy and the two-thirds of the group that were not Diana Ross, see Posner, *Motown,* 138–149, 187–193.

46. Angela Davis, *Blues Legacies and Black Feminism* (New York: Vintage, 1998), 3–11.

47. Quoted in Hirshey, *Nowhere to Run,* 170.

48. Brenda Lee, telephone interview, July 19, 2002.

49. Gaar, *She's a Rebel,* 23.

50. Judith Butler, *Gender Trouble: Feminism and the Subversion of Identity* (New York: Routledge, 1990), 136.

51. "Feminism, Marxism, and the State," in *Feminism and Sexuality: A Reader,* eds. Stevi Jackson and Sue Scott (New York: Columbia University Press, 1996), 182–190.

52. Kate Campbell, interview, Minneapolis, October 4, 2002.

53. June Millington, interview, Guerneville, California, September 22, 2001.

54. Jean Millington, telephone interview, October 16, 2001.

55. McDonnell and Wessel, "Joan Jett," 147.

56. *Dreamworlds II,* dir. Sut Jhally (Northampton, MA: Media Education Foundation, 1995).

57. Indigo Girls, interview, Vienna, Virginia, August 7, 2001.

58. Kate Schellenbach, interview, Los Angeles, August 29, 2001.

59. Melissa Auf der Maur, telephone interview, August 13, 2001.

60. Rana Ross, interview, Los Angeles, August 29, 2001. Ross died in May 2003 of a chronic liver disease. In the last months of her life, she devoted what energy she could to working on a solo album that was near and dear to her heart.

61. See, for example, Adrienne Rich, "Compulsory Heterosexuality and Lesbian Existence," in *Blood, Bread and Poetry* (London: Virago, 1978), 23–75; Monique Wittig, *Feminist Issues* (London: Harvester Wheatsheaf, 1992); Cheryl Clarke, "Lesbianism: An Act of Resistance," in *This Bridge Called My Back,* 2nd ed., eds. Cherie Moraga and Gloria Anzaldúa (New York: Kitchen Table: Women of Color Press, 1981), 128–137.

62. Janis Ian, telephone interview, September 24, 2002.

63. "It's Alright." Words and music by Emily Saliers. Used by permission.

64. Luce Irigaray, *This Sex Which Is Not One*, trans. Catherine Porter with Carolyn Burke (Ithaca, NY: Cornell University Press, 1985), 76.

65. Ibid. Similarly, feminist theorist Judith Butler suggests "parody" as a practice to undermine gendered practices that are assumed to be natural and invisible. *Gender Trouble*, 142–149.

66. Sheila Whiteley, *Women and Popular Music: Sexuality, Identity and Subjectivity* (London: Routledge, 2000), 164.

67. O'Brien, *She Bop*, 63.

68. Gaar, *She's a Rebel*, 59.

69. O'Brien, *She Bop*, 64.

70. Robin Renée, interview, Asheville, North Carolina, November 13, 2001.

71. Quoted in Ria Roncales Goodwin, interview with Magdalen Hsu-li, *The Asian Reporter* (May 1999) on http://www.magdalenhsuli.com/interviews/int7.shtml.

72. Michael Eric Dyson, *Reflecting Black: African-American Cultural Criticism* (Minneapolis: University of Minnesota Press, 1993), 3.

73. Tricia Rose, *Black Noise: Rap Music and Black Culture in Contemporary America* (Hanover, NH: Wesleyan University Press, 1994), 2.

74. For example, see popular press articles: Brent Staples, "How Long Can Rap Survive?" *New York Times*, September 22, 1996; Richard S. Dunham and Michael Oneal, "Gunning for the Gangstas," *Business Week* 3429 (June 19, 1995): 41; Yelena Dynnikova, "Women are Under a Rap Attack," *Harvard Educational Review* 65, 2 (Summer 1995): 271–273; "Women and 'Gangsta' Rap," editorial, *Glamour* 92, 6 (June 1994): 93; Nathan McCall, "My Rap Against Rap," *Reader's Digest* 44, 865 (May 1994): 63–66; Donald M. Suggs, "Gangsta Rap—a Wake-up Call," *Crisis* 101, 2 (Feb/Mar 1994): 3; J. Leo, "Polluting Our Popular Culture," *U.S. News & World Report* 109, 1 (July 2, 1990): 15.

75. For more on the origins and meanings of rap, see Cheryl L. Keyes, "The Meaning of Rap Music in Contemporary Black Culture," in *The Triumph of the Soul: Cultural and Psychological Aspects of African American Music*, ed. Ferdinand Jones and Arthur C. Jones (Westport, CT: Praeger, 2001), 153–179. For an examination of rap's transformation and commodification within the music industry, see Adam Krims, *Rap Music and the Poetics of Identity* (Cambridge: Cambridge University Press, 2000).

76. Marla L. Shelton, "Can't Touch This! Representations of the African American Female Body in Urban Rap Videos," *Popular Music and Society* 21 (Fall 1997): 107–116.

77. Patricia Hill Collins, *Black Feminist Thought: Knowledge, Consciousness and the Politics of Empowerment* (Boston: Unwin, 1990), 28–29. See also Murray Forman, " 'Movin' Closer to an Independent Funk': Black Feminist Theory, Standpoint, and Women in Rap," *Women's Studies* 23 (1994): 35–55.

78. J. R. Reynolds, "Women Rap for Dignity," *Billboard* 106 (March 26, 1994): 5–6.

For more, see Terry Gross's interview with Queen Latifah, National Public Radio, *Fresh Air,* WHYY-FM, Philadelphia, January 10, 2003. Original interview recorded in 1999.

79. Rose, *Black Noise*, 147.

80. Quoted in J. R. Reynolds, "Women Rap for Dignity," 5–6.

81. Quoted in ibid.

82. For more analysis of women in rap, see Robin Roberts, "Sisters in the Name of Rap: Rapping for Women's Lives," in *Black Women in America,* ed. Kim Marie Vaz (Thousand Oaks, CA: Sage, 1995), 323–333.

83. Quoted in Joy Bennett Kinnon, "Sisters of Rap," *Ebony* (November 1999): 92–94.

84. Quoted in Gerri Hirshey, "Rhymes & Misdemeanors," *Rolling Stone* 816/817 (July 8/22, 1999): 55–58.

85. Quoted in *Ebony* (November 1999): 107.

86. "The Bad Girls of Hip-Hop," *Essence* 27 (March 1997): 76–78.

87. Brenda Lee, telephone interview, July 19, 2002.

88. Ibid.

Chapter 3

The Joni Mitchell epigraph to this chapter is drawn from Alice Echols, *Shaky Ground: The Sixties and Its Aftershocks* (New York: Columbia University Press, 2002).

1. David Wild, "Joni Mitchell," *Rolling Stone* (October 10, 2002); also recounted by Alice Echols, *Shaky Ground,* 219; she quotes Dylan at greater length.

2. Echols, *Shaky Ground,* 219.

3. Carolyn Keating, " 'chelle Shocked," *Women Who Rock,* 2, 2 (Summer 2002): 31.

4. Keating, *Women Who Rock,* 31; see also www.michelleshocked.com for biographical information.

5. Pirkko Moisala and Beverley Diamond, "Introduction," *Music and Gender* (Chicago: University of Illinois Press, 2000), 9.

6. Quoted in David Fricke, "Patti Smith," *Rolling Stone* 738–739 (July 11, 1996–July 25, 1996): 43–50.

7. Roger Deitz, "Female Folk Artists Fight Pigeonholing," *Billboard* 107 (November 11, 1995): 13–14. See also Susan McClary, "Women and Music on the Verge of the New Millenium," *Signs: Journal of Women in Culture and Society* 25 (2000): 1283–1286.

8. D. DiPrimi and L. Kennedy, "Beat the Rap," *Mother Jones* 15 (September/October 1990): 32–39.

9. Quoted in Timothy White, "Morissette's New 17-Cut Set is All It's 'Supposed' to Be," *Billboard* 110 (October 3, 1998): 1–4.

10. bell hooks defines feminism as "the struggle to end sexist oppression." *Feminist Theory: From Margin to Center* (Cambridge, MA: South End Press, 1984);

see also her *Feminism is for Everybody: Passionate Politics* (Cambridge, MA: South End Press, 2000). On the discrepancy between feminist identity and acknowledgment of feminist issues, see Rachel Williams and Michele Andrisin Wittig, " 'I'm not a feminist, but . . .': Factors contributing to the discrepancy between pro-feminist orientation and feminist social identity," *Sex Roles* 37 (1997): 885–904; Susan J. Douglas, "I'm Not a Feminist, But . . . ," in *Where the Girls Are: Growing Up Female with the Mass Media* (New York: Times Books, 1995); Susan Faludi, "I'm Not a Feminist But I Play One on TV," *Ms.* 5 (March/April 1995): 30–39. Gail B. Griffin, "Orphans of the Storm: The F-Word and the Post-Feminist Generation," *Calling: Essays in Teaching in the Mother Tongue* (Pasadena, CA: Triology, 1992). For an excellent work on young women's relationship to feminism, see Jennifer Baumgardner and Amy Richards, *Manifesta: Young Women, Feminism, and the Future* (New York: Farrar, Straus, & Giroux, 2000).

11. "(R)evolution Now," in *Sexing the Groove: Popular Music and Gender,* ed. Sheila Whiteley (London: Routledge, 1997), 61–62.

12. Quoted in Laura Jamison and Sheila Metzner, "Me'Shell Ndegeocello," *Rolling Stone* 773 (November 13, 1997): 161.

13. Quoted in Shirley Liu, "Basking in the Indiglow," *Curve* 8 (March 1998): 20–21, 31.

14. Mary Wilson, telephone interview, October 16, 2001.

15. Quoted in Katherine Dieckman and Mary Ellen Mark, "Etta James," *Rolling Stone* 773 (November 13, 1997): 152–153.

16. Quoted in Laura Jamison and Dana Lixenberg, "Ruth Brown," *Rolling Stone* 773 (November 13, 1997): 103.

17. Quoted in Dunn and Sirota, "Courtney Love," 164–166.

18. Quoted in Elysa Gardner and Peggy Sirota, "Bonnie Raitt," *Rolling Stone* 773 (November 13, 1997): 157.

19. Quoted in Ann Cvetkovich and Gretchen Phillips, "Revenge of the Girl Bands," *Nation* 271 (July 10, 2000): 16–17. See also Hillary Frey, "Kathleen Hanna's Fire," *Nation* 276 (January 13, 2003): 27–28.

20. See the classics in this area: Mary Belenky, Blythe Clinchy, Nancy Golderberger, and Jill Tarule, *Women's Ways of Knowing: The Development of Self, Voice, and Mind* (New York: Basic Books, 1997); Carol Gilligan, *In a Different Voice: Psychological Theory and Women's Development* (Cambridge: Harvard University Press, 1983); Mary Bray Pipher, *Reviving Ophelia: Saving the Selves of Adolescent Girls* (New York: Ballantine Books, 1995).

21. Ferron, telephone interview, July 10, 2002. For biographical details, see also Laura Post, AMG Biography of Ferron, www.allmusic.com.

22. Ferron, telephone interview, July 10, 2002.

23. Toure, "The power and the passion," *Rolling Stone* 685 (June 30, 1994): 66.

24. Udovitch, "Mothers of Invention," 49.

25. One source that discusses "Me and a Gun" is Simon Reynolds and Joy

Press, *The Sex Revolts: Gender, Rebellion, and Rock 'n' Roll* (Cambridge: Harvard University Press, 1995), 266–269.

26. Karen Ocamb, "Melissa Etheridge Sheds Her Skin," *Lesbian News* 26, 12 (July 2001): 30ff.

27. Jonatha Brooke, in *Solo: Women Singer-Songwriters in Their Own Words,* ed. Marc Woodworth (New York: Delta Trade Paperbacks, 1998), 45.

28. Ibid., 47–48.

29. Jonatha Brooke, interview, Portland, Oregon, September 2002.

30. June Millington, interview, Guerneville, California, September 22, 2001.

31. Jonatha Brooke, interview, Portland, Oregon, September 2002.

32. Leah Hinchcliff, interview, Portland, Oregon, August 23, 2001.

33. Scarlet Rivera, telephone interview, July 31, 2001.

34. Indigo Girls, interview, Vienna, Virginia, August 7, 2001.

35. Bitch and Animal, interview, New York City, September 6, 2001.

36. Indigo Girls, interview, Vienna, Virginia, August 7, 2001.

37. Kate Campbell, interview, Minneapolis, October 4, 2002.

38. Shortly after self-publishing her first CD, Kate spent two years as a songwriter for Fame Music in Muscle Shoals, Alabama. She was playing at a coffee shop in Huntsville, Alabama, when a man approached her and said he knew the folks at Fame, and he would like to take them Kate's CD, *Songs from the Levee*. Kate says at first she figured he was just trying to get a free CD, but she gave it to him anyway. A couple of weeks later, she got phone calls from Walt Aldridge and Rick Hall inviting her to come to Muscle Shoals and talk. She spent a full day in Hall's gold-record-covered office and ended up signing a publishing deal with Fame. She says she was the first woman songwriter the studio had signed in seven or eight years. She says that in her two years with Fame, she learned more about songwriting and recording than she ever would have dreamed. She continues to build on the relationships she established there. Kate Campbell, interview, Minneapolis, October 4, 2002.

39. In the context of popular music, to "cover" a song means to perform a song written by someone else.

40. Paul Zollo, *Songwriters on Songwriting* (Cincinnati: Writer's Digest Books, 1991), 41.

41. Susan Cheever, "Tori Amos," *Rolling Stone* 773 (November 13, 1997): 101.

42. Paul Zollo, "Riding on the Horses: Rickie Lee Jones," in *Songwriters on Songwriting* (Cincinnati: Writer's Digest Books, 1991), 134.

43. Jonatha Brooke, interview, Portland, Oregon, September 2002.

44. Mary Chapin Carpenter, in *Solo,* ed. Marc Woodworth, 130–131.

45. Lynn Ann Witting, email interview, August 17, 2001.

46. Campbell's inspiration for this song was Dennis Covington's account, *Salvation on Sand Mountain: Snake Handling and Redemption in Southern Appalachia* (New York: Penguin, 1996).

47. Holly Palmer, in *Solo,* ed. Marc Woodworth, 179–180.

48. For more on music and the Civil Rights Movement, see Kerran L. Sanger, *"When the Spirit Says Sing!": The Role of Freedom Songs in the Civil Rights Movement* (New York: Garland, 1995).

49. For more on music and social movements, see Rob Rosenthal, "Serving the Movement: The Role(s) of Music," *Popular Music & Society* 25 (Fall/Winter 2001): 11–24; Rob Eyerman and Andrew Jamison, *Music and Social Movements: Mobilizing Traditions in the Twentieth Century* (Cambridge: Cambridge University Press, 1998); Reebee Garofalo, ed., *Rockin' the Boat: Mass Music and Mass Movements* (Boston: South End, 1992); Robin Denselow, *When the Music's Over: The Story of Political Pop* (London: Faber and Faber, 1989); John Street, *Rebel Rock: The Politics of Popular Music* (Oxford: Basil Blackwell, 1986); R. Serge Denisoff, *Sing a Song of Social Significance,* 2nd ed., (Bowling Green, OH: Bowling Green State University Popular Press, 1983).

50. Ron Eyerman and Andrew Jamison, "Social Movements and Cultural Transformation: Popular Music in the 1960s," *Media, Culture & Society* 17 (1995): 449–468. For more on the folk revival, see Ronald D. Cohen, *Rainbow Quest: The Folk Music Revival and American Society, 1940–1970* (Amherst: University of Massachusetts Press, 2002).

51. Eyerman and Jamison, "Social Movements and Cultural Transformation," 458.

52. Charlie Gillett, *Sounds of the City* (London: Souvenir, 1970), 297.

53. Eyerman and Jamison, "Social Movements and Cultural Transformation," 459–460.

54. Shelly Romalis, *Pistol Packin' Mama: Aunt Molly Jackson and the Politics of Folksong* (Chicago: University of Illinois Press, 1998).

55. O'Brien, *She Bop,* 366.

56. "The Songwriter," www.peggyseeger.com (cited June 16, 2003).

57. Recorded on *An Odd Collection.*

58. "The Singer," www.peggyseeger.com (cited June 16, 2003).

59. Joan Baez, *And A Voice to Sing With: A Memoir* (New York: Summit, 1987), 117.

60. In 1939 Anderson was denied use of Constitution Hall because she was black.

61. For an excellent history of the women's movement, see Ruth Rosen, *The World Split Open: How the Modern Women's Movement Changed America* (New York: Penguin, 2001).

62. Quoted in O'Brien, *She Bop,* 248.

63. Quoted in Mike Ragogna, "Biography," CD booklet of *The Essential Helen Reddy Collection,* June 1998.

64. See Gloria T. Hull, Patricia Bell Scott, and Barbara Smith, eds., *All the Women are White, All the Blacks are Men, but Some of Us are Brave: Black Women's Studies* (Old Westbury, NY: Feminist Press, 1982). Patricia Hill Collins coined the term "matrix of domination" to describe the ways that various forms of oppression

interlock and shape one another in such a way that, for example, black women cannot separate their experiences of racism from their experiences of sexism. Rather, they experience their blackness and their femaleness as interrelated factors in a single identity. Collins, *Black Feminist Thought.*

65. Bernice Johnson Reagon, *If You Don't Go, Don't Hinder Me: The African American Sacred Song Tradition* (Lincoln: University of Nebraska Press, 2001), 100.

66. Bernice Johnson Reagon, " 'Let Your Light Shine'—Historical Notes," in *We Who Believe in Freedom: Sweet Honey in the Rock . . . Still on the Journey,* ed. Bernice Johnson Reagon (New York: Anchor, 1993), 38.

67. Ibid., 31.

68. For more on lesbian history, see Lillian Faderman, *To Believe in Women: What Lesbians Have Done for America—A History* (Boston: Houghton Mifflin, 1999); Diane Helene Miller, *Freedom to Differ: The Shaping of the Gay and Lesbian Struggle for Civil Rights* (New York: New York University Press, 1998); Arlene Stein, *Sex and Sensibility: Stories of a Lesbian Generation* (Berkeley: University of California Press, 1997); Neil Miller, *Out of the Past: Gay and Lesbian History from 1869 to the Present* (New York: Vintage Books, 1995).

69. For more about the intersections of black oppression and lesbian/gay oppression, see Johnetta B. Cole and Beverly Guy-Sheftall, *Gender Talk: The Struggle for Women's Equality in African American Communities* (New York: One World: Ballantine Books, 2003) and Keith Boykin, *One More River to Cross: Black and Gay in America* (New York: Anchor Books/Doubleday, 1996).

70. Quoted in Deitz, "Female Folk Artists Fight Pigeonholing," 13–14.

71. O'Brien, *She Bop II,* 191.

72. R. Givens, "Armatrading's Romantic Truth," *Newsweek,* 132, 11 (September 12, 1998): 72.

73. Quoted in Anthony De Curtis, "Tracy Chapman's Black and White World," *Rolling Stone* 529 (June 30, 1988): 44–46.

74. J. R. Reynolds, "Women Rap for Dignity," 1. This article also suggests, cannily, that artists like Chapman, Ben Harper, and Babyface in his acoustic/folk incarnation have had a difficult time finding an audience because marketers and radio do not know where to position them. Race and musical style are still linked, usually with a repressive effect.

75. Hirshey, *We Gotta Get Out of This Place,* 194.

76. Quoted in Michael Paoletta, "Premier Storyteller Tracy Chapman Spins New Tales on Elektra Set," *Billboard* 112 (February 12, 2000): 11.

77. For an analysis of Chapman's self-titled album, see Sheila Whiteley, "Talkin' 'Bout a Revolution: Tracy Chapman, Political Uprisings, Domestic Violence and Love," in Whitely, *Women and Popular Music,* 171–195.

78. Kate Campbell, interview, Minneapolis, October 4, 2002.

79. For more information, visit the Feminist Majority's Web site at feminist.org.

80. Jann Arden, telephone interview, September 18, 2002.

81. Indigo Girls, interview, Vienna, Virginia, August 7, 2001.

82. As Buffy Childerhose notes, this was the term Sarah McLachlan used initially to refer to her vision. *From Lilith to Lilith Fair: The Authorized Story* (New York: St. Martin's Griffin, 1998), 19. While Lollapalooza, the multi-artist music festival that began with a seventeen-city tour in 1991, was not completely male, it was decidedly male dominated.

83. Quoted in ibid., 18–19.

84. Find this and more statistics at www.lilithfair.com.

85. "Lilith Fair: Sarah McLachlan Live" found at http://surrender.e-vapor .net/live/lf.html (cited March 10, 2003).

86. Childerhose, *From Lilith to Lilith Fair,* 26–27.

87. Sarah Vowell, "Throwing Ovaries: The Second-Grade Sensibility of the Pseudo-Feminist Lilith Fair," *Salon* (July 11, 1997), found at http://www.salon.com/ july97/columnists/vowell970711.html (cited March 12, 2003).

88. Quoted in Childerhose, *From Lilith to Lilith Fair,* 113, 114.

89. Quoted in Donna Freydkin, "Lilith Fair: Lovely, Lively, and Long Overdue," Special to CNN Interactive, July 28, 1998, found at http://cgi.cnn.com/SHOW-BIZ/Music/9807/28/lilith.fair/ (cited March 12, 2003).

90. "Dissing" means "disrespecting"; Baumgardner and Richards, *Manifesta,* 63.

91. See Christopher John Farley et al., "Galapalooza," *Time* 150, 3 (July 21, 1997): 60–64.

92. O'Brien, *She Bop II,* 472.

93. Vowell, "Throwing Ovaries."

94. Quoted in Childerhose, *From Lilith to Lilith Fair,* 71.

95. J. M. Smith, "Parents' Alert: Secrets of the Lilith Fair," *National Liberty Journal* (June 1999), found at http://www.liberty.edu/chancellor/nlj/June1999/ lilith.htm (cited March 10, 2003).

96. Ann Powers, "Girl Power Takes on Rock's Challenges," *New York Times,* August 9, 1999, section E.

97. "Lilith Fair Performers, Attendees Achieve Largest-Ever Synchronized Ovulation," *The Onion* 43, 4 (August 27, 1998), found at http://www.theonion.com/ onion3404/lilithfair.html (cited March 10, 2003).

98. Karen Thompson, "The Beauty of Bitter," *Lesbian News* 24, 12 (July 1999): 22.

99. Various media reported this after a panel discussion by some of the artists before the 1998 tour. See Daniel Frankel, "Lilith Shows Off Real Girl Power," *E! Online* (April 17, 1998), found at http://movies.eonline.com/News/Items/ 0%2C1%2C2866%2C00.html.

100. Quoted in Freydkin, "Lilith Fair."

101. See Lorraine Ali, "Backstage at Lilith," *Rolling Stone* 768 (September 4, 1997): 23–33.

102. Childerhose, *From Lilith to Lilith Fair,* 67.

103. O'Brien, *She Bop II*, 472.

104. Michelle Goldberg, "The Lilith Fair Quiet Grrrls: Lilith Fair at the Shoreline Amphitheater, Mountain View, Calif., July 8, 1997," *Salon* (July 11, 1997), found at http://www.salon.com/july97/entertainment/lilith970711.html (cited March 12, 2003).

105. Hirshey, *We Gotta Get Out of This Place*, 194.

106. Ibid., 173.

107. Baumgardner and Richards, *Manifesta*, 15.

108. For more on social learning theory and modeling, see Albert Bandura, *Social Learning Theory* (Englewood Cliffs, NJ: Prentice-Hall, 1977) and Albert Bandura, ed., *Self-Efficacy in Changing Societies* (New York: Cambridge University Press, 1997).

Chapter 4

The Deborah Frost epigraph to this chapter is drawn from an interview, New York City, September 6, 2001.

1. Deborah Frost, interview, New York City, September 6, 2001.

2. On women in the professional job market in the 1960s, see, for example, Sara M. Evans, "Sources of the Second Wave: The Rebirth of Feminism," in *Long Time Gone: Sixties America Then and Now,* ed. Alexander Bloom (New York: Oxford University Press, 2001), 192–193.

3. Deborah Frost, interview, New York City, September 6, 2001.

4. See, for example, Blanche Linden-Ward, *American Women in the 1960s: Changing the Future* (New York: Twayne, 1993).

5. Quoted in Joan Morrison and Robert K. Morrison, *From Camelot to Kent State: The Sixties Experience in the Words of Those Who Lived It* (New York: Oxford University Press, 1987), 182.

6. Andrea Dworkin, *Heartbreak: The Political Memoir of a Feminist Militant* (New York: Basic Books, 2002), 129–131.

7. Quoted in Alice Echols, *Scars of Sweet Paradise: The Life and Times of Janis Joplin* (New York: Metropolitan Books, 1999), 14.

8. Ibid., 30–31.

9. Ibid., 46–49.

10. O'Brien, *She Bop*, 104.

11. Brita Rae Borough, email interview, December 4, 2002.

12. Jill Sobule, telephone interview, July 17, 2002. For more information on the artist, see www.jillsobule.com.

13. Bitch and Animal, interview, New York City, September 6, 2001. For more information on the artists, see www.bitchandanimal.com.

14. Paula Spiro, telephone interview, October 10, 2001. For more information on Paula Spiro and the Female Drummers Workshop, see www.drummergirl.com/interviews/spiro.html.

15. Melissa Auf der Maur, telephone interview, August 13, 2001. For more

information on the artist and her work with Hole, see www.absolutedivas.com/
melissa/biography.shtml.

16. Paz Lenchantin, interview, New York City, September 7, 2001.

17. Stacey Board, email interview, August 8, 2001.

18. Lynn Frances Anderson, interview, Corvallis, Oregon, May 2001.

19. Rose Polenzani, interview, Chicago, August 17, 2001.

20. Rana Ross, interview, Los Angeles, August 29, 2001.

21. For an excellent sociological study of women's entrance into bands and
performance in the U.K. from the 1970s to the 1990s, see Mavis Bayton, *Frock Rock:
Women Performing Popular Music* (Oxford: Oxford University Press, 1998).

22. See, for example, Sheila Whiteley's essay on Annie Lennox's androgyneity
in her *Women and Popular Music,* 119–135.

23. Indigo Girls, interview, Vienna, Virginia, August 7, 2001.

24. Sarah Dash, telephone interview, October 14, 2002.

25. Leah Hinchcliff, interview, Portland, Oregon, August 23, 2001; Jill Gewirtz,
email interview, July 29, 2001.

26. Jann Arden, telephone interview, September 18, 2002.

27. Jonatha Brooke, interview, Portland, Oregon, September 2002.

28. Niki Lee, email interview, August 3, 2001.

29. Lynn Witting, email interview, August 17, 2001.

30. Indigo Girls, interview, Vienna, Virginia, August 7, 2001.

31. Kate Campbell, interview, Minneapolis, October 4, 2002.

32. Lynn Frances Anderson, interview, Corvallis, Oregon, May 2001.

33. Brenda Lee, telephone interview, July 6, 2002.

34. Jean Millington, telephone interview, October 16, 2001.

35. Shirley Alston Reeves, interview, Brevard, North Carolina, August 10, 2001.

36. Leah Hinchcliff, interview, Portland, Oregon, August 23, 2001.

37. Rana Ross, interview, Los Angeles, August 29, 2001.

38. Reynolds and Press, *The Sex Revolts,* 233–234.

39. Quoted in O'Brien, *She Bop,* 139.

40. "Red Blue Jeans: Wanda Jackson and Grace Slick," in *Trouble Girls,* ed.
Barbara O'Dair, 150.

41. Gaar, *She's a Rebel,* 277.

42. Rana Ross, interview, Los Angeles, August 29, 2001.

43. Kitzie P. Stern, interview, Corvallis, July 24, 2001.

44. Erin O'Hara, interview, New York City, September 8, 2001.

45. Quoted in Gaar, *She's a Rebel,* 278.

46. Quoted in ibid., 279–280.

47. O'Brien, *She Bop,* 126.

48. Ann Hornaday, "Cyndi Lauper," *Ms.* 13 (January 1985): 47.

49. Melissa Auf der Maur, telephone interview, August 13, 2001.

50. Carol Kaye, interview, Los Angeles, August 27, 2001. On women in big
bands, see Sherrie Tucker, *Swing Shift* (Durham, NC: Duke University Press, 2000).

51. Deborah Frost, interview, New York City, September 6, 2001.

52. Quoted in Gaar, *She's a Rebel*, 256.

53. Interview in Laura Post, *Backstage Pass: Interviews with Women in Music* (Norwich, VT: New Victoria, 1997), 221.

54. Scarlet Rivera, telephone interview, July 31, 2001.

55. Wilfred Mellers, "From Folk Fiddle to Jazz Violin," in *The Book of the Violin*, ed. Dominic Gill (New York: Phaidon Press, 1984), 228.

56. Scarlet Rivera, telephone interview, July 31, 2001.

57. Kate Schellenbach, interview, Los Angeles, September 29, 2001.

58. Jean Millington, telephone interview, October 16, 2001.

59. Quoted in Gaar, *She's a Rebel*, 416.

60. Deborah Frost, "Garageland," in *Trouble Girls*, ed. Barbara O'Dair, 416.

61. Quoted in *The New Rolling Stone Encyclopedia of Rock & Roll*, ed. Patricia Romanowski and Holly George-Warren (New York: Fireside, 1995), 326.

62. Gaar, *She's a Rebel*, 220.

63. Frost, "Garageland," 420.

64. Quoted by Gavin Martin, "Whomping the Suckers with a Superball," *New Musical Express* (April 10, 1982), cited in Lucy O'Brien, *She Bop II*, 122.

65. Frost, "Garageland," 420.

66. Quoted in McDonnell and Wessel, "Joan Jett," 147.

67. Gaar, *She's a Rebel*, 271–273.

68. Quoted in Gaar, *She's a Rebel*, 273.

69. Quoted in O'Brien, *She Bop*, 152.

70. Quoted in Hirshey, *We Gotta Get Out of This Place*, 125.

71. Leah Hinchcliff, interview, Portland, Oregon, August 23, 2001.

72. Ann Powers, "Bohemian Rhapsodies," in *Trouble Girls*, ed. Barbara O'Dair, 326.

73. Quoted in Garr, *She's a Rebel*, 222.

74. Quoted in ibid., 225.

75. Quoted in Hirshey, *We Gotta Get Out of This Place*, 136.

76. "Heart" found at www.annandnancy.com (cited February 10, 2003).

77. Ray Waddell, "Venue Views," *Billboard* 115 (May 31, 2003): 36.

78. Jancee Dunn, "True Confessions: Alternative Sounds," in *Trouble Girls*, ed. Barbara O'Dair, 518.

79. O'Brien, *She Bop*, 178.

80. Ibid.

81. Michael Azerrad, "The Real New Deal," *Rolling Stone* 668 (October 28, 1993): 18.

82. Dunn and Sirota, "Courtney Love," 164.

83. The name of the band comes from a line in Euripides's *Medea*. "It's about the abyss that's inside," said Love. Quoted in O'Brien, *She Bop II*, 166.

84. This movement describing a musical genre, a women's band, a feminist zine, and a feminist category will be explored further in this chapter.

85. Christopher John Farley with Lisa McLaughlin, "Rock Goes Coed," *Time* 144, 6 (August 8, 1994): 62.

86. Kylie Murphy, " 'I'm Sorry—I'm Not Really Sorry': Courtney Love and Notions of Authenticity," *Hecate* 27, 1 (2001): 139.

87. Nisha Gopalan, "Riot Girls Unite on a Smaller Scale," *The Daily Bruin* (1996), found at http://www.dailybruin.ucla.edu/db/issues/96/1.18/ae.riotgrrrl.html.

88. Quoted in Dunn and Sirota, "Courtney Love," 166.

89. *Merriam-Webster's Collegiate Dictionary, 11th Edition* (Springfield, MA: Merriam-Webster, 2003).

90. Joy Press, "Shouting Out Loud: Women in U.K. Punk," in *Trouble Girls,* ed. Barbara O'Dair, 301.

91. Ibid., 463.

92. Farai Chideya and Melissa Rossi, "Revolution, Girl Style," *Newsweek* 120, 21 (November 23, 1992): 84.

93. Hirshey, *We Gotta Get Out of This Place,* 161.

94. O'Brien, *She Bop,* 167.

95. Hirshey, *We Gotta Get Out of This Place,* 161.

96. Evelyn McDonnell, "Rebel Grrls," in *Trouble Girls,* ed. Barbara O'Dair, 461; Le Tigre probably would not be happy with this, yet another, book on women and rock. As Lucy O'Brien points out, in 2000 while the group was onstage, they chanted, "Not another book about women in rock!" Quoted in O'Brien, *She Bop,* 1.

97. Hillary Frey, "Kathleen Hanna's Fire," *Nation* 276, 2 (January 13, 2003): 27.

98. You pass under the road while driving between Portland and Olympia; if you are a music fan first and a traveler second, it hits you by surprise. "Oh, how nice that they named the road after that great band!"

99. Ann Cvetkovich and Gretchen Phillips, "Revenge of the Girl Bands," *Nation* 271, 2 (July 10, 2000): 16; Hirshey, *We Gotta Get Out of This Place,* 232.

100. Donna Freydkin, "Punk Trio Sleater-Kinney Keeps on Digging with Fourth Album," Special to CNN Interactive, March 23, 1999, found at www.cnn.com/SHOWBIZ/Music/9903/23/sleater-kinney/ (cited March 15, 2003).

101. Charles R. Cross, "Sleater-Kinney," *Rolling Stone* 908 (October 31, 2002): 57.

102. Benjamin Nugent, "Olympia Ladystyle," *Time* 156, 6 (August 7, 2000): 82.

103. Robin Renée, interview, Asheville, North Carolina, November 13, 2001. See also Anthony DeCurtis, "Is Rock 'n Roll a White Man's Game?" *Time* 147 (April 29, 1996) and the forthcoming book by Maureen Mahon, *Black Rock Sisters: Notes on Race, Gender, and Rock,* to be published by Duke University Press.

Chapter 5

The title for this chapter comes from a well-known song of 1976 by Holly Near that became an anthem of the women's music movement. The Margie Adam epigraph to this chapter is drawn from "Thoughts on Women's Music," http://www.margieadam.com/info/thoughts.htm.

1. Deborah Frost, interview, New York City, September 6, 2001.

2. June Millington, interview, Guerneville, California, September 22, 2001.

3. Quoted in L. Margaret Pomeroy, "The Soul of the Changer," *Echo* (October 2000), found at http://www.leftbankreview.com/echo/2ndQtr-00/page2.html.

4. Romanowski and George-Warren, *New Rolling Stone Encyclopedia*; Martin C. Strong, *The Great Rock Discography* (New York: Times Books, 1998).

5. Bonnie Morris, "Happy 25th Anniversary, 'Angry Atthis,'" *Hot Wire* 10, 3 (September 1994): 10.

6. The identification of "Leaping Lesbians" with Meg Christian became a sore point with Sue Fink and her collaborators, because Christian generally omitted the writing credit when she performed the song. She rectified that lapse in etiquette in the mid-1980s. See Toni Armstrong Jr., "True Life Adventures in Women's Music: Sue Fink," *Hot Wire* 7, 2 (May 1991): 2.

7. Olivia Records Timeline, http://www.olivia.com/about/timeline.html; Kay Gardner, "Early East Coast Women's Music and the Squirrel," in *Lesbian Culture: An Anthology*, ed. Julia Penelope and Susan Wolfe (Freedom, CA: The Crossing Press, 1993), 377.

8. L. Margaret Pomeroy, "The Song and Soul of the Changer," *Echo*, found at http://www.leftbankreview.com/echo/2ndQtr-00/page2.html (cited March 1, 2003).

9. "DIY" means "do-it-yourself."

10. On the making of women's communities and lesbians' group identity, see, for example, Elizabeth Lapovsky Kennedy and Madeline D. Davis, *Boots of Leather, Slippers of Gold: The History of a Lesbian Community* (New York: Routledge, 1993); Esther Newton, *Cherry Grove, Fire Island: Sixty Years in America's First Gay and Lesbian Town* (Boston: Beacon Press, 1993). It is very important to note that there were positive, even in some cases life-saving dimensions to the lesbian bars for some people, and that the bars have offered a variety of atmospheres, rules, and clienteles. For a wonderful video history of the place of a bar in a lesbian community, see *Last Call at Maud's* (1993), directed by Paris Poirer. For more on lesbian history, see Leila J. Rupp, *A Desired Past: A Short History of Same-Sex Love in America* (Chicago: University of Chicago Press, 2002); Lillian Faderman, *Surpassing the Love of Men: Romantic Friendship and Love between Women from the Renaissance to the Present,* reissue ed. (New York: Perennial, 2001); *Odd Girls and Twilight Lovers: A History of Lesbian Life in Twentieth Century America* (New York: Penguin, 1992).

11. Sue Fink and Toni Armstrong, "True Life Adventures in Women's Music," in *Lesbian Culture: An Anthology: The Lives, Work, Ideas, Art and Visions of Lesbians Past and Present*, ed. Julia Penelope and Susan J. Wolfe (Berkeley, CA: Crossing Press, 1993), 397–398.

12. Bonnie J. Morris offers an excellent historical summary of these political conflicts in *Eden Built by Eves: The Culture of Women's Music Festivals* (Los Angeles: Alyson Books, 1999), 147–176. She also argues that the conflicts, while sometimes hurtful or regrettable, are potentially a "positive learning experience."

13. Holly Pruett, "The Michigan Women's Music Festival: 25 Years," *Lesbian News*, 26, 1 (August 2000): 24.

14. http://www.michfest.com/General/general.htmper.

15. Deborah R. Lewis, "The Original Womyn's Woodstock: Michigan Womyn's Music Festival," in *The Woman-Centered Economy: Ideals, Reality, and the Space In Between*, ed. Loraine Edwalds and Midge Stocker (Chicago: Third Side Press, 1995), 167–178.

16. Quoted in Morris, *Eden Built by Eves*, 46.

17. Interview in *Backstage Pass: Interviews with Women in Music*, ed. Laura Post (Norwich, VT: New Victoria, 1997), 217.

18. Ibid., 218.

19. Interview in ibid., 116.

20. For an excellent discussion of the intersections of gender, race, and sexuality, see Audre Lorde, *Sister Outsider* (Freedom, CA: Crossing, 1984).

21. Toni Armstrong Jr., "A Taste of the Canadian Prairies: Heather Bishop," *Hot Wire* 6, 2 (May 1990): 2–3.

22. Otto Luck, "Mistress Helga and other tough femmes at the Lilith Fair," *NY Rock*, August 1999, http://www.nyrock.com/lilithfair/080799.htm.

23. Tret Fure, telephone interview, August 28, 2001.

24. "Holly Near," http://www.hollynear.com/bio.html (cited March 5, 2003).

25. Harriet L. Schwartz, "Holly Near's Heart Song," *Lesbian News* 23, 10 (May 1998): 36.

26. "Holly Near," http://www.hollynear.com/bio.html (cited March 5, 2003).

27. Holly Near, email interview, August 20, 2001.

28. Nancy S. Love, " 'Singing for Our Lives': Women's Music and Democratic Politics," *Hypatia* 17, 4 (Fall 2002): 86.

29. Holly Near with Derk Richardson, *Fire in the Rain . . . Singer in the Storm: An Autobiography* (New York: William Morrow and Company, 1990), quoted in Nancy S. Love, "Singing for Our Lives," 72.

30. Terri Sutton, "Fierce Folkies: Contemporary Roots Music," in *Trouble Girls*, ed. Barbara O'Dair, 482.

31. Indigo Girls, interview, Vienna, Virginia, August 7, 2001.

32. Ferron, telephone interview, July 10, 2002.

33. Lori Medigovich, "Still Riot," *Lesbian News* 22, 1 (August 1996): 15.

34. Ferron, telephone interview, July 10, 2002.

35. Will Grega, *Billboard* 107 (May 25, 1995): 6. Sometimes the perception of a market is as important as the market itself. These numbers are hard to believe.

36. Scott Alarik, *Boston Sunday Globe*, October 1, 2000, found at http://www.criswilliamson.com/news.htm.

37. Ferron, telephone interview, July 10, 2002.

38. Lori Medigovich, "Still Riot," 15.

39. Margie Adam, "Thoughts on Women's Music," found at http://www.margieadam.com/info/thoughts.htm.

40. Bonnie J. Morris, "Long Before Lilith—and After," *Advocate* 785 (May 11, 1999): 57.

41. For more on coming out, see Laura A. Markowe, *Redefining the Self: Coming Out as a Lesbian* (Cambridge, England: Polity, 1996).

42. "Androgyny Goes Pop: But Is It Lesbian Music?" *Out/Look* 12 (Spring 1991): 26–33.

43. "Crossover Dreams: Lesbianism and Popular Music Since the 1970s," in *The Good, the Bad and the Gorgeous: Popular Culture's Romance with Lesbianism,* ed. Diane Hamer and Belinda Budge (London: Pandora, 1994), 15–27.

44. Quoted in Richard Natale, "Music Biz Hears New Songs of Openness," *Daily Variety* 269 (October 11, 2000): A14.

45. Quoted in Mim Udovitch, "k.d. lang," *Rolling Stone* 662 (August 5, 1993): 54–57.

46. Steve Jensen, quoted in Natale, "Music Biz," A14.

47. For more on lesbian stardom and fandom, see Louise Allen, *The Lesbian Idol: Martina, kd, and the Consumption of Lesbian Masculinity* (London: Cassell, 1997).

48. Martha Mockus, "Queer Thoughts on Country Music and K. D. Lang," in *Queering the Pitch: The New Gay and Lesbian Musicology,* ed. Philip Brett, Elizabeth Wood, and Gary C. Thomas (New York: Routledge, 1994), 268.

49. Lily Braindrop, "Pop Goes Queer," *The Advocate* 587 (October 8, 1991): 37.

50. Holly George-Warren, "Melissa Etheridge," *Rolling Stone* 908 (October 31, 2002): 124.

51. Karen Ocamb, "Melissa Etheridge: Daring to Tell the Truth," *Lesbian News* 25 (January 2000): 24–25.

52. Quoted in Rich Cohen, "Melissa Etheridge," *Rolling Stone* 698/699 (December 29, 1994–January 12, 1995): 110–115.

53. Quoted in Anne Stockwell, "Melissa Etheridge," *Advocate* 876 (November 12, 2002): 54–55.

54. Quoted in Cohen, "Melissa Etheridge."

55. Quoted in Holly Crenshaw, "Indigo Girls: Unplugged . . . and Outspoken," *Out* (April 1994), found at http://www.lifeblood.net/articles/1994/9404xx.html.

56. Ibid.

57. Quoted in Deb Taylor, "She Speaks," *The Flint Hills [Michigan] Observer,* May 1998, found at http://www.debtaylor.com/fho/059802.html.

58. Lynn Frances Anderson, interview, Corvallis, Oregon, May 2001.

59. The word "queer" has in the last decade become the self-definer of choice for a large portion, though *not* all, of the anglophone homosexual population. Using "queer" (like "dyke" in our next sentence) serves as an appropriation of the language of the oppressor as well as a move toward linguistic efficiency, bypassing the strained inclusiveness of "gay, lesbian, bisexual, transsexual, transgendered,"

and so forth. The list goes on. We add that for many older lesbians and gay men, the word "queer" still sparks such painful personal memories that its use is unacceptable. See further in this chapter for an expanded discussion of "queer" politics.

60. Bitch and Animal, interview, New York City, September 6, 2001.

61. For more on sexual identities, see Butler, *Gender Trouble*; "Imitation and Gender Insubordination," in *Inside/Out: Lesbian Theories, Gay Theories,* ed. Diana Fuss (London: Routledge, 1991); *Bodies that Matter: On the Discursive Limits of 'Sex'* (London: Routledge, 1993); Teresa De Lauretis, *The Practice of Love: Lesbian Sexuality and Perverse Desire* (Bloomington: Indiana University Press, 1994).

62. See, for example, Vera Whisman, "Identity Crises: Who is a Lesbian Anyway?" in *Sisters, Sexperts, Queers: Beyond the Lesbian Nation,* ed. Arlene Stein (New York: Plume 1993), 47–60.

63. "Compulsory Heterosexuality and Lesbian Existence," in *Blood, Bread and Poetry* (London: Virago, 1978), 130–143.

64. Marcia Diehl and Robyn Ochs, "Biphobia," *Empathy* 2 (1989/1990): 15–19.

65. Quoted in Laura Jamison and Sheila Metzner, "Me'Shell Ndegeocello," *Rolling Stone* 773 (November 13, 1997): 161.

66. Quoted in McLean Greaves, "Me'Shell Ndegeocello: A Sista from Another Planet," *Essence* 27 (September 1996): 95–96.

67. Quoted in Achy Obejas, "Both Sides Now," *The Advocate* 748 (December 9, 1997): 26–27.

68. Quoted in Matthew Rothschild, "Ani DiFranco," *The Progressive* (May 2000): 32–38.

69. For more on queer identity and queer history, see Joan Nestle, Riki Wilchinc, and Clare Howell, eds., *Genderqueer: Voices from Beyond the Sexual Binary* (Los Angeles: Alyson, 2002); Allida M. Black, ed., *Modern American Queer History* (Philadelphia: Temple University Press, 2001); Dawn Atkins, ed., *Looking Queer: Body Image and Identity in Lesbian, Bisexual, Gay, and Transgender Communities* (Binghamton, NY: Harrington Park, 1998); Carol Queen and Lawrence Schimel, eds., *Pomosexuals: Challenging Assumptions about Gender and Sexuality* (San Francisco: Cleis, 1997); Elizabeth Weed and Naomi Schor, eds., *Feminism Meets Queer Theory* (Bloomington: Indiana University Press, 1997).

70. Quoted in Obejas, "Both Sides Now," 26.

71. For more on queer history, see Craig Rimmerman, *From Identity to Politics: The Lesbian and Gay Movements in the United States (Queer Politics, Queer Theories)* (Philadelphia: Temple University Press, 2001); Allida M. Black, ed., *Modern American Queer History* (Philadelphia: Temple University Press, 2001).

72. Peter Brooker, *A Concise Glossary of Cultural Theory* (London: Hodder Arnold, 1999).

73. Simon Watney, "Queer Epistemology: Activism, 'Outing,' and the Politics of Sexual Identities," in *Critical Quarterly* 36 (1994): 13–27.

74. Quoted in T. A. Gilmartin, "The Butchies are Fightin' the Power," *Lesbian News* 26 (August 2000): 42.

75. Ibid.

76. Michael du Plessis and Kathleen Chapman, "Queercore: The Distinct Identities of Subculture," *College Literature* 24 (February 1997): 45–58.

Queercore band Tribe 8 played the Michigan Womyn's Music Festival in 1994, and many within the lesbian community complained about the band's confrontational politics. Bassist Lynn Payne explains, "The main argument was between the cultural feminists and the radical pro-sex feminists. We didn't walk out of that meeting [with Festival attendees uncomfortable with the band's show] with any sense of agreement, but at least we gave each other the room to discuss the situation." Brett Atwood, "Queercore Punk Rock Ready to Face Market," *Billboard* 107 (May 6, 1995): 1–3.

77. Quoted in Todd Wiese, "Tribe 8 Interview," found at www.theroc.org/roc-mag/textarch/roc-18/roc18-08.htm.

78. Robert Dechaine, "Mapping Subversion: Queercore Music's Playful Discourse of Resistance," *Popular Music and Society* 21 (Winter 1997): 7–37.

79. Larry Flick and Michael Paoletta, "Albums: Pop, The Butchies," *Billboard* 113, 17 (April 28, 2001): 37.

80. Karen Iris Tucker, "Born to Be Butchie," *Advocate* 838 (May 22, 2001): 65.

81. Available at http://www.bitchandanimal.com.

82. Robert Hilburn, "The Freshman Class of 2001," *Los Angeles Times,* December 9, 2001, found at http://www.bitchandanimal.com/press.html (cited March 5, 2003).

Chapter 6

The Margot Mifflin epigraph to this chapter is drawn from "The Fallacy of Women in Rock," in *Rock She Wrote: Women Write about Rock, Pop, and Rap,* ed. Evelyn McDonnell and Ann Powers (New York: Delta, 1995), 76–79.

1. Lynn Frances Anderson, interview, Corvallis, Oregon, May 2001.

2. Rose Weitz, ed., *The Politics of Women's Bodies: Sexuality, Appearance, and Behavior* (New York: Oxford University Press, 2003), 133.

3. Tom McGrath, *MTV: The Making of a Revolution* (Philadelphia: Running Press, 1996), 72.

4. Wanda Jackson, telephone interview, September 18, 2001.

5. "Women and Their Hair: Seeking Power through Resistance and Accommodation," in Rose Weitz, ed., *The Politics of Women's Bodies,* 135.

6. Ibid., 148.

7. Shirley Alston Reeves, interview, Brevard, North Carolina, August 10, 2001.

8. Indigo Girls, interview, Vienna, Virginia, August 7, 2001.

9. It is unfortunate that there is a social foundation for the growing number of books examining the dilemma of adolescent girls' loss of self-esteem and often damaged self-image. Among the most prominent works examining these problems, from a range of disciplinary perspectives, are Joan Jacobs Brumberg, *The*

Body Project: An Intimate History of American Girls (New York: Random House, 1997); Carol Gilligan, Nona P. Lyons, and Trudy J. Hanmer, eds., *Making Connections: The Relational Worlds of Adolescent Girls at Emma Willard School* (Cambridge: Harvard University Press, 1990); Mary Pipher, *Reviving Ophelia: Saving the Selves of Adolescent Girls* (New York: Putnam Publishing Group, 1994); Peggy Orenstein, *Schoolgirls: Young Women, Self-Esteem, and the Confidence Gap* (New York: Doubleday, 1994). Several of these studies were energized by the 1990 study by the American Association of University Women, published as *How Schools Shortchange Girls* by Marlowe & Company in 1995. That study, conducted at the Wellesley College Center for Research, distilled twenty years of research on school-age girls to conclude that structural gender bias continued to present barriers to girls' self-image, aspirations, and achievements.

10. Indigo Girls, interview, Vienna, Virginia, August 7, 2001.

11. Holly Near, email interview, August 20, 2001.

12. Three excellent videos on this topic are: *Dying to Be Thin,* dir. Larkin McPhee (South Burlington, VT: WGBH Video, 2000); *Killing Us Softly 3,* dir. Sut Jhally (Northampton, MA: Media Education Foundation, 2000); *Beyond Killing Us Softly,* dir. Margaret Lazareus and Renner Wunderlich (Cambridge, MA: Cambridge Documentary Films, 2000).

13. For more on the connection between body image and eating disorders, see Michael J. Devlin, "Body Image in the Balance," *JAMA: Journal of the American Medical Association* 286 (November 7, 2001): 2159. See also Alison E. Field, "Media Influence on Self-Image: The Real Fashion Emergency," *Healthy Weight Journal* (November/December 2000): 88–89, 95.

14. A number of studies have demonstrated that for Western women the ideal body type is ectomorphic. See, for example: Kathryn Graff, et al., "Internalization of the Thin Ideal: Weight and Body Image Concerns," *Social Behavior and Personality* 31 (2003): 81–90; Jacqueline N. Standford and Martia P. McCabe, "Body Image Ideal among Males and Females: Sociocultural Influences and Focus on Different Body Parts," *Journal of Health Psychology* 7 (November 2002): 675–684; J. Robyn Goodman, "Flabless is Fabulous: How Latina and Anglo Women Read and Incorporate the Excessively Thin Body Ideal into Everyday Experience," *Journalism & Mass Communication Quarterly* 79 (Autumn 2002): 712–727; J. C. Butler and R. M. Ryckman, "Perceived and Ideal Physiques in Male and Female University Students," *The Journal of Social Psychology* 133 (1993): 751–752; L. D. Cohn and N. E. Adler, "Female and Male Perceptions of Ideal Body Shapes: Distorted Views among Caucasian College Students," *Psychology of Women Quarterly* 16 (1992): 69–79.

15. Gerri Hirshey, "Women Who Rocked the World," *Rolling Stone* 773 (November 13, 1997): 81.

16. Adena Young, "Battling Anorexia: The Story of Karen Carpenter," found at http://atdpweb.soe.berkeley.edu/quest/Mind&Body/Carpenter.html (cited June 2003).

17. Barbara O'Dair, "Kim Gordon," *Rolling Stone* 773 (November 13, 1997): 144.

18. Hirshey, "Women Who Rocked the World," 81.

19. On Mama Cass, see Lucy O'Brien, *She Bop II,* 212.

20. Hirshey, "Women Who Rocked the World," 81.

21. Ibid.

22. Echols, *Scars of Sweet Paradise,* 12.

23. Michael P. Levine argues that media messages implicitly or explicitly suggest that "(1) beauty is a woman's principal project in life; (2) slenderness is crucial for success and goodness; (3) 'image' is really substance; (4) women are naturally self-conscious about and bound up with their bodies; (5) 'fat' announces your personal responsibility for weakness, failure, and helplessness; and (6) a 'willing' and 'winning' woman can transform and renew herself through the technology of fashion, dieting, and rigorous exercise." "Mass Media and Body Image: A Brief Review of the Research," *Healthy Weight Journal* (November/December 2000): 84–85, 95. See also S. Almond, "The Influence of Media on Eating Disorders," *Journal of Human Nutrition & Dietetics* 13 (October 2000): 363–371; Eaaron Henderson-King and Donna Henderson-King, "Media Effects on Women's Body Esteem: Social and Individual Difference Factors," *Journal of Applied Social Psychology* 27 (March 1997): 399–413.

24. Quoting Simon Cowell, *American Idol,* Fox Broadcasting Company (February 18, 2003).

25. Quoted in "Simon Says and Vanessa Does," *Entertainment Tonight Online,* February 28, 2003, found at http://www.etonline.com/celebrity/a14701.htm (cited March 14, 2003).

26. Jann Arden, telephone interview, September 18, 2002.

27. See David Elkind, *All Grown Up and No Place to Go: Teenagers in Crisis* (Reading, MA: Addison-Wesley, 1984), 33–36.

28. According to some scholars, "Objectified Body Consciousness" is a result of internalized cultural body standards that demand women "learn to view their bodies as if they were outside observers." OBC reflects the cultural norm that female bodies are objects to be looked at. Nita Mary McKinley and Janet Shibley Hyde, "The Objectified Body Consciousness Scale: Development and Validation," *Psychology of Women Quarterly* 29 (1996): 181–215.

29. Elkind, *All Grown Up,* 35.

30. Shirley Alston Reeves, interview, Brevard, North Carolina, August 10, 2001.

31. Gerri Hirshey, "Tina Turner," *Rolling Stone* 773 (November 13, 1997): 118.

32. Holly Near, email interview, August 20, 2001.

33. Janis Ian, telephone interview, September 24, 2002.

34. Bitch and Animal, interview, New York City, September 6, 2001.

35. Hirshey, "Tina Turner," 120. bell hooks suggests that the image of Tina Turner, created by Ike and then inverted by Tina once she had escaped him, reifies the racist stereotype of the black woman as a "wild sexual savage." She argues that the image of a powerful black woman in control of her sexuality that Turner tries

to present in videos such as "What's Love Got To Do With It" remains "rooted in misogynist notions. Rather than being a pleasure-based eroticism, it is ruthless, violent; it is about women using sexual power to do violence to the male Other." In "Selling Hot Pussy: Representations of Black Female Sexuality in the Cultural Marketplace," in Rose Weitz, ed., *The Politics of Women's Bodies.*

36. One could contend that this baby doll image is also one that has been eroticized in this and other cultures. But without detracting from the complexities of this fact, we might also observe that there are clinical labels for adult individuals who choose children as sexual objects.

37. Hirshey, "Tina Turner," 118.

38. Ibid.

39. "Tina Turner," found at http://www.tvtome.com/tvtome/servlet/PersonDetail/personid-52278 (cited March 16, 2003). These are just a few of her many television appearances.

40. Hirshey, "Tina Turner," 120.

41. "Tina Turner," found at http://www.swinginchicks.com/tina_turner.htm (cited March 16, 2003).

42. Collins, *Black Feminist Thought,* 163–180. See also bell hooks, *Black Looks: Race and Representation* (Boston: South End, 1992).

43. Gaar, *She's a Rebel,* 78.

44. Mary Wilson, telephone interview, October 16, 2001.

45. Sarah Dash, telephone interview, October 14, 2002.

46. Jann Arden, telephone interview, September 18, 2002.

47. Susan Douglas, *Where the Girls Are: Growing Up Female with the Mass Media* (New York: Times Books, 1995), 303.

48. Lisa A. Lewis, *Gender Politics and MTV: Voicing the Difference* (Philadelphia: Temple University Press, 1990), 38.

49. Ibid., 40–41. See also Livingston A. White, "A Re-Investigation of Sex-Role Stereotyping in MTV Music Videos," *Women & Language* 25 (Spring 2001): 45; Joe Gow, "Reconsidering Gender Roles on MTV: Depictions in the Most Popular Music Videos of the Early 1990s," *Communication Reports* 9 (Summer 1996): 152–162. For an excellent video, see *Dreamworlds 2,* dir. Sut Jhally.

50. Joan Morgan, "Sex, Lies and Videos," *Essence* (June 2002): 120–124.

51. Ibid.

52. Lewis, *Gender Politics and MTV,* 217–222.

53. Robin Roberts, " 'Sex as a Weapon': Feminist Rock Music Videos," *NWSA Journal* 2 (Winter 1990): 1–15.

54. Holly Near, email interview, August 20, 2001.

55. O'Brien, *She Bop,* 107.

56. Hirshey quoting S. S. Fair in *We Gotta Get Out of This Place,* 137.

57. McDonnell and Wessel, "Joan Jett," 147.

58. Sarah Dash, telephone interview, October 14, 2002.

59. Quoted in Gaar, *She's a Rebel,* 198–199.

60. Sarah Dash, telephone interview, October 14, 2002.

61. Ting Yu, et al., "They Stole Cher's Hair!" *People* 59, 11 (March 24, 2003): 20.

62. Quoted in O'Brien, *She Bop II*, 242.

63. Ibid., 243.

64. Quoted in Yu et al., 20.

65. Hirshey, "Women Who Rocked the World," 79.

66. Quoted in Gerri Hirshey, "Madonna," *Rolling Stone* 773 (November 13, 1997): 100.

67. Ibid., 98.

68. Ibid.

69. Quoted in ibid., 100.

70. The complete CNN "Larry King Live" interview can be found at http://www.cnn.com/SHOWBIZ/Music/9901/19/madonna.lkl/.

71. *Larry King Live*, CNN (October 10, 2002).

72. These are the items of transformation Murphy cleverly seized upon in her perceptive treatment of Love's musical and iconic evolution; see "I'm Sorry," 152.

73. Quoted in Dunn and Sirota, "Courtney Love," 166.

74. Ibid., 164.

75. Ginia Bellafante, "Feminism: It's All About Me," *Time* 151, 25 (June 29, 1998): 54.

76. Katherine Dieckmann, "Courtney Love," in *Trouble Girls,* ed. Barbara O'Dair, 468.

77. Dunn and Sirota, "Courtney Love," 166.

78. Quoted in Dieckmann, "Courtney Love," 473.

79. Ibid., 472.

80. Kylie Murphy, 155, citing Susan Bordo, "Reading the Slender Body," in Mary Jacobus, Evelyn Fox Keller, and Sally Shuttleworth, eds., *Body/Politics: Women and the Discourses of Science* (London: Routledge, 1990), 83–113.

81. Marlien Rentmeester, "Courtney Love's Body," *Women's Sports & Fitness* 1, 10 (July/August 1998): 57.

82. Murphy, "I'm Sorry," 139.

83. "Beyond Belief!" (cover story) *People* 56, 12 (September 17, 2001): 160.

84. O'Brien, *She Bop II*, 246.

85. Jann Arden, telephone interview, September 18, 2002.

86. Hirshey, *We Gotta Get Out of This Place,* 135.

87. Ibid., 130.

88. Quoted in ibid., 134.

89. O'Brien, *She Bop II*, 267.

90. O'Dair, "Kim Gordon," 144.

91. Childerhose, *From Lilith to Lilith Fair,* 90.

92. Bitch and Animal, interview, New York City, September 6, 2001.

Chapter 7

The Sheryl Crow epigraph to this chapter is drawn from Jill Hamilton and Peggy Sirota, "Sheryl Crow," *Rolling Stone* 773 (November 13, 1997): 108ff. The Liz Phair epigraph to this chapter is drawn from Neva Chonin and Guzman, "Liz Phair," *Rolling Stone* 773 (November 13, 1997): 111.

1. Scarlet Rivera, telephone interview, July 31, 2001.

2. Brenda Lee, telephone interview, July 19, 2002.

3. The Beatles even opened for *her* in Germany and England in the 1960s. "They were very nice boys," Lee told Mobile's *The Harbinger* years later. "Very down to earth. Very normal, no matter how they looked. Very, very talented, of course. I liked 'em a lot. John and I probably talked more than the rest of 'em." She was so impressed with them, she says, "I even took a tape back to my record company to see if I could get 'em a record deal." Later, John Lennon repaid the compliment, saying Brenda Lee had "the greatest rock 'n' roll voice of them all." Quotes from Gary James, "Brenda Lee Interview," *The Harbinger,* Mobile, Alabama, May 12, 1998, found at http://www.theharbinger.org/xvi/980512/james.html (cited January 31, 2003).

4. Janis Ian, telephone interview, September 24, 2002.

5. Interview with Shadow Morton in "More with George: Shadow Morton," found at http://www.lirock.com/shadow09.html (cited September 26, 2002).

6. Janis Ian, telephone interview, September 24, 2002.

7. Interview with Shadow Morton in "More with George: Shadow Morton," found at http://www.lirock.com/shadow09.html (cited September 26, 2002).

8. Janis Ian, telephone interview, September 24, 2002.

9. James Dickerson, *Women On Top: The Quiet Revolution That's Rocking the American Music Industry* (New York: Billboard Books, 1998), 67.

10. Janis Ian, "The Death of Independence: A Rant," *Performing Songwriter,* 8, 47 (July/August 2000), 74.

11. Dickerson, 68–74; Veronika Kalmar, *Label Launch: A Guide to Independent Record Recording, Promotion, and Distribution* (New York: St. Martin's Griffin, 2002), 2–6.

12. Carol Kaye, interview, Los Angeles, August 27, 2001; Linda Tomasello, "Ace of Bass," *Venus Zine* 14 (Winter 2002): 26–27.

13. Carol Kaye, interview, Los Angeles, August 27, 2001; see also Tomasello, "Ace of Bass," 26.

14. Carol Kaye, interview, Los Angeles, August 27, 2001.

15. Melissa Auf der Maur, telephone interview, August 13, 2001.

16. Ibid.

17. Bill DeMain, "Aimee Mann Finds Her Second Act," *Performing Songwriter,* 9, 62 (June 2002), 56.

18. Amy Schroeder, "Aimee Mann in All Modesty," *Venus Zine* 14 (Winter 2002): 51.

19. DeMain, "Aimee Mann Finds Her Second Act," 57.

20. Laura Kiritsy, "Melissa Ferrick," *Performing Songwriter* 9, 58 (Winter 2001): 27–31.

21. Erin O'Hara, interview, New York City, September 8, 2001.

22. Ann Powers, Eddie Vedder, Boots Riley, Amy Ray, Carrie Brownstein, and Tom Morello, "The Power of Music," *Nation* 276, 2 (January 13, 2003): 11.

23. Holly Crenshaw, "Amy Ray and the Founding, Operation, and Mission of Her Label: Daemon Records," *Performing Songwriter* 10, 66 (December 2002): 44–45.

24. Ann Powers, Eddie Vedder, Boots Riley, Amy Ray, Carrie Brownstein, and Tom Morello, "The Power of Music," 14.

25. Crenshaw, "Amy Ray," 43–45.

26. Amy Ray, "About Daemon" at the Daemon Records Web site, http://www.daemonrecords.com/beta/about/index.htm (cited March 21, 2003).

27. Dylan Siegler, "Daemon's Belloluna Carves a Fresh Style in Family Atmosphere," *Billboard* 110, 50 (December 12, 1998): 12.

28. Michael Hubbard, "Indigo Girls—On Records, Recording and the Recording Industry," March 2002, found at http://www.musicomh.com/interviews/indigo-girls-2.htm (cited March 21, 2003).

29. Rose Polenzani, interview, Chicago, August 17, 2001.

30. Quoted in Brooke Shelby Biggs, "Amy Ray Does It Her Way: The Brunette Indigo Shows Her Punk Roots," *Girlfriends* (April 10, 2001), found at http://www.alternet.org/members/story.html?StoryID=10696 (cited March 21, 2003).

31. Larry Flick, "Indigo Girl Amy Ray Goes 'Stag' Via Her Daemon Imprint," *Billboard* 113, 11 (March 17, 2001): 11.

32. Ann Powers, Eddie Vedder, Boots Riley, Amy Ray, Carrie Brownstein, and Tom Morello. "The Power of Music," 14. For more on the difficulty of maintaining independent alternative music, see Thomas L. Bell's discussion of Sub Pop Records in "Why Seattle? An Examination of an Alternative Rock Culture Hearth," *Journal of Cultural Geography* 18 (Spring/Summer 1999): 35–47.

33. Jill Pesselneck, "DiFranco's Righteous Babe Grows Up with Ambitious Expansion, Double CD," *Billboard* 31, 12 (March 24, 2001): 5.

34. Marilyn A. Gillen, "Ani DiFranco: Envisioning a Future That Makes Artistic Integrity a Top Priority and Puts Black Ink on the Bottom Line," *Billboard* 112, 2 (January 8, 2000): 160.

35. Michael Hubbard, "Indigo Girls," found at http://www.musicomh.com/interviews/indigo-girls-2.htm (cited March 23, 2003).

36. Jann Arden, telephone interview, September 18, 2002.

37. Ferron, telephone interview, July 10, 2002.

38. Madeline Puckette, interview, Corvallis, Oregon, July 24, 2001.

39. Ferron, telephone interview, July 10, 2002.

40. O'Dair, "Kim Gordon," 143.

41. Janis Ian, "The Death of Independence," 74.

42. Leah Hinchcliff, interview, Portland, Oregon, August 23, 2001.

43. Mary Wilson, telephone interview, October 16, 2001.

44. "Full Inductee List" found at http://www.rockhall.com/hof/allinductees.asp (cited March 24, 2003).

45. Mary Wilson, telephone interview, October 16, 2001.

46. Ingrid Sischy, "Madonna," *Interview* (March 2001): 155.

47. Mary Wilson, telephone interview, October 16, 2001.

48. Janet Penfield, "What's a Nice Woman Like You Doing in a Male-Dominated Church Like This?" *The Christian Century* 98 (1981): 493–494.

49. Quoted in Sischy, "Madonna," 155.

50. Quoted by Jewel in Janeane Garofalo, "Jewel," *Rolling Stone* 773 (November 13, 1997): 162. Here Phair is referring to the album cover of the Go-Go's 1982 *Vacation.*

51. Woodworth, *Solo,* 16–17.

52. Childerhose, *From Lilith to Lilith Fair,* 61.

53. Gerri Miller, "Branded Female," *Billboard* 113, 48 (December 21, 2001): 26.

54. Ann Powers quoted in a PBS "Frontline" interview found at http://www.pbs.org/wgbh/pages/frontline/shows/cool/interviews/powers.html (cited February 28, 2002).

55. Freydkin, "Lilith Fair." Also see Brian Fenton and William Livingstone, "And the Buyers Are . . . ," *Stereo Review* 63, 6 (June 1998): 6.

56. This was down slightly from 51.2 percent in 2001. Total dollars spent on music was also down to $12.6 billion in 2002 from a high of $14.6 billion in 1999. The Recording Industry Association of America, "2002 Consumer Profile." www.riaa.com (cited May 22, 2003).

57. In 2002, 3.4 percent of music purchases were via the Internet. Although this number is relatively small, it represents a steady increase each year since 1997. Another trend is the decreasing number of sales in record stores (from 56.2 percent in 1993 to 36.8 percent in 2002) and the corresponding increase of sales in other kinds of stores (from 26.1 percent in 1993 to 50.7 percent in 2002). Ibid.

58. Tara J. Fenwick, "Lady, Inc.: women learning, negotiating subjectivity in entrepreneurial discourses," *International Journal of Lifelong Education* 21 (March–April 2002): 162–177.

59. Jann Arden, telephone interview, September 18, 2002.

60. Quoted in Hirshey, *We Gotta Get Out of This Place,* 188.

61. Jann Arden, telephone interview, September 18, 2002.

62. Sischy, "Madonna," 158.

63. Steve Daly, "Britney Spears: Inside the Heart and Mind (and Bedroom) of America's New Teen Queen," (cover story), *Rolling Stone* 810 (April 15, 1999): 60.

64. Ibid.

65. Rebecca Boone, "Britney and the Backlash," *Off Our Backs* 32 (January–February 2002): 48–49.

66. Quoted in Sischy, "Madonna," 158.

67. Lorraine Ali and Vanessa Juarez, "Hit or Miss," *Newsweek* 141, 3 (January 20, 2003): 73.

68. Ibid. This reaction was similar to that of teens in the 1970s toward a chubby Poly Styrene of X-Ray Spex, who wore braces and had short, frizzy hair and considered herself a misfit.

69. See Tom Beaudoin, *Virtual Faith: The Irreverent Spiritual Quest of Generation X* (San Francisco: Jossey-Bass, 1998).

70. Ann Powers quoted in a PBS "Frontline" interview found at http://www.pbs.org/wgbh/pages/frontline/shows/cool/interviews/powers.html (cited February 28, 2002).

71. Ali and Juarez, "Hit or Miss," 73. Also see Oren Harari, "You Say You Want a Revolution?" *Management Review* 88 (November 1999): 30–33; "Music Business: U.S. Album Sales Down for Second Straight Year," dated January 2003, found at http://www.ejazznews.com/modules.php?op=modload&name=News&file=article&sid=61.

72. Shirley Alston Reeves, interview, Brevard, North Carolina, August 10, 2001.

73. Ann Powers quoted in a PBS *Frontline* interview found at http://www.pbs.org/wgbh/pages/frontline/shows/cool/interviews/powers.html (cited February 28, 2002).

74. Shirley Alston Reeves, interview, Brevard, North Carolina, August 10, 2001.

75. Jann Arden, telephone interview, September 18, 2002.

76. Ibid.

77. Martha Reeves, telephone interview, October 5, 2001.

78. Erik Erikson, *Identity: Youth and Crisis* (New York: W.W. Norton and Company, 1968), 138.

Chapter 8

The Stevie Nicks epigraph to this chapter is drawn from David Wild, "Stevie Nicks," *Rolling Stone* 872 (July 5, 2001): 44ff.

1. Janis Ian, telephone interview, September 24, 2002.

2. Rana Ross, interview, Los Angeles, August 29, 2001.

3. Research suggests that girls and women, in particular, struggle with issues of self-esteem. Often, women feel that they are "impostors" when they are successful and imagine that it is only a matter of time until they are found out. For more, see Mary Bray Pipher, *Reviving Ophelia: Saving the Selves of Adolescent Girls* (New York: Ballantine, 2001); Deborah Y. Anderson and Christopher L. Hayes, *Gender, Identity, and Self-Esteem: A New Look at Adult Development* (New York: Springer, 1996); Peggy Orenstein, *Schoolgirls: Young Women, Self-Esteem, and the Confidence Gap* (New York: Doubleday, 1994); Janet Malone, "The Self-Esteem of Women," *Human Development* 17 (Summer 1996): 5–7; Pauline Rose Clance and Debbara Dingman, "Imposter Phenomenon in an Interpersonal/Social Context: Origins and Treatment," *Women & Therapy* 16 (1995): 79–96.

4. Rana Ross, interview, Los Angeles, August 29, 2001; Rana Ross Web site, http://www.bassgirl.com/; *Bassics* Web site, http://www.bassics.com/pages/issues.html.

5. Web page, Rana Ross, http://www.bassgirl.com/.

6. Rana Ross, interview, Los Angeles, August 29, 2001.

7. For more on the importance of the mentoring relationship, see Ronald J. Burke and Carol A. McKeen, "Gender Effects in Mentoring Relationships," *Journal of Social Behavior & Personality* 11 (December 1996): 91–104; Mayra Bloom, "Multiple Roles of the Mentor Supporting Women's Adult Development," *New Directions for Adults & Continuing Education* 65 (Spring 1995): 63–72; G. F. Dreher and R. A. Ash, "A Comparative Study of Mentoring among Men and Women in Managerial, Professional and Technological Positions," *Journal of Applied Psychology* 75 (1990): 539–546; B. R. Ragins and D. B. McFarlin, "Mentor Roles: An Investigation of Cross-Gender Mentoring Relationships," Washington, DC: Academy of Management Best Paper Proceedings, 1989; A. M. Morrison, R. P. White, and E. Van Velsor, *Breaking the Glass Ceiling* (Reading, MA: Addison-Wesley, 1987).

8. See the Carol Kaye Web site, http://www.carolkaye.com/www/catalog/index.htm.

9. Rana Ross, interview, Los Angeles, California, August 29, 2001.

10. Melissa Auf der Maur, telephone interview, August 13, 2001.

11. *Lilith Fair* (2000).

12. Laya Fisher, email interview, September 10, 2001.

13. Erin O'Hara, interview, New York City, September 8, 2001.

14. Lynn Frances Anderson, interview, Corvallis, Oregon, May 2001.

15. Jonatha Brooke, interview, Portland, Oregon, September 2002.

16. Lynn Frances Anderson, interview, Corvallis, Oregon, May 2001.

17. Ferron, telephone interview, July 10, 2002.

18. Institute for the Musical Arts Web site, http://www.ima.org/.

19. As of mid-2003, under new management as Filter.

20. Ellen Rosner, interview, Chicago, August 18, 2001.

21. Erin O'Hara, interview, New York City, September 8, 2001.

22. Ibid.

23. Erin O'Hara, "Indestructible Joy," from the album *Indestructible Joy,* c. 2001, mother trucker records. Used by permission of the artist.

24. Janis Ian biography, on www.janisian.com.

25. Janis Ian, "Take No Prisoners," c. Rude Girl Publishing. Used by permission of the artist.

26. Jill Sobule, telephone interview, July 17, 2002.

27. Ibid.

28. Mark Woodlief, "Jill Sobule Returns with Playful, Eclectic *Pink Pearl,*" VH1.com, Friday, April 21, 2000, www.vh1.com/artists/news/821303.04212000/sobule_jill.jhtml.

29. Jill Sobule, telephone interview, July 17, 2002.

30. Shirley Alston Reeves, interview, Brevard, North Carolina, August 10, 2001.

31. Ferron, telephone interview, July 10, 2002.

32. Patricia Romanowski, "Bonnie Raitt," in *Trouble Girls,* ed. Barbara O'Dair, 192–195.

33. Quoted in Gardner and Sirota, "Bonnie Raitt," 157.

34. Romanowski, "Bonnie Raitt," 193, 195.

35. Gaar, *She's a Rebel,* 190–191.

36. Romanowski, "Bonnie Raitt," 193.

37. James Henke, "Bonnie Raitt, the *Rolling Stone* Interview," *Rolling Stone* 3 (May 1990), cited in Lucy O'Brien, *She Bop II,* 130.

38. Romanowski, "Bonnie Raitt," 194–196.

39. John Kehe, "It's Like Running Away with the Circus," *Christian Science Monitor* 91, 196 (September 3, 1999): 17.

40. Quoted in Paul Verna, Dylan Siegler et al., "The Long Road Pays Off for Columbia's Colvin," *Billboard* 110, 11 (March 14, 1998): 1.

41. Michael Hall, "Shawn Colvin," *Texas Monthly* 26, 9 (September 1998): 128.

42. Lydia Hutchinson, "Shawn Colvin Through One Small Year," *Performing Songwriter* 8 (March/April 2001), 54.

43. Ibid., 55–56.

44. Ibid., 52.

45. Ibid., 55.

46. Jonatha Brooke, interview, Portland, Oregon, September 2002.

47. See Abraham Maslow, *Toward a Psychology of Being,* 3rd edition (New York: John Wiley & Sons, 1998); *The Farther Reaches of Human Nature (An Esalen Book)* (London: Arkana, 1993).

48. Shirley Alston Reeves, interview, Brevard, North Carolina, August 10, 2001.

49. Carol Kaye, interview, Los Angeles, August 27, 2001.

50. Holly Near, email interview, August 20, 2001.

51. Kitzie P. Stern, interview, Corvallis, Oregon, July 24, 2001.

52. Bitch and Animal, interview, New York City, September 6, 2001

53. Paz Lenchantin, interview, New York City, September 7, 2001.

54. Brenda Lee, telephone interview, July 19, 2002.

55. Wanda Jackson, telephone interview, September 18, 2001.

56. Janis Ian, telephone interview, September 24, 2002.

57. Carey Colvin, email interview, September 27, 2001.

58. Lynn Frances Anderson, interview, Corvallis, Oregon, May 2001.

59. Emily White, email interview, May 7, 2002.

60. Rose Polenzani, interview, Chicago, August 17, 2001.

61. Rana Ross, interview, Los Angeles, August 29, 2001.

62. Kate Schellenbach, interview, Los Angeles, August 29, 2001.

63. Mary Wilson, telephone interview, October 16, 2001.

64. Melissa Auf der Maur, telephone interview, August 13, 2001.

65. Robin Renée, interview, Asheville, North Carolina, November 13, 2001.
66. Indigo Girls, interview, Vienna, Virginia, August 7, 2001.
67. Leah Hinchcliff, interview, Portland, Oregon, August 23, 2001.
68. Quotation found at http://indiegrrl.com/joinPerforming.html.

SOURCES CONSULTED AND FURTHER READING

A Note on Internet Sources

The World Wide Web continues to be wonderfully kaleidoscopic, its geography shifting and impermanent. Rather than cite specific sites, only to have them disappear or morph into unrecognizable entities, we recommend that readers use Google or another search engine to locate up-to-date information on artists, periodicals, recordings, and institutions.

Print Periodicals

Acoustic Guitar
The Advocate
Billboard
Curve
Hot Wire
Hypatia
Lesbian News
Ms.
Off Our Backs
Performing Songwriter
Popular Music
Popular Music and Society
Rockrgrl
Rolling Stone
Spin
Variety
Venus Zine
Women Who Rock

Films

Beyond Killing Us Softly, directed by Margaret Lazareus and Renner Wunderlich (Cambridge, MA: Cambridge Documentary Films, 2000).

Dying to Be Thin, directed by Larkin McPhee (South Burlington, VT: WGBH Video, 2000).

Killing Us Softly 3, directed by Sut Jhally (Northampton, MA: Media Education Foundation, 2000).

Last Call at Maud's, directed by Paris Poirer (1993).

Radical Harmonies, directed by Dee Mosbacher (San Francisco: Woman Vision, 2002).

Welcome to the Club—The Women of Rockabilly, produced by Beth Harrington (2002).

Books on Music

Bacon, Tony. *History of the American Guitar.* New York: Friedman/Fairfax, 2001.

Balfour, Victoria. *Rock Wives: The Hard Lives and Good Times of the Wives, Girlfriends, and Groupies of Rock and Roll.* Reprint edition. New York: William Morrow & Company, 1987.

Bayton, Mavis. *Frock Rock: Women Performing Popular Music.* New York: Oxford University Press, 1999.

Brett, Philip, Elizabeth Wood, and Gary C. Thomas, eds. *Queering the Pitch: The New Gay and Lesbian Musicology.* New York: Routledge, 1994.

Buell, Bebe, with Victor Bockris. *Rebel Heart: An American Rock 'n' Roll Journey.* New York: St. Martin's, 2001.

Butler, Judith. *Gender Trouble: Feminism and the Subversion of Identity.* New York: Routledge, 1990.

Caponi, Gena Dagel, ed. *Signifyin(g), Sanctifyin', and Slam Dunking: A Reader in African American Expressive Culture.* Amherst: University of Massachusetts Press, 1999.

Carter, Walter. *Gibson Guitars: 100 Years of an American Icon.* Miami: Warner Brothers, 2003.

Childerhose, Buffy. *From Lilith to Lilith Fair: The Authorized Story.* New York: St. Martin's Griffin, 1998.

Clemente, John. *Girl Groups: Fabulous Females that Rocked the World.* Iola, Wisconsin: Krause Publications, 2000.

Cohen, Ronald D. *Rainbow Quest: The Folk Music Revival and American Society, 1940-1970.* Amherst: University of Massachusetts Press, 2002.

Davis, Angela. *Blues Legacies and Black Feminism.* New York: Vintage, 1998.

Denisoff, R. Serge. *Sing a Song of Social Significance.* 2nd ed. Bowling Green, OH: Bowling Green State University Popular Press, 1983.

Denselow, Robin. *When the Music's Over: The Story of Political Pop.* London: Faber and Faber, 1989.

Des Barres, Pamela. *I'm With the Band: Confessions of a Groupie*. Beech Tree Books, 1987.

Dickerson, James. *Women On Top: The Quiet Revolution That's Rocking the American Music Industry*. New York: Billboard Books, 1998.

Echols, Alice. *Scars of Sweet Paradise: The Life and Times of Janis Joplin*. New York: Metropolitan Books, 1999.

———. *Shaky Ground: The Sixties and its Aftershocks*. New York: Columbia University Press, 2002.

Evans, Liz, ed. *Girls Will Be Boys: Women Report on Rock*. Chicago: Independent Publishers Group, 1999.

———, ed. *Women, Sex, and Rock 'N'Roll: In Their Own Words* (A Pandora Book). Chicago: Independent Publishers Group, 1994.

Evans, Tom and Mary Anne. *Guitars: Music, History, Construction, and Players from the Renaissance to Rock*. New York: Facts on File, 1977.

Eyerman, Rob, and Andrew Jamison. *Music and Social Movements: Mobilizing Traditions in the Twentieth Century*. Cambridge: Cambridge University Press, 1998.

Friedlander, Paul. *Rock and Roll: A Social History*. Boulder, Colorado: Westview Press, 1996.

Gaar, Gillian. *She's a Rebel: The History of Women in Rock & Roll*. Seattle: Seal Press, 1992.

Garofalo, Reebee, ed. *Rockin' the Boat: Mass Music and Mass Movements*. Boston: South End, 1992.

Gillett, Charlie. *Sounds of the City*. London: Souvenir, 1970.

Hirshey, Gerri. *Nowhere to Run: The Story of Soul Music*. New York: Times Books, 1984.

———. *We Gotta Get Out of This Place: The True, Tough Story of Women in Rock*. New York: Atlantic Monthly Press, 2001.

Jackson, Stevi, and Sue Scott, eds. *Feminism and Sexuality: A Reader*. New York: Columbia University Press, 1996.

Jones, Hettie. *Big Star Fallin' Mama: Five Women in Black Music*. New York: Viking, 1974.

Juno, Andrea, and V. Vale, eds. *Angry Women in Rock*. San Francisco: RE Search Publications, 2000.

Kalmar, Veronika. *Label Launch: A Guide to Independent Record Recording, Promotion, and Distribution*. New York: St. Martin's Griffin, 2002.

Karlen, Neal. *Babes in Toyland: The Making and Selling of a Rock and Roll Band*. New York: Times Books, 1994.

Krims, Adam. *Rap Music and the Poetics of Identity*. Cambridge: Cambridge University Press, 2000.

Lewis, Lisa A. *The Adoring Audience*. London: Routledge, 1992.

McDonnell, Evelyn, and Ann Powers, eds. *Rock She Wrote: Women Write About Rock, Pop, and Rap*. New York: Delta, 1995.

McGrath, Tom. *MTV: The Making of a Revolution*. Philadelphia: Running Press, 1996.

McNutt, Randy. *We Wanna Boogie: An Illustrated History of the American Rockabilly Movement*. Np: Hamilton Hobby Press Books, 1988.

Miller, James. *Flowers in the Dustbin: The Rise of Rock and Roll, 1947-1977*. New York: Simon & Schuster, 1999.

Moisala, Pirkko, and Beverley Diamond, eds. *Music and Gender*. Chicago: University of Illinois Press, 2000.

Morris, Bonnie J. *Eden Built by Eves: The Culture of Women's Music Festivals*. Los Angeles: Alyson Books, 1999.

Morrish, John, ed. *The Classical Guitar: A Complete History*. San Francisco: Backbeat Books, 2002.

Morrison, Craig. *Go Cat Go! Rockabilly Music and its Makers*. Reissue edition. Urbana: University of Illinois Press, 1999.

Morton, Laura, and Melissa Etheridge. *The Truth Is... My Life in Love and Music*. New York: Villard Books, 2001.

Near, Holly, with Derk Richardson. *Fire in the Rain...Singer in the Storm: An Autobiography*. New York: William Morrow and Company, 1990.

O'Brien, Lucy. *She-Bop: The Definitive History of Women in Rock, Pop, and Soul*. New York: Penguin, 1995.

———. *She Bop II: The Definitive History of Women in Rock, Pop, and Soul*. London/New York: Continuum, 2002.

O'Dair, Barbara, ed. *The Rolling Stone Book of Women in Rock: Trouble Girls*. New York: Rolling Stone Press, 1997.

Pendle, Karin, ed. *Women and Music: A History*. Bloomington: Indiana University Press, 2001.

Posner, Gerald. *Motown: Music, Money, Sex, and Power*. New York: Random House, 2002.

Post, Laura. *Backstage Pass: Interviews with Women in Music*. Norwich, VT: New Victoria, 1997.

Raphael, Amy, ed. *Grrrls: Viva Rock Divas*. New York: St. Martin's Griffin, 1995.

Reagon, Bernice Johnson. *If You Don't Go, Don't Hinder Me: The African American Sacred Song Tradition*. Lincoln: University of Nebraska Press, 2001.

———, ed. *We Who Believe in Freedom: Sweet Honey in the Rock . . . Still on the Journey*. New York: Anchor, 1993.

Reed, Teresa L. *The Holy Profane: Religion in Black Popular Music*. Lexington: The University Press of Kentucky, 2002.

Reynolds, Simon, and Joy Press. *The Sex Revolts: Gender, Rebellion, and Rock 'n'Roll*. Cambridge: Harvard University Press, 1995.

Romalis, Shelly. *Pistol Packin' Mama: Aunt Molly Jackson and the Politics of Folksong*. Chicago: University of Illinois Press, 1998.

Romanowski, Patricia, and Holly George-Warren, eds. *The New Rolling Stone Encyclopedia of Rock & Roll*. New York: Fireside, 1995.

Sanger, Kerran L. *"When the Spirit Says Sing!" The Role of Freedom Songs in the Civil Rights Movement.* New York: Garland, 1995.

Savage, Ann M. *They're Playing Our Song: Women Talk about Feminist Rock Music.* Westport, CT: Praeger Publishers, 2003.

Schwerin, Jules. *Got To Tell It: Mahalia Jackson, Queen of Gospel.* New York: Oxford University Press, 1992.

Shaw, Arnold. *Black Popular Music in America: From the Spirituals, Minstrels, and Ragtime to Soul, Disco, and Hip-Hop.* New York: Schirmer Books, 1986.

Sherman, Dale. *20th Century Rock and Roll: Women in Rock.* Burlington, Ontario: Collector's Guide Publishing, 2001.

Spector, Ronnie. *Be My Baby: How I Survived Mascara, Miniskirts, and Madness or My Life as a Fabulous Ronette.* New York: Harmony Books, 1990.

Street, John. *Rebel Rock: The Politics of Popular Music.* Oxford: Basil Blackwell, 1986.

Strong, Martin C. *The Great Rock Discography.* New York: Times Books, 1998.

Tucker, Sherrie. *Swing Shift.* Durham: Duke University Press, 2000.

Tyler, James. *The Guitar and Its Music: From the Renaissance to the Classical Era.* Oxford: Oxford University Press, 2002.

Waksman, Steve. *Instruments of Desire: The Electric Guitar and the Shaping of Musical Experience.* Cambridge, MA: Harvard University Press, 1999.

Ward-Royster, Willa, and Toni Rose. *How I Got Over: Clara Ward and the World-Famous Ward Singers.* Philadelphia: Temple University Press, 1997.

Whiteley, Sheila, ed. *Sexing the Groove: Popular Music and Gender.* London: Routledge, 1997.

Wilson, Mary. *Dreamgirl: My Life as a Supreme.* New York: St. Martin's Press, 1986.

Woodworth, Marc, ed. *Solo: Women Singer-Songwriters in Their Own Words.* New York: Delta Trade Paperbacks, 1998.

Young, Alan. *Woke Me Up This Morning: Black Gospel Singers and the Gospel Life.* Jackson: University Press of Mississippi, 1997.

Zollo, Paul. *Songwriters on Songwriting.* Cincinnati: Writer's Digest Books, 1991.

Zwonitzer, Mark. *Will You Miss Me When I'm Gone? The Carter Family and Their Legacy in American Music.* New York: Simon & Schuster, 2002.

Books on Women, Gender, and Social History

Allen, Louise. *The Lesbian Idol: Martina, kd, and the Consumption of Lesbian Masculinity.* London: Cassell, 1997.

American Association of University Women. *How Schools Shortchange Girls.* Np: Marlowe & Company, 1995.

Anderson, Deborah Y., and Christopher L. Hayes. *Gender, Identity, and Self-Esteem: A New Look at Adult Development.* New York: Springer, 1996.

Atkins, Dawn, ed. *Looking Queer: Body Image and Identity in Lesbian, Bisexual, Gay, and Transgender Communities.* Binghamton, NY: Harrington Park, 1998.

Baumgardner, Jennifer, and Amy Richards. *Manifesta: Young Women, Feminism, and the Future.* New York: Farrar, Straus, & Giroux, 2000.

Beaudoin, Tom. *Virtual Faith: The Irreverent Spiritual Quest of Generation X.* San Francisco: Jossey-Bass, 1998.

Belenky, Mary, Blythe Clinchy, Nancy Golderberger, and Jill Tarule. *Women's Ways of Knowing: The Development of Self, Voice, and Mind.* New York: Basic Books, 1997.

Black, Allida M., ed. *Modern American Queer History.* Philadelphia: Temple University Press, 2001.

Bloom, Alexander, ed. *Long Time Gone: Sixties America Then and Now.* New York: Oxford University Press, 2001.

Boykin, Keith. *One More River to Cross: Black and Gay in America.* New York: Anchor Books/Doubleday, 1996.

Brooker, Peter. *A Concise Glossary of Cultural Theory.* London: Hodder Arnold, 1999.

Brownmiller, Susan. *Femininity.* New York: Fawcett Columbine, 1984.

Brumberg, Joan Jacobs. *The Body Project: An Intimate History of American Girls.* New York: Random House, 1997.

Butler, Judith. *Bodies that Matter: On the Discursive Limits of 'Sex.'* London: Routledge, 1993.

———. *Gender Trouble: Feminism and the Subversion of Identity.* London: Routledge, 1990.

Cole, Johnnetta B., and Beverly Guy-Sheftall. *Gender Talk: The Struggle for Women's Equality in African American Communities.* New York: One World: Ballantine Books, 2003.

Collins, Mary. *The Essential Daughter: Changing Expectations for Girls at Home, 1797 to Present.* Westport, CN: Praeger, 2002.

Collins, Patricia Hill. *Black Feminist Thought: Knowledge, Consciousness and the Politics of Empowerment.* Boston: Unwin, 1990.

De Lauretis, Teresa. *The Practice of Love: Lesbian Sexuality and Perverse Desire.* Bloomington: Indiana University Press, 1994.

Douglas, Susan J. *Where the Girls Are: Growing Up Female with the Mass Media.* New York: Times Books, 1995.

Dworkin, Andrea. *Heartbreak: The Political Memoir of a Feminist Militant.* New York: Basic Books, 2002.

Dyson, Michael Eric. *Reflecting Black: African-American Cultural Criticism.* Minneapolis: University of Minnesota Press, 1993.

Elkind, David. *All Grown Up and No Place to Go: Teenagers in Crisis.* Reading, Massachusetts: Addison-Wesley, 1984.

Erikson, Erik. *Identity: Youth and Crisis.* New York, W.W. Norton and Company, 1968.

Faderman, Lillian. *Odd Girls and Twilight Lovers: A History of Lesbian Life in Twentieth Century America.* New York: Penguin, 1992.

———. *To Believe in Women: What Lesbians Have Done for America—a History.* Boston: Houghton Mifflin, 1999.

————. *Surpassing the Love of Men: Romantic Friendship and Love between Women from the Renaissance to the Present.* Reissue edition. New York: Perennial, 2001.

Forman-Brunell, Miriam, ed. *Girlhood in America: An Encyclopedia.* Santa Barbara: ABC-CLIO, 2001.

Fuss, Diana, ed. *Inside/Out: Lesbian Theories, Gay Theories.* London: Routledge, 1991.

Gilligan, Carol. *In a Different Voice: Psychological Theory and Women's Development.* Cambridge, Massachusetts: Harvard University Press, 1983.

Gilligan, Carol, Nona P. Lyons, and Trudy J. Hanmer, eds. *Making Connections: The Relational Worlds of Adolescent Girls at Emma Willard School.* Cambridge: Harvard University Press, 1990.

Hamer, Diane, and Belinda Budge, eds. *The Good, the Bad and the Gorgeous: Popular Culture's Romance with Lesbianism.* London: Pandora, 1994.

hooks, bell. *Black Looks: Race and Representation.* Boston: South End, 1992.

————. *Feminist Theory: From Margin to Center.* Cambridge, MA: South End Press, 1984.

————. *Feminism is for Everybody: Passionate Politics.* Cambridge, MA: South End Press, 2000.

Hull, Gloria T., Patricia Bell Scott, and Barbara Smith, eds. *All the Women are White, All the Blacks are Men, but Some of Us Are Brave: Black Women's Studies.* Old Westbury, NY: Feminist Press, 1982.

Jackson, Stevi, and Sue Scott, eds. *Feminism and Sexuality: A Reader.* New York: Columbia University Press, 1996.

Jacobus, Mary, Evelyn Fox Keller, and Sally Shuttleworth, eds. *Body/Politics: Women and the Discourses of Science.* London: Routledge, 1990.

Kennedy, Elizabeth Lapovsky, and Madeline D. Davis. *Boots of Leather, Slippers of Gold: The History of a Lesbian Community.* New York: Routledge, 1993.

Kimmel, Michael S. *Manhood in America: A Cultural History.* New York: Free Press, 1996.

Lewis, Lisa A. *Gender Politics and MTV: Voicing the Difference.* Philadelphia: Temple University Press, 1990.

Linden-Ward, Blanche. *American Women in the 1960s: Changing the Future.* New York: Twayne, 1993.

Lorde, Audre. *Sister Outsider.* Freedom, CA: Crossing, 1984.

Markowe, Laura A. *Redefining the Self: Coming Out as a Lesbian.* Cambridge, UK: Polity, 1996.

Maslow, Abraham. *The Farther Reaches of Human Nature (An Esalen Book).* London: Arkana, 1993.

————. *Toward a Psychology of Being.* 3rd edition. New York: John Wiley & Sons, 1998.

Miller, Diane Helene. *Freedom to Differ: The Shaping of the Gay and Lesbian Struggle for Civil Rights.* New York: New York University Press, 1998.

Miller, Neil. *Out of the Past: Gay and Lesbian History from 1869 to the Present.* New York: Vintage Books, 1995.

Morrison, A. M., R. P. White, and E. Van Velsor. *Breaking the Glass Ceiling.* Reading, MA: Addison-Wesley, 1987.

Morrison, Joan, and Robert K. Morrison. *From Camelot to Kent State: The Sixties Experience in the Words of Those Who Lived It.* New York: Oxford University Press, 1987.

Nestle, Joan, Riki Wilchinc, and Clare Howell, eds. *Genderqueer: Voices from Beyond the Sexual Binary.* Los Angeles: Alyson, 2002.

Newton, Esther. *Cherry Grove, Fire Island: Sixty Years in America's First Gay and Lesbian Town.* Boston: Beacon Press, 1993.

Orenstein, Peggy. *Schoolgirls: Young Women, Self-Esteem, and the Confidence Gap.* New York: Doubleday, 1994.

Penelope, Julia, and Susan Wolfe, eds. *Lesbian Culture: An Anthology.* Freedom, CA: The Crossing Press, 1993.

Pipher, Mary Bray. *Reviving Ophelia: Saving the Selves of Adolescent Girls.* New York: Putnam Publishing Group, 1994.

Queen, Carol, and Lawrence Schimel, eds. *Pomosexuals: Challenging Assumptions about Gender and Sexuality.* San Francisco: Cleis, 1997.

Rich, Adrienne. "Compulsory Heterosexuality and Lesbian Existence." In *Blood, Bread and Poetry.* London: Virago, 1978.

Rimmerman, Craig. *From Identity to Politics: The Lesbian and Gay Movements in the United States.* Philadelphia: Temple University Press, 2001.

Rosen, Ruth. *The World Split Open. How the Modern Women's Movement Changed America.* New York: Penguin, 2001.

Rupp, Leila J. *A Desired Past: A Short History of Same-Sex Love in America.* Chicago: University of Chicago Press, 2002.

Shandler, Sara. *Ophelia Speaks: Adolescent Girls Write About Their Search for Self.* New York: HarperCollins, 1999.

Stein, Arlene. *Sex and Sensibility: Stories of a Lesbian Generation.* Berkeley: University of California Press, 1997.

———, ed. *Sisters, Sexperts, Queers: Beyond the Lesbian Nation.* New York: Plume, 1993.

Vaz, Kim Marie, ed. *Black Women in America.* Thousand Oaks, CA: Sage, 1995.

Weed, Elizabeth, and Naomi Schor, eds. *Feminism Meets Queer Theory.* Bloomington: Indiana University Press, 1997.

Weisman, Leslie K. *Discrimination by Design: A Feminist Critique of the Man-Made Environment.* Chicago: University of Illinois Press, 1994.

Weitz, Rose, ed. *The Politics of Women's Bodies: Sexuality, Appearance, and Behavior.* New York: Oxford University Press, 2003.

Wittig, Monique. *Feminist Issues.* London: Harvester Wheatsheaf, 1992.

INDEX